D1220792

XML and FrameMaker

KAY ETHIER

Apress™

XML and FrameMaker
Copyright © 2004 by Kay Ethier

All rights reserved. No part of this work may be reproduced or transmitted in any form or by any means, electronic or mechanical, including photocopying, recording, or by any information storage or retrieval system, without the prior written permission of the copyright owner and the publisher.

ISBN-13 (pbk): 978-1-59059-276-2

ISBN-10 (pbk): 1-59059-276-X

Printed and bound in the United States of America (POD)

Trademarked names may appear in this book. Rather than use a trademark symbol with every occurrence of a trademarked name, we use the names only in an editorial fashion and to the benefit of the trademark owner, with no intention of infringement of the trademark.

Technical Reviewer: Chris Despopoulos

Editorial Board: Dan Appleman, Craig Berry, Gary Cornell, Tony Davis, Steven Rycroft, Julian Skinner, Martin Streicher, Jim Sumser, Karen Watterson, Gavin Wray, John Zukowski

Assistant Publisher: Grace Wong

Project Manager: Kylie Johnston

Copy Editor: Lynanne Fowle

Compositor: Robert Kern

Proof Reader: A. Khedron de León

Indexer: Ariel Tuplano

Production Manager: Kari Brooks

Production Services: *TIPS* Technical Publishing, Inc.

Cover Designer: Kurt Krames

Manufacturing Manager: Tom Debolski

Distributed to the book trade in the United States by Springer-Verlag New York, Inc., 233 Spring Street, 6th Floor, New York, NY, 10013 and outside the United States by Springer-Verlag GmbH & Co. KG, Tiergartenstr. 17, 69112 Heidelberg, Germany.

In the United States, phone 1-800-SPRINGER, email orders@springer-ny.com, or visit http://www.springer-ny.com. Outside the United States, fax +49 6221 345229, email orders@springer.de, or visit http://www.springer.de.

For information on translations, please contact Apress directly at 2855 Telegraph Avenue, Suite 600, Berkeley, CA 94705. Phone 510-549-5930, fax: 510-549-5939, email info@apress.com, or visit http://www.apress.com.

The information in this book is distributed on an "as is" basis, without warranty. Although every precaution has been taken in the preparation of this work, neither the author nor Apress shall have any liability to any person or entity with respect to any loss or damage caused or alleged to be caused directly or indirectly by the information contained in this work.

The source code for this book is available to readers at http://www.apress.com in the Source Code/Downloads section.

To Mom and Dad, whose support I value to this day;
and to J, Ri, and Nad, without whom life would be meaningless.

Contents at a Glance

Contents

Acknowledgments

I need to acknowledge those who helped me make this book possible.

First and foremost, I thank Bob Kern for believing in me and giving this book a chance. In 1999, I met with Bob and he asked me about what I wanted to write. Over sushi, I explained that what I really wanted to write was a book about XML and Adobe FrameMaker. XML was in its infancy, FrameMaker books were few and far between, and Bob thought (and rightly so) that it wasn't the right time for such a topic.

Then, in 2002, almost three years from that initial meeting, he and I met again (with sushi close at hand), and this time he handed me the contracts to write this book. The time had come, it seemed. Bob, you are the best! Thank you for the years of professional support and the other books along the way.

Along with Bob, a big thank you goes to Gary Cornell, Martin Streicher, and Kylie Johnston of Apress. They believed in me and the proposed content. Without them, this book's time might not have come.

Thank you, too, to Lynanne Fowle, Chris Mills, and Chris Despopoulos for their editing of this book. I was glad to have three such masters of their crafts providing me with feedback and suggestions.

Another thank you goes to Alan Houser for helping me become an author in the first place. I enjoyed working with Alan on the *XML Weekend Crash Course*, and his company and counsel were definitely missed on this book. Thank you, too, to Bernard Aschwanden for sharing his insights on structure and the future of publishing.

Thank you to my colleagues at Bright Path Solutions for supporting me and helping me free up the time needed to write this book. Special thanks to Vicky Rosenthal and George Luke, with whom I work on a daily basis—you two make every day feel more like play than work!

On the personal side, I want to acknowledge my parents for their unending support. Thanks go to them and to my sister Kim for taking such good care of my youngest children while I was writing. Thank you, too, to my oldest for supporting me from far away, and to son Riley and daughter Nadia—thank you for being quiet sometimes when I was writing at home. *(You three guys are my life.)* Also, thank you to Denis for helping out when he could.

Much appreciation goes to my dear friend, Candace, for her guidance, and many—but not too many—years of good advice from junior high school days to today.

And a final, tiny, personal thanks to John Mellencamp, whose background music makes writing that much easier.

About the Author

KAY ETHIER, a native of Pittsburgh, Pennsylvania, is currently based in the Research Triangle Park area of North Carolina. Ms. Ethier is an *Adobe Certified Expert* in FrameMaker (versions 7, 6, and 5.5) and FrameMaker+SGML 6. She is also a certified trainer with the Quadralay *WebWorks University* program.

In 2000, Ms. Ethier coauthored *XML Weekend Crash Course* with Alan Houser. Kay has most recently been the lead author on *Advanced FrameMaker*, published by TIPS Technical Publishing. As an expert in both XML and FrameMaker, Ms. Ethier instructs training classes, performs consulting services, and provides hotline support for clients in a variety of industries. In her position with BrightPath Solutions, Ms. Ethier supports clients in the United States, Canada, the United Kingdom, and beyond.

As of the publication of this book, Ms. Ethier lives in Cary, North Carolina, with her two youngest children; her parents and siblings close at hand. She misses her oldest child, who at 18 is already famous and working far from home as a software engineer.

Preface

This book is about XML and, specifically, Adobe® FrameMaker® 7.x. If you are working with a later version of FrameMaker, some procedures or settings shown in this text may need to be adjusted. This book was also written and edited using FrameMaker 7.0 and 7.1.

XML is a technology buzzword and a format that definitely offers opportunities. Companies that are generating content for publishing, enterprise systems, catalogs, or the Web are looking for a way to make the content more reusable. Some companies are also interested in ways to get their information out in multiple formats to their clients. Adobe noticed this interest and has been modifying their Adobe FrameMaker software since 1998 to become a "multichannel publishing solution." With FrameMaker 7.0, Adobe implemented round-trip XML and opened a new door for enterprise information management. Not only can users Open and Save As XML, but an additional XML-creation tool called Quadralay® WebWorks® Publisher Standard Edition is included in every FrameMaker 7.x installation to allow easy XML/XSL creation.

FrameMaker 7.x's round-trip XML capability means that, in addition to the technical publishing groups that have been using FrameMaker for years, XML producers and information managers can now also use this tool. Fitting nicely into an enterprise workflow, FrameMaker 7.x allows users to bring in their raw XML to create documents, cell phone output (WML), PDA-friendly output (lit), PDF, and HTML. It also permits extraction of XML, allowing users to make changes and then ship the XML back to the database—or folder—from whence it came.

XML can be difficult to work with. FrameMaker is high-end and requires a moderate level of technical skill to use properly. Combine these two difficulties and you have a puzzle. This book serves to help you piece together that puzzle by taking an applied approach to both XML and FrameMaker. Concepts are illustrated using a series of projects completed over the course of the book. Part I introduces the concepts for these projects. Part II moves the reader through these projects, showing them the possibilities and putting the pieces together for them. Part III then shows the reader how to extend the projects presented and begin their own projects.

The projects that are presented beginning in Part II and moving into Part III include the following:

- A document, using a simplified XDocBook Application, which will be output to several formats and used to demonstrate structure using this well-known DTD

- A cookbook with recipes that can be saved to XML for Web posting or database use, then opened up again in FrameMaker for paper and PDF publishing

- A new portrait document, well known to FrameMaker users, which will also be used to show a very simple document and how it may be moved to XML

A brief description of each chapter is provided below. This should give you an idea what you can expect from this book.

Part I: Understanding the XML Capabilities of FrameMaker

Chapter 1—Introduction to XML

This book is geared to XML users who wish to learn about publishing with Adobe FrameMaker. Because many FrameMaker users will also read this book to learn about publishing with XML, the book begins with an overview of XML. Learning XML is a good starting point for FrameMaker users, and may be skipped by those who are already XML savvy.

Chapter 2–Introduction to Adobe FrameMaker

THIS BOOK IS GEARED to XML users who wish to learn about publishing with Adobe FrameMaker. This chapter provides a starting point for those who are familiar with XML but not as familiar with FrameMaker. For those familiar with FrameMaker, this chapter provides information on Structured FrameMaker. You may skip this chapter if you are familiar with FrameMaker and its structured document publishing capabilities.

Chapter 3–Understanding and Creating FrameMaker Templates

THIS CHAPTER IS DESIGNED to give you a better understanding of the parts of FrameMaker templates. It is designed for those who have come to FrameMaker from an XML background, although it can serve as a review for FrameMaker users who have not recently created a template.

Chapter 4–Reviewing the FrameMaker Connection to XML

IN THIS CHAPTER, we review the importing and exporting of XML—with and without an Application setup to automate your XML round trip. This should give you an understanding of the FrameMaker–XML dynamic.

Chapter 5–Reviewing Multichannel Publishing Output Options

IN THIS CHAPTER, you will discover the potential outputs from your FrameMaker documents.

Part II: Using Applications for XML Publishing

Chapter 6–Preparing to Perform the Exercises

THIS CHAPTER PROVIDES an overview of the setup for using this book's example files. You need to perform this setup if you wish to use the example files covered in this part of the book.

Chapter 7–Exploring a Structured Document

THIS CHAPTER DESCRIBES structured documents and the procedures for maneuvering in structure. You will learn how the structure tools are used. You will be walked through editing documents to ensure you are comfortable with structure. You will also learn where the structure comes from. Understanding this will help you better understand how to produce your own structure later.

Chapter 8–Importing XML to Create Structured FrameMaker Documents

THIS CHAPTER DESCRIBES how XML becomes a FrameMaker structured document and some of the controls behind the scenes. The results are explored in this chapter.

Chapter 9–Using Style Sheets and Namespaces in XML

IF YOU PLAN TO USE cascading style sheets (CSS) or Extensible Stylesheet Language (XSL) to format XML produced from FrameMaker documents, then you may find it helpful to have FrameMaker provide a starting point on your style sheets. The options available with FrameMaker and with Quadralay WebWorks Publisher are described in this chapter. XML namespace support in FrameMaker is also discussed in this chapter.

Chapter 10–Working with EDDs and Structured Documents

THIS CHAPTER EXPLORES the structure of FrameMaker documents, walking you through a structured document and its corresponding Element Definition Document (EDD).

Part III: Breaking Apart the XML Round-Trip Process

Chapter 11–Exploring the FrameMaker Application File

IN THIS CHAPTER, the Structured Application Definitions file is checked out, its components explained, and options for adjusting and adding Structured Applications noted.

Chapter 12–Creating Your Structure (EDD Development)

THIS CHAPTER OUTLINES potential workflows for moving into the publishing of structured documents. Included are descriptions of the FrameMaker EDD's structure and the EDD authoring process.

Chapter 13–Understanding Read/Write Rules

This chapter explores the Read/Write rules file. This file, sometimes used with an XML Application, allows you to adjust the way FrameMaker imports or exports structured content.

Chapter 14–Steps to Creating Your XML Application

FrameMaker structured Applications may be created fairly easily once you have a template and DTD available—even if they are still being refined. To adjust the Import and Export functions, you may need to create an Application designed specifically for your documents. XML Application creation is detailed in this chapter.

Chapter 15–Resources for XML and Structured FrameMaker

THIS CHAPTER INCLUDES websites and other resources that relate to XML, FrameMaker, or both. These may help you expand on your knowledge as you move forward.

PART I

Understanding the XML Capabilities of FrameMaker

CHAPTER 1

Introduction to XML

THIS BOOK IS GEARED to XML users who wish to learn about publishing with Adobe FrameMaker. Because many FrameMaker users will also read this book to learn about publishing with XML, the book begins with an overview of XML. Learning XML is a good starting point for FrameMaker users, and may be skipped by those who are already XML savvy.

Understanding Markup Languages

XML stands for Extensible Markup Language, which is sometimes written as eXtensible Markup Language (either is appropriate). XML is named and defined by the World Wide Web Consortium (W3C). XML's specifications are set by the W3C and any revisions come through them.

> W3C=World Wide Web Consortium, the governing body for web technologies. Further details may be found on the **w3c.org** website

A markup language is not a language in the way C++ and COBOL are languages. The *markup* is the key. It means that tags are put around your content—marking it with delimiters.

Reviewing the Evolution of XML

XML has its roots in another markup language—Standard Generalized Markup Language (SGML). SGML is a very complex markup language used by government and industry to share content in simple, ASCII-format files. Because files are a combination of tags (elements) and content, they can be understood fairly well when read from printouts. One advantage the government saw in this was that if a computer system was lost, the *data* in print could still be understood from its tags. SGML, however, turned out to be just the beginning.

Because of its complexity, a simpler markup language was thought to be needed—one that was both easier to use and optimized for the Internet. So, SGML was used to create Hypertext Markup Language, or HTML. Being a very small set of tags, HTML was more manageable and easier to learn and use. The results of HTML's rollout can be seen in the explosion of HTML content (the Web) during the 1990s.

HTML, however, had limitations. Because it was a specific list of tags, there was no good way to represent pieces of information. Something tagged with an <H1> HTML tag could be displayed as a heading, but could not be further delineated. Was it merely a heading above content, or was it a part within a catalog, or a document section, or a person's name? Companies were screaming for more and better markup options, with tags that they could use based on information types. Consequently, a scaled-down version of SGML was created that was called XML. XML overcame HTML's limitations, and has the functionality to let companies create tags as needed.

XML is not the only technology overseen by the W3C. Many technologies exist that interact with XML and HTML. These include CSS and XSLT, which are discussed in Chapter 9.

In the W3C's XML 1.0 Recommendation, the W3C describes its goals for XML. These design goals, as stated on the W3C website, are:

- XML shall be straightforwardly usable over the Internet

- XML shall support a wide variety of applications

- XML shall be compatible with SGML

- It shall be easy to write programs which process XML documents

- The number of optional features in XML is to be kept to the absolute minimum—ideally zero

- XML documents should be human-legible and reasonably clear

- The XML design should be prepared quickly

- The design of XML shall be formal and concise

- XML documents shall be easy to create

- Terseness in XML markup is of minimal importance

The bottom line is that *XML* was designed to fit where *HTML* was falling short in both extensibility and reusability. For some applications (uses), HTML just did not offer enough flexibility. Web designers and information managers (among others) wanted more from a markup language, but didn't want to work with SGML. The end result is that XML is a simpler, yet still powerful, alternative.

A Review of Basic Terminology

Before getting into the rules of XML, it is important for you to be familiar with XML terms. Many are evocative of a family tree, alluding to the *Tree View* many tools use to display XML documents. It may help to refer to Figure 1–1 when reviewing these terms.

Element

When working within XML, you have beginning and end tags around your content—for example, `<Recipe>` and `</Recipe>`. These tags form an element, into which you may enter content or even other elements. In FrameMaker, elements can be displayed in a *Structure View* as rectangles with the element name inside the rectangle, or you can display the element boundaries as tags so you can see the beginning and end of each element in your content. You can also display the element boundaries as square brackets, although this is not as clearly descriptive as the using the tags.

Element names can be created by each individual company, and the rules about how the elements fit together can be crafted for specific needs. Essentially, a set of elements is created for each type of document that is published—with some companies working with several DTDs—to produce several different document types.

```
<?xml version="1.0" encoding="UTF-8"?>
<Recipe Category="Other">
   <Name>French Baguettes</Name>
   <Ingredients>
      <Item><Quantity>1</Quantity><Unit> cup</Unit>
         <ItemName> water</ItemName></Item>
      <Item><Quantity>3</Quantity><Unit> cups</Unit>
         <ItemName> flour</ItemName></Item>
      <Item><Quantity>1 1/2</Quantity><Unit> tsp</Unit>
         <ItemName> bread machine yeast </ItemName></Item>
      <Item><Quantity>1 </Quantity><Unit></Unit>
         <ItemName>egg yolk </ItemName></Item>
      <Item><Quantity>1</Quantity><Unit> tsp</Unit>
         <ItemName> water </ItemName></Item>
   </Ingredients>
<Procedure><Step><Para>Measure carefully, and place 1 cup water,
bread flour, sugar, salt, and yeast into bread machine pan in the
order recommended by manufacturer. Select Dough/Manual cycle.</Para></Step>
<Step><Para>Place dough in a greased bowl, turning to coat all sides.
Cover. Let rise in a warm place for about 30 minutes, or until doubled
in bulk. Dough is ready if indentation remains when touched.</Para></Step>
<Step><Para>Punch down dough. Roll into a 16 x 12 inch rectangle
on a lightly floured surface. Cut dough in half, creating two 8
x 12 inch rectangles. Roll up each half of dough tightly, beginning
at 12 inch side. Roll gently back and forth to taper end. Place
3 inches apart on a greased cookie sheet. Make 1/4 inch deep diagonal
slashes across loaves every 2 inches, or make one lengthwise slash
on each loaf. Cover. Let rise in a warm place for 30 to 40 minutes,
or until doubled in bulk. </Para></Step>
<Step><Para>Heat oven to 375 degrees F (190 degrees C). Mix egg
yolk with 1 tablespoon water; brush over tops of loaves. </Para></Step>
```

Figure 1–1. This shows an XML sample with element nesting.

Attribute

Extra information may be attached to an element as an *attribute*. Attributes can add information regarding the element's content. They can also be used by software applications and style sheets to adjust formatting. An example of an attribute for a chapter element is an Author attribute. In Figure 1–1, you can see a Category attribute with a value of Other within the `<Recipe>` element.

The Category attribute provides additional data about the `Recipe`. It may be used to select an image when the XML is displayed, or it may be excluded in the resulting FrameMaker document's display.

Attributes have a *name-value pair*, meaning that they have a name and a value to go with that name. For instance, if an *author* attribute is created for a *chapter* element, the value would be the *author's name*. The value is inserted by the document's creator, although some limitations on the value can be designed into the attribute definition.

Attributes are created along with the elements, and formatting rules based on the attribute values can be written inside the FrameMaker element definitions.

DTD

An acronym for Document Type Definition, the DTD is the list of elements, attributes, and other constructs that are used to create XML structure.

The DTD specifies the elements that can be used in an XML document. The DTD also contains rules regarding how frequently an element can be used, when elements can be used, the order in which elements must be used, what attributes the elements must have, which attributes have to be given values, and what elements can be used inside other elements.

You can either use a DTD that is created specifically for your company's documents, or an industry standard DTD. DocBook is one such standard, as is XHTML. If different types of documents are being created, then a company may decide to work with multiple DTDs.

Brought into FrameMaker, a DTD becomes an EDD and may then be edited to add formatting. A DTD can also be created from a FrameMaker EDD, if that is what you have to work with.

NOTE   An EDD is a FrameMaker document that includes DTD-like element information alongside formatting rules.

If an XML document or Structured FrameMaker document is following all of the rules of a DTD, then that document is considered to be *valid.* If it is not following all of the rules (using an element, for example, in a location where it is not specified in the DTD that it can be used) but it is following all of the rules of XML, then it is considered to be *well-formed.*

Schema

A DTD describes a set of elements and attributes for a document type, and a schema does pretty much the same thing. A schema, unlike a DTD, is an XML document. The elements, attributes, and other information in schema are defined using XML syntax. As with a DTD, you may validate a document against a schema.

As of FrameMaker 7.1, schema are not supported for use with XML documents. If you have a schema, you may be able to convert it to a DTD for use with FrameMaker.

NOTE   Tools such as TurboXML™ allow you to open a schema and save it as a DTD. Some also allow you to take a DTD and save it as a schema, should you need to do so.

Nesting

This refers to the way XML tags envelope other tags. A parent may contain—between its beginning and end tags—a child element's beginning and end tags. It may even contain multiple child elements, each beginning and ending in turn.

Hierarchy

Similar to a family tree, elements in an XML file have relationships to each other. Referring to the example in Figure 1–1, you can see that the elements in the XML instance are nested, with some elements inside others. You can refer to Figure 1–1 as you review the hierarchical terms *parent, child, sibling, descendent,* and *ancestor.* The example may help you to better understand their meaning.

Parent

An element that contains another element is the *parent* of the second element. In Figure 1-1, you see the parent element <Recipe>, which contains elements such as <Name>, <Ingredients>, and <Procedure>.

Child

An element contained inside another element is a *child* of the element that contains it. In the example in Figure 1–1, <Name>, <Ingredients>, and <Procedure> are children of <Recipe>.

Sibling

Two elements that are contained inside the same parent are considered *siblings*. In Figure 1–1, <Name>, <Ingredients>, and <Procedure> are siblings.

Ancestor

Any elements which are hierarchically above an element in the Tree View are the ancestors of that element. <Recipe>, for example, is the ancestor of all elements (as such, it is the document root element, which is described further in the next section on XML rules). When viewed in tag mode, an ancestor would be the tags before and after an element.

Descendent

Any elements that are hierarchically inside an element (wrapped inside its beginning and end tags) are the descendants of that element. <Quantity> is one of many descendents of <Recipe>.

Style sheet

A style sheet is a document outside the XML that can be used to format it. You may be familiar with the cascading style sheets (CSS) used with HTML. There are also XSL style sheets, XSLT (a subset of XSL) style sheets, and more.

DOCTYPE

The *doc*ument *type* (DOCTYPE) is sometimes included in XML documents and refers to the specific DTD to be used for that document. For example, underneath your XML declaration (*Line 1*) you might have a DOCTYPE naming your DTD by filename (*Line 2*).

```
<?xml version="1.0"?>                                    Line 1
<!DOCTYPE UserManual SYSTEM "manual.dtd">                Line 2
```

Validate

The process of validation checks your document's structure against the rules defined in the DTD (outside FrameMaker) or EDD (inside FrameMaker). In FrameMaker, there is a Validate tool which moves you from error to error—if you have any errors—within your structured document or structured book.

If any content inside FrameMaker is not following the structure rules, red symbols or red dashed lines will appear to help you see the errors. It then tells you when your documents are valid. In other words, it tells you whether or not the documents follow all the rules of the DTD.

If you do not correct the errors, you cannot produce *valid* XML but you can still produce *well-formed* XML. Well-formed means that your documents follow all the rules of XML but do not necessarily confirm to a DTD or schema. Depending on what you are doing with your XML, you may be able to work with well-formed XML. If you plan to reuse, store, and share content, however, you may need to aim toward valid XML.

Understanding XML Rules

What do you need to do to create an XML document? At the simplest level, you need a text editor in which you can type. On the other end of the spectrum, you may need an XML editing program; a validation tool; a DTD and DTD editor; XSL or CSS for formatting; and a repository for storage, tracking, and retrieval.

In this section, I cover simple rules that XML documents need to follow. Examples in this section serve to clarify the rules of XML, with each addressing a specific aspect of XML. The numbering on the rules (Rule 1, Rule 2, …) is just to help you in your reading.

If you follow XML rules when writing HTML, you are actually creating XHTML!

Rule 1: If you have an XML declaration, it must be the first line of the document.

While an XML declaration is not required, it can be helpful when bringing XML into different tools. The XML declaration is located at the top of your XML file and helps tools (and readers) identify the file as XML, rather than SGML or some other markup. An XML declaration may look like this:

```
<?xml version="1.0"?>
```

If you have many small XML documents—XML fragments—that you plan to store and assemble, you might want to omit the declaration. That way, you do not end up with multiple declarations in an assembled file. This scenario will cause an error, since the declaration cannot occur below any content.

If you plan to produce valid XML, please note that you must have a declaration for an XML document to be valid.

Rule 2: All XML documents must have a root element.

In the example below, the root element is `<zoo>`. This root element begins the XML and its corresponding end tag `</zoo>` comes after all the content in the document, as shown in the following code:

```
<?xml version="1.0"?>
<zoo>
Zoo Document Content
</zoo>
```

Rule 3: All XML elements must be properly nested within the root element.

Items are nested inside the `<zoo>` root, as shown in the following code. These nested items include an `<animals>` child element. Inside this child element are additional elements called `<cat>` and `<reptile>`. These are nested child elements.

```
<?xml version="1.0"?>
<zoo>
   <animals>
      <cat>Leo</cat>
      <reptile>Pudgie</reptile>
   </animals>
</zoo>
```

NOTE   Spaces in front of the lines of code, as used in examples, are to help you see the beginning and end tags and the element nesting. This spacing is not required.

The preceding code snippet shows proper nesting. The tags begin and end without *intermingling* with other tags. An improper version might look like the following code:

```
<?xml version="1.0"?>
<zoo>
   <animals>
      <cat>Leo
      <reptile>Pudgie</cat></reptile>
   </animals>
</zoo>
```

What is incorrect is that the `</cat>` end tag is inside the reptile start and end tags. The nesting is incorrect because the tags cannot fold inside other tags unless they do so completely. Mathematically speaking, it is the equivalent of mixing up parentheses in a grouping, as illustrated in the following example:

$(x + y)/z$

does not have the same meaning as

$(x + y/z)$

In these equations, having the parentheses in different locations changes what is divided by z and thereby change the value of the equation. In the first equation, x + y is divided by z, while in the second equation y alone is divided by z and then the result is added to x. So, placement of parentheses is important to getting the correct result. As with the equation above, to produce appropriate structure in XML it is necessary to properly nest the beginning and end tags.

Rule 4: Tag names can include underscores, letters, and numbers, but not spaces.

In the following accounting-related example, <acctg> is the root element. This example shows a variety of element names, including names with underscores and numbers. Spaces are not allowed in the element names.

Later in this book, you'll look at FrameMaker naming and refer to the issue of spaces inside element names.

```
<?xml version="1.0"?>
<acctg>
    <invoice>
        <inv_num>123</inv_num>
        <client>
            <company_name>Alliance Corporation</company_name>
            <contact_name>Nancy</contact_name>
            <address1>4601 Creekstone Drive, Suite 112</address1>
            <address2>PO Box 14265</address2>
            <city>Research Triangle Park</city>
            <state>NC</state>
            <zip_plus4>27709-4265</zip_plus4>
        </client>
        <amount>55,400.00</amount>
        <due_date>2003/11/02</due_date>
    </invoice>
</acctg>
```

It is also important to note that XML is case sensitive, unlike HTML, which allows you to mix case (see following code).

```
<p>This is a small paragraph of text.</P>
```

XML beginning and end tags must match in case (see following code).

```
<Body>This is a small paragraph of text.</Body>
```

If the case does not match, then you may get an error when attempting to use or view the XML. Internet Explorer, for example, will not display the file content if case is mismatched. Instead, it displays a message that the end tag does not match the beginning tag.

Rule 5: Except for empty elements, XML elements must have beginning and end tags.

Spaces are not allowed because it causes confusion. Because of the way element attributes are separated by spaces, any tool or human moving through the XML will see a space and assume "attribute."

What else might be in an XML document? Well, you might have empty tags. Empty tags may be used in place of beginning and end tags for your elements that have no content. To use some HTML examples to clarify this, in HTML you might have:

```
<img src="corplogo.gif">
```

or perhaps

The <hr> is the HTML element for a horizontal rule.

```
<hr>
```

These are tags with no content, but they are serving some specific function. The equivalents expressed in XML, with the ending slash, are:

```
<img src="corplogo.gif"/>
```

and

```
<hr/>
```

NOTE   You might need to type a space in front of the empty element's ending slash or your documents may not display in some browsers. This is good practice, and does not cause any issues.

In this next XML document example, <doc> is the root element. An image-type element is used, although in this case it is called <figure>. If you wish to use the more familiar <img> in your XML documents, that is your choice. Again, spacing is used to show the nesting.

```
<?xml version="1.0"?>
<doc>
   <chapstart>
      <title>Buying a Car</title>
      <author>
         <name>John Doe</name>
         <figure source="doe02.svg" />
      </author>
   </chapstart>
   <section>
      <title>Selecting a Body Type</title>
      <para>Some text would be here.</para>
      <para>Some text would be here.</para>
   </section>
   <section>
      <title>Selecting a Manufacturer</title>
      <para>Some text in here as well.</para>
   </section>
</doc>
```

One important comment on the preceding example documents: because the tags denote where pieces of information start and stop, you can display XML in several ways.

You can display a document with spacing, as shown in the following code:

```
<?xml version="1.0"?>
<acctg>
   <invoice>
      <inv_num>123</inv_num>
      <client>
         <company_name>Alliance Corporation</company_name>
         <contact_name>Nancy</contact_name>
         <address1>4601 Creekstone Drive, Suite 112</address1>
         <address2>PO Box 14265</address2>
         <city>Research Triangle Park</city>
         <state>NC</state>
         <zip_plus4>27709-4265</zip_plus4>
      </client>
      <amount>55,400.00</amount>
      <due_date>2003/11/02</due_date>
   </invoice>
</acctg>
```

You can also display the XML without indents, as shown in the following code:

```
<?xml version="1.0"?>
<acctg>
<invoice>
<inv_num>123</inv_num>
<client>
<company_name>Alliance Corporation</company_name>
<contact_name>Nancy</contact_name>
<address1>4601 Creekstone Drive, Suite 112</address1>
<address2>PO Box 14265</address2>
<city>Research Triangle Park</city>
<state>NC</state>
<zip_plus4>27709-4265</zip_plus4>
</client>
<amount>55,400.00</amount>
<due_date>2003/11/02</due_date>
</invoice>
</acctg>
```

Displaying it with or without indents is the same as the code in the following sample:

```
<?xml version="1.0"?><acctg><invoice><inv_num>123</inv_num><client>
<company_name>Alliance Corporation</company_name><contact_name>Nancy
</contact_name><address1>4601 Creekstone Drive, Suite
112</address1><address2>PO Box 14265</address2><city>Research
Triangle Park</ city><state>NC</state><zip_plus4>27709-
4265</zip_plus4></client><amount>55,400.00</amount>
<due_date>2003/11/02</due_date></invoice></acctg>
```

The line breaks are used mostly to make it easier on human editors and readers. All *views* are equivalent XML, but some are easier to read.

NOTE   When importing XML into FrameMaker, FrameMaker does not filter out white space. Depending on whether the spaces (or tabs) are inside or between elements, you can end up with unwanted <WHITESPACE> elements that must be cleaned out. To avoid this, do not use spaces/tabs within your XML.

Rule 6: Attribute values must always be quoted.

Attributes in XML documents must be properly quoted. This is also a rule for HTML documents, although browsers have been designed to be forgiving on this point. HTML documents that have unquoted attributes will usually still display. XML documents with unquoted attributes are not well-formed. Remember to quote your attribute values. For example,

> Attributes must consist of a name-and-value pair, such as draft="final"

```
<figure source="doe02.svg" />
```

or

```
<recipe type="dessert">
```

Rule 7: All entities and special characters must be used properly.

Special characters must be defined and used properly. An ampersand (&), for example, cannot be typed directly into your content. It must be set up as an entity.

Beyond these simple rules, you have a lot of free reign as to what elements your XML documents can contain. Quite honestly, if you don't have a specific purpose or method in mind, it will not matter what you include in your XML.

Looking at XML with Quality Checking

At this point, it probably looks like XML is easy. Well, it is and it isn't. You can follow the preceding rules and make up the tags as you go, but that will not do much for you. If you really get into reusing your information and making good use of XML, you will want to specify a list of the elements and how they can be used.

This becomes imperative as you move forward and begin formatting, reusing, and sharing your XML. Tools—and people—need to know what elements and structure to expect.

In our accounting example (see page 11), there are many tags that make up an invoice. These include <inv_num>, <client>, <amount>, <due_date>, and many others.

In an ideal situation, you would have a list of all these elements and how they can be used. This list would then be put into a format that allows a machine or a software package to check the XML for you (eliminating errors by human editors). Such a list is called a DTD.

As mentioned in the terminology section, the DTD lists the elements and a *rule* about how the element can be used. The process of checking your XML documents against the rules to check compliance is called validation (also mentioned in the terminology section). Documents that follow the DTD content rules are valid. Documents which do not follow the rules of a DTD, but follow the rules of XML, are well-formed.

Valid documents are always well-formed, but well-formed documents are not necessarily valid.

For example, you can define the tag <invoice> and state in its rule that it always has to have <client>, <amount>, and <due_date>, but doesn't always have to have an <inv_num>. You can then use a software package that checks the XML against the DTD and validates it to make sure that all the invoices have the appropriate information.

Some software can even show you where there are missing pieces so the XML can be fixed. You'll see this in FrameMaker, which displays missing pieces as red symbols in a *Structure View*.

Looking at XML with Formatting

You can also use style sheets to format your XML (make it display a certain way). XML can be formatted using several methods.

- You can bring XML into tools to change the way it looks

- You can use style sheets to format XML

- You can use the XML formatting and transforming language, called XSLT, to adjust XML

XSLT allows you to use the tags within your XML document to create formatted output. The formatting could be as simple as adding bold to an object with a `<company_name>` tag. The formatting can also be as complex as telling all the invoice pieces to go into a table and become sortable.

XSLT is written in XML

Getting Started with a Pilot Project

How do you get started with XML? You now have an idea about what is in an XML document. You have a basic understanding of the purpose of DTDs and XSLT.

There are actually better questions that you should try to answer for yourself. For what do you want to use XML? It can be used to do many different things. What issues are you facing that have sent you searching for a better alternative? Start with answers to these questions and then move forward.

Once you finish implementing XML to fix a specific problem, you will start to see other places where it can fit into your environment.

Still don't know where to start? Then start small! Pick a pilot or pet project and give XML a whirl. Find a list, a directory, or some other information that has a pattern to it. Take that and try to duplicate it in XML, creating a structure based on the pattern. You may need some help from your Webmaster or a developer (if you can get your hands on one).

XML fits into a lot of places. It can replace or work with other technologies. It can be used instead of scripts or to supplement them. It can work with databases or on its own to store content. Before you dive into what XML might do, it can help if you learn more about what it can do for you.

Summary

In closing, let me reiterate that understanding XML's rules is not difficult. Typing an XML document is also not difficult. What *is* difficult is figuring out what to do with XML.

If you feel that you need more information on XML before proceeding into FrameMaker, there are many, many resources available for XML, DTDs, and XSLT. Start with www.w3.org. Then, to figure out what that site is really talking about, go to www.w3schools.com.

You might also pick up an XML book at www.amazon.com, www.fatbrain.com, or your local bookstore. Try the *XML Weekend Crash Course*, if you are really starting from scratch, or visit www.apress.com to learn more about books by the company that published this one. And, once you feel comfortable with XML, try moving on to a book on XSLT.

CHAPTER 2

Introduction to Adobe FrameMaker

THIS BOOK IS GEARED to XML users who wish to learn about publishing with Adobe FrameMaker. This chapter provides a starting point for those who are familiar with XML but not as familiar with FrameMaker. For those familiar with FrameMaker, this chapter provides information on Structured FrameMaker. You may skip this chapter if you are familiar with FrameMaker and its structured document publishing capabilities.

Understanding FrameMaker

Adobe FrameMaker provides a strong feature set for publishing to both paper and electronic formats. FrameMaker is one of the leading tools for "single source" publishing. This includes publishing with XML. Several of FrameMaker's strengths are explored below in "Formatting Capabilities and Other Strong Points."

Single Source = A system in which content is authored one time and then used to create multiple documents/outputs.

FrameMaker's formatting engine allows users to do complex text formatting and page layout. FrameMaker has the ability to create PDF and to output online formats including XML, HTML, XHTML, online help, and SGML.

Formatting Capabilities and Other Strong Points

In this section, you will review FrameMaker's features for formatting your content. If you plan to use FrameMaker as your tool for publishing XML to paper and PDF, it is important for you to know what it brings to the table.

FrameMaker allows you to create templates that contain settings that can be used for all of your documents. For now, let's look at some of the specific aspects of these templates.

Text Formatting

Text formatting in FrameMaker is accomplished at two levels. Formatting is first set for entire paragraphs and then for select words or phrases within the paragraph. This is how you make words and phrases stand out in bold, for example. When you bring your XML into FrameMaker, you will be able to design some elements to create paragraphs, while other elements become text ranges inside those paragraphs.

Paragraph formats are created using the Paragraph Designer. This Designer is shown in Figure 2–1.

There are six sheets of properties that may be set for each paragraph format (seen on the tabs at the top of the Paragraph Designer). Only one of these properties sheets is shown in Figure 2–1. The other sheets control appearance, page position, autonumbering, advanced text adjustments, and behavior within tables.

Character formats are set in the Character Designer. Similar to the Paragraph Designer, the Character Designer controls text properties. The Character Designer—much simpler than the Paragraph Designer—only has one properties sheet, which is shown in Figure 2–2.

Table Placement and Formatting

FrameMaker allows you to create pages and pages of tables easily. Tables can spread across many pages—even 50 pages or more. FrameMaker includes a Table Designer for creating table formats. These formats include settings for properties such as rules, shading, and indents. These stored formats can be used to create many, many tables, and the formats may be invoked by elements in your XML

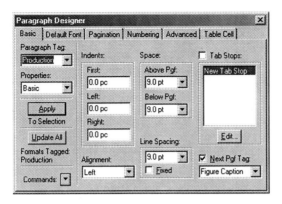

Figure 2–1.   The Paragraph Designer is used to create and manage paragraph formats.

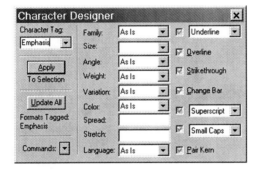

Figure 2–2.   The Character Designer is used to create and manage character formats.

round trip. This allows you to turn different *types* of XML data into tables with different appearances.

There are three sheets of properties in the Table Designer, one of which is shown in Figure 2–3. If you create sample tables in a FrameMaker template, and use the Table Designer to Update All, additional data will be stored with the table format. These include column width settings and paragraph formats used in cells. Even though these are not listed within the table format's properties in the Designer, they are stored with the format.

FrameMaker's table management is very stable. There are certain FrameMaker-specific rules about table construction that must be followed, and these should be taken into account when you design your XML elements. If a table has a title, for example, it must be the first

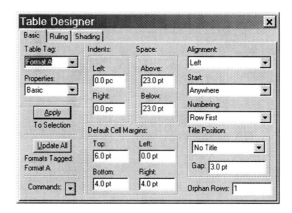

Figure 2–3.   The Table Designer is used to create and manage table formats.

element inside the table structure (the first child of the table-start element). This rule and others are explored further in Chapter 10.

Figure Placement and Settings

Along with its ability to handle lots of text and long tables, FrameMaker also handles graphics—even many graphics of varied types. FrameMaker gives you options for linking with graphics or embedding them in your documents.

You can also choose on a graphic-by-graphic basis whether you want a graphic to be anchored to a specific point on a page or attached to a specific piece of text within the document's flow.

NOTE   When working with XML, you can only attach graphics to text because graphics attached to the page will not transfer out to XML.

As each graphic is attached to text, its position can be set to produce a desired look. For example, the graphic can be set up to *Run into paragraph* so that the text wraps around its edges. The graphic can also be set as *Below current line* to get it to drop beneath the text to which it is attached. There are many other settings that provide a wide variety and the potential for using different settings for each occurrence of a graphic.

Cross-References

In this era of interactive documents, having pieces of cross-linked data and the ability to move between them is imperative. FrameMaker provides an easy-to-use interface for linking one piece of content to another—or one element to another within an XML-based structured document.

Once transferred out of FrameMaker, these links can be *hot links* and provide users with navigation without requiring you to go through any extra hoops in FrameMaker. The hot links are created automatically when a cross reference is created. When the document is turned into PDF, HTML, or some other online format, the links become *live* (they may also be activated using shortcuts in FrameMaker, thereby allowing you to test links or even navigate while editing).

When working with XML, FrameMaker includes the link identification numbers as attributes within your XML, along with references to those identification numbers saved as attributes. You can then use XSLT to make the links perform within a browser or other XML-based delivery system, such as a cell phone using Wireless Markup Language (WML).

Markers

Markers may require some explanation if you are not used to working in a document publishing tool. Markers are FrameMaker objects that contain text but keep that text from appearing in the documents. If desired, the markers' content can be extracted and used to produce other documents, such as indexes or glossaries.

Markers can be an effective way of holding onto XML elements that you need within your XML but don't want to appear where they are placed in your published documents. Marker content can include process instructions or even code.

Variables

FrameMaker variables come in two flavors: system and user. System variables are maintained by FrameMaker, although they can be adjusted from one document (template) to another. Some examples of system variables are *Current Date* and *Current Page Number(#)*.

User variables are created by template designers and are used for text that is typed often, or must be adjusted on the fly. Some examples of user variables are *ProductName*, *ProjectNumber*, and *Company*. When designing a template, you can create many of these, name them whatever you want, and then define the text that you want FrameMaker to drop in when they are used.

When sending data out to XML, text from variables may be sent out as straight text (PCDATA) within your XML. You can also set variables up as entities so that they go out to XML as entities and can come back in as variables. If not set up this way, variables become text when sent to XML and remain just text when the XML returns to FrameMaker—they are no longer variables.

Page Layout

FrameMaker moves beyond the capabilities of word processors in that it provides powerful page layout capabilities. Limited margin settings and headers/footers found in other tools are replaced by the drawing of frames wherever you want them on the page—possibly explaining the name *Frame*Maker. You can draw header, footer, and other *background* frames wherever you want them on the page. You can even make them turn sideways or at an angle, which is very helpful for watermarks. You also draw the typing area that you want exactly where you want it to be.

It is important for you to note that nothing related to the page layout travels with your XML. Page layout is specific to your documents while you are working within FrameMaker and is irrelevant to the XML.

NOTE   This is true of both XML and HTML. Whether saving directly or using WebWorks Publisher, FrameMaker leaves its page layout behind.

Master Pages

Assuming that you may be new to FrameMaker and need some basics on creating page layouts, this next section will briefly explore the page layout options known as *master pages.*

When working in a FrameMaker document, you are normally on the *body pages.* This is where the majority of the document content exists: the text, graphics, tables, and other items that make up the entire document flow. Behind these, in every FrameMaker file, is a set of master pages. The master pages hold the layout, including background items like headers and footers. An example master page is shown in Figure 2–4.

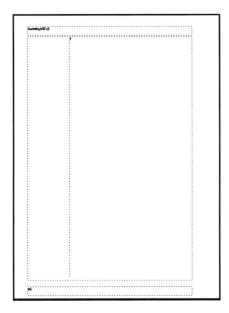

Figure 2–4.   This is a master page.

A body page corresponding to the master page shown in Figure 2–4 can be seen in Figure 2–5.

As you can see in these figures, the body page only has the frame showing for the typing area. This is the area that can be edited to create documents. The background frames are visible on the master pages and can only be edited on the master pages. Therefore, their frames don't show on the body pages, even if their content does.

You create text frames on the master page with one of the graphics tools—the Text Frame tool. The Text Frame tool is shown

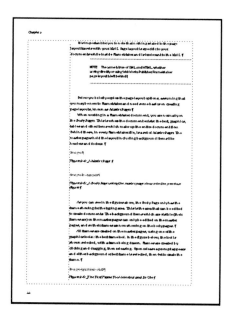

Figure 2–5.   *This is a body page using the master page shown in Figure 2-4.*

circled in Figure 2–6. Frames are created by clicking and dragging, then releasing. Upon release, an Add New Text Frame prompt appears. You can select either *Background Frame* or *Template for Body Page Text Frame* and click Set to create the frame.

Once frames are drawn on the master pages and set up as body page text frames, content may be added on the body pages. The content will fit within the created frames.

PDF Creation

FrameMaker has the ability to output high quality PostScript. Because PostScript is used to create PDFs, FrameMaker creates high quality PDFs. It can create PDFs with special features like bookmarks, articles, and hypertext links.

PDF files are created using printer drivers. The printer drivers that come with Acrobat vary depending on the version, but may include PDFWriter and Acrobat Distiller (in Acrobat version 6 called Adobe PDF Printer Driver). Acrobat Distiller works with FrameMaker and creates a PostScript file that can be run through the Distiller component. PDFWriter creates PDFs directly and is best used for software

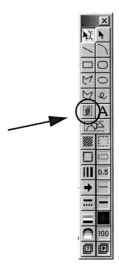

Figure 2–6.   The Text Frame tool is circled.

packages that cannot produce PostScript. This is discussed in more detail in Chapter 5.

Content Sharing across the Enterprise

FrameMaker provides word-processing capability, and enables you to make documents of all types and lengths—from small memos to large books. FrameMaker not only allows you to create content, but it can also use content created by other software tools and then return that content to those tools.

A FrameMaker (*filename.fm*) file can be opened using the version of FrameMaker with which it was created, or using a later version. You may also save a document in Maker Interchange Format (MIF, an ASCII-based format that fully describes a FrameMaker file) if you need to open the document in an *earlier* version of FrameMaker (or a version on another platform). Therefore, version compatibility is not a limiting factor.

NOTE MIF is a form of markup specific to FrameMaker. Some users work in MIF rather than in the software interface. Programs like Quadralay's WebWorks Publisher convert FrameMaker documents to MIF so that they can scan through them to extract/use content.

Importing

When you think of "word processing," you may envision an administrator working in Microsoft® Word® or Corel WordPerfect®. Word processing is computer-based preparation of text for printing. It is a phrase that came about before the phrase, "desktop publishing."

Files in many other formats can be imported into FrameMaker. This may be helpful if you are coming to FrameMaker from other tools. In addition to allowing import of XML, FrameMaker opens other types of files including: Rich Text Format, Word, WordPerfect, Interleaf ASCII, and text.

Exporting

You may reuse FrameMaker content in multiple documents to extend your publishing. Some features even allow you to produce content that is personalized for each deliverable, so making manuals geared toward a specific client can be easily done.

FrameMaker has its own proprietary format for saving files, which is a pretty standard practice with software tools. FrameMaker, however, allows you to move out of its proprietary format and into a long list of other formats.

FrameMaker outputs to many formats, including XML and many of the formats that it imports. To ensure that you can share documents, FrameMaker can Save As through filters to produce documents in formats for other software tools. The available filters include (but are not limited to):

- Microsoft RTF (Rich Text Format) and RTF Japanese

- Word

- WordPerfect

- HTML

- XML

- XHTML

- SGML

- MIF

- Text

Once a document—even a document collection—is saved as another file type, it can be shared more easily than the proprietary FrameMaker files. Of course, this kind of data sharing is a major goal of XML and SGML, and FrameMaker is particularly well suited for that.

Understanding FrameMaker Templates

Many of the formats and special features discussed herein are components of FrameMaker templates. Their place within FrameMaker, and the role they play in creation of your documents, is explained in this section.

What Is a Template?

In FrameMaker, a template is a file that contains formatting and layout information for text, tables, graphics, and pages. Often when new files are created, the author uses a template to ensure the new document matches other documents of that type. Some companies use several templates.

A template contains a set of formats, all designed to work together and create a specific type of document. Some templates are included in the FrameMaker installation, although the majority of companies create their own templates to suit their needs. Components that make up a template are:

- Paragraph formats

- Character formats

- Master page layouts

- Table formats

- Color definitions

- Document properties (this includes a variety of settings, including zoom percentage, pagination, numbering, and text options)

- Reference pages

- Variable definitions

- Cross-reference formats

- Conditional text settings

- Math definitions

While you may not need to use all of these functions (for example, you can skip math definitions if you are not creating equations), you must set up some text formatting and page layouts at a minimum. The process for producing a template is something like this:

1. Analyze your documents and determine the formats needed to create the look and feel you want.

2. Create your FrameMaker template, creating the necessary formats.

3. Save the template in a safe place.

4. Open the template each time you need to create a new document, and *Save As* a new name in whatever folder is appropriate.

What is a Structured Template?

A structured template is a FrameMaker template into which element definitions (EDD information) have been imported.

While a regular FrameMaker template deals only with formatting, structured templates also deal with issues of structure and rules of content. These templates have information in them that is similar to the information you would find in a DTD.

The process for producing a structured template is something like this:

1. Analyze your documents and determine the formats needed to create the look and feel you want.

2. Analyze your document content to determine the structure required to produce the necessary XML. You can also import your DTD to provide FrameMaker with the information about your structure.

3. Create your FrameMaker template with the necessary formats.

4. You create elements and attributes as needed to produce appropriate XML. You can also add formatting and feature information to your DTD to tie FrameMaker functions to your existing elements and attributes.

5. Save the template in a safe place.

6. Configure FrameMaker to use the template when it opens an XML file.

7. Open the template each time you need to create a new document, and *Save As* a new name in whatever folder is appropriate. If importing XML, you can also select the configuration that includes the template so that FrameMaker uses it automatically.

A template that contains formatting information plus the element information from the EDD is referred to as a structured template.

The structured templates certainly require more time and thought. While issues in formatting are easy to clear up in FrameMaker templates, problems with structure may not be so easy to fix—especially if you plan to export XML for use by other tools, you need to structure your content as correctly as possible on the first pass. You can always extend a structure, but major rework could render existing documents invalid.

The file in which you create your structure and add the tie-ins to FrameMaker's formatting engine is called an Element Definition Document (EDD). As mentioned in the terminology section, this is the list of FrameMaker elements and attributes. The EDD contains information on how often elements can be used, what elements must be present, and what elements can be used inside other elements. It also contains formatting information for each element. This is what differentiates it from a Document Type Definition (DTD), and what makes it possible for the elements to tie into FrameMaker's formatting features. Once it is exported from FrameMaker, the formatting information is dropped and the EDD becomes a DTD.

Once you have your structured template created, you can begin publishing structured documents. In many cases, you will have additional files that will interact with—and augment—your structured template. A few of these are described in the next sections.

Understanding Structured FrameMaker Basics

Document Window and Structure View

You need to be aware that you can view documents in a *document window* to see the printable document, or in a *Structure View window* to see the way the elements are structured.

The document window is where you see your content (text, graphics, and tables). When you author a document, you are typing and entering content into the document window. This is also what you see when you print.

The Structure View is opened by clicking the Structure View button (▣), located in the upper right corner of your documents. The Structure View shows you the structure tree within your structured document or imported XML file. You will see all of the elements and their attributes (but the attributes are not seen within the document window).

Element Catalog

The Element Catalog acts as your guide through any structure, displaying elements that may be inserted as you author.

Read/Write Rules

The read/write rules are written and stored in an optional, separate file. These rules may be added to an XML round-trip setup to adjust element names (change case, shorten, lengthen), adjust the nesting

Figure 2–7.   The Element Catalog displays elements you can use in your document.

of elements, or drop and add elements as XML is imported (read) into FrameMaker or exported (written) from FrameMaker.

XML does not specify element types, for example, yet FrameMaker designates element types (containers, tables, graphics, cross-references, footnotes, and more). It may be desirable to create rules that add an element type as XML is imported.

A second example is that you might use a rule to change a FrameMaker element *Chapter Title*, which contains a space, to *ChapterTitle* in XML, to eliminate the space that XML will not allow. This example rule could even be modified to make the XML element name *chaptitle* if desired.

Read/write rules are discussed in more detail in Chapter 13.

Application

You may hear the term *application* when someone is referring to a software product. For example, FrameMaker may be called an application. This is not the Application that is referred to in regard to structured document publishing.

An Application in the structured-documents context is a set of files given a name and designed to work together. You can have multiple Applications, and they might be either XML Applications or SGML Applications.

NOTE A *capital "A"* will be used on *Application* in this chapter to help you make the distinction. It does not need to be capitalized, although you may note that its element name is capitalized within the FrameMaker setup.

The name of an Application is given by its creator. The files that work together include (but are not limited to) a structured template, read/write rules, a DTD, and a style sheet (all of these are described within the terminology section).

The Applications that install with FrameMaker (except the UNIX version) are DocBook, XDocBook, and XHTML. Some of these Applications are XML and others are SGML.

A round-trip Application allows you to perform importing (XML to FrameMaker) and exporting (FrameMaker to XML). The XML Application must be set up within FrameMaker on each machine that will work with the XML. You provide the name and the pointers (or paths) to the documents that work together (DTD, template, and so forth).

An XML Application can be set up to allow you to publish fully-formatted documents—formatting being one of FrameMaker's strengths—and to produce XML for use by other systems and departments within your enterprise.

Looking at Round Trip XML Benefits

In this section, several of the *XML round-trip* benefits are examined. Other parts of this book deal with *structured document publishing* benefits (consistency, validation, and guided writing among others). There may be—and should be—some overlap with the structured document publishing benefits.

Multichannel Publishing

One benefit of round-trip publishing with FrameMaker is that you can access all of FrameMaker's capabilities for multichannel publishing (publishing to many formats). Multichannel publishing is not easily accomplished with XML alone, or with any other single tool. FrameMaker's ability to format documents for press, output high-quality PDF, and output to HTML and online help, will allow you to do more with your XML.

You may also single source those components into documents with completely different appearances by using multiple templates. XML being what it is, there is no formatting to get in the way of adjusting the content to look the way that you want it to look. You can set up multiple XML Applications, each using a different FrameMaker template.

Content Sharing and Reuse with XML

XML allows you to reference XML fragments together to form complete documents. This means you can reuse XML in multiple documents by referencing them. The concept is similar to FrameMaker's text inset feature.

Not only can you pull together content from multiple XML documents, you can also share your XML throughout your enterprise. The XML created by FrameMaker—like XML created in Notepad—has no formatting. You are producing data that is not in a proprietary format, but is basically ASCII text. You can easily use your FrameMaker-exported XML with other tools. Those within your organization using FrameMaker can certainly use your XML. Those who are using other XML-ready tools may use it also! You are not limiting access to your data—you are opening up access to it.

NOTE   Tools such as TEXTML® by IXIASOFT (*www.ixiasoft.com*) allow you to store XML and other files with metadata about each file. You can then search, retrieve, and reuse from the data in the XML server. This tool is mentioned specifically because it was designed for XML, yet has a software *bridge* to work with FrameMaker 7.x.

Metadata

Store metadata along with your content to make your data more flexible and reusable. Instead of just storing your content (text, images, and so forth), you include data about your content—metadata—by using elements and attributes. Attributes provide information about each element's content.

In creating a catalog, for example, you might type your catalog data within a structure that describes the data (item, price, and so forth) and has attributes with additional data (category, weight, requirements, and so forth).

You may even set up database connectivity—including database connectivity for content management—if you have a database that can handle XML.

Extensibility

By definition and name, XML is extensible. This means you can add elements and attributes as needed. This is advantageous if you wish to get a system in place and working before expanding it to suit other needs. For example, a system may be designed and rolled out for one department, and then extended to add components desired by other departments to create the complete system.

Summary

FrameMaker provides you with what you need to create documents of all sizes. It is designed to handle complex documents with consistent, repeating formatting and layouts.

FrameMaker is template based, with formats for everything from text to tables to page layouts.

FrameMaker is useful for creating XML. Its strength is in being able to combine content from multiple sources and do single sourcing—producing good-looking documents in multiple formats.

CHAPTER 3

Understanding and Creating FrameMaker Templates

THIS CHAPTER IS DESIGNED to give you a better understanding of the parts of FrameMaker templates. It is designed for those who have come to FrameMaker from an XML background, although it can serve as a review for FrameMaker users who have not recently created a template.

Reviewing a FrameMaker Document and Its Formats

Before walking you through creating a template, this chapter will review some of the components that make up a FrameMaker template—such as paragraph formats, character formats, master page layouts, and cross-reference formats. The following sections provide background data on these and other template parts.

In the real world, planning and upfront design is needed before you create a template. We will not walk you through that process here, but we will point out the following two paths to the template:

- If you are coming at XML from the publishing side, you must first examine the documents you want to make. Determine what text styles you will have, what page layouts you need, and so forth. Also think about the structure (elements) that you will need

- If you are coming at publishing from the XML side, you will need to determine your text styles, page layouts, and so on, and will need to sort out how these fit with your existing XML elements

As you determine what you need to have in your template, formulate the naming conventions that you will use. The following are a few things you should keep in mind regarding the naming of your FrameMaker formats:

- Avoid including special characters in the format names

- FrameMaker is case sensitive—as is XML. Standardize your naming to make it easier to manage and troubleshoot

- Avoid using spaces in element names. While FrameMaker does not mind spaces in format names or element names, XML does not like spaces and you might have to remove them from your elements later

- Use logical names

These tips are emphasized in the following sections, which provide you with an overview of several important template parts.

NOTE   A FrameMaker template is not a different format from other FrameMaker documents. This means that, in a pinch, any FrameMaker document may be used as a template.

Paragraph Formats

A paragraph format contains settings for how the text looks and how it fits with other things on the page. Paragraph formats are created with the Paragraph Designer, which is opened by clicking *Format>Paragraphs>Designer.*

Paragraph formats are the basis of document formatting in unstructured FrameMaker documents. Paragraph formats can also be the basis of document formatting in structured FrameMaker documents. The template setup described in this chapter assumes that the paragraph formats will be used with structured documents.

NOTE   You will learn in Chapter 10 that formatting structured FrameMaker documents can be done several ways. Formatting via paragraph formats is usually considered to be the most effective means of formatting by the author, since it lends itself better to single sourcing and exporting to formats like Microsoft Word.

The paragraph designer consists of six sheets of properties. The first is the *Basic* properties sheet, shown in Figure 3–1.

As you can see, Basic properties affect things like spacing and indents. This gives you control over how your paragraphs fit along the page margins and from line to line. Also on this sheet is *Space Above Pgf* (paragraph) and *Space Below Pgf*, which let you put padding between paragraphs. These particular settings, used properly, avoid empty *returns* on the page to adjust spacing. All spacing is consistently inserted as needed.

The second property sheet is labeled *Default Font*, as shown in Figure 3–2.

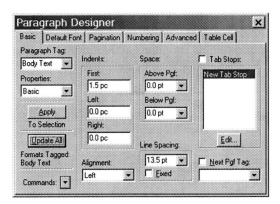

Figure 3–1.   The Paragraph Designer Basic properties sheet is one of six.

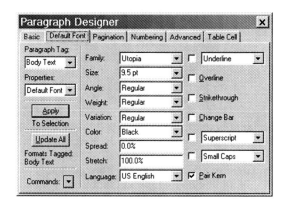

Figure 3–2.   Paragraph Designer Default Font properties sheet is displayed.

Default Font settings affect the appearance of your text. Some of these warrant extra explanation.

- *Spread*   This allows you to adjust the spacing between words and characters. If you type a negative value for the Spread, the characters in the paragraph will move closer together. If you type a positive value, extra spacing is added between the characters.

- *Stretch*   By replacing the 100% with a greater percentage value (for example, 110%), you can stretch the characters (*a*, *b*, *c*, etc.) to make them wider. Replacing with a lesser percentage value (for example, 75%) would make the characters thinner.

NOTE   Because Stretch manipulates the font, it can cause problems with search-ability in any resulting PDF documents. It is suggested that you use this setting sparingly.

- *Language*   This selection affects the Spell Check dictionary used on the text. Changing this to *None* for any paragraph format means that text using that format cannot be spell checked. This can save you time by letting you bypass code, for example, during a spell check.

NOTE You can still use *Find/Change* to find content in a paragraph with language set to *None*. In fact, there does not seem to be a way to keep language-free text out of the *Find* stream.

- *Numeric Underline* (instead of *Underline*) Creates an underline on the text that adjusts based on the font size, which makes the underlining look a bit better than with the *Underline* setting.

The next sheet in the Paragraph Designer is the Pagination properties sheet, which is shown in Figure 3–3.

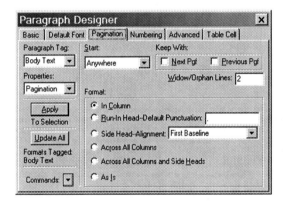

Figure 3–3. The Paragraph Designer Pagination properties sheet is displayed.

Pagination settings allow a paragraph to do things like move to the top of the next page, or *stick* to a paragraph just above (*Previous*) or below (*Next*).

Within the *Format* settings (bottom right on the Pagination properties sheet), there are options for placement of text. These require some clarification, as the terms are somewhat FrameMaker specific.

- *In Column* This means that the text flows in columns— whether the page has a single column, two columns, or more— and each new paragraph is positioned below the one that comes before it. With an *In Column* paragraph, pressing *Enter* gives you a new paragraph just below it.

- *Run-In Head*   This special setting allows a paragraph set to *Run-In Head* to pull the following paragraph up in its baseline. With this, you can have two separate paragraphs existing on the same line. This is often used with lower level headings. It can also be used when you have text in one font that you need positioned next to text in another font and you want to save time in formatting.

  For example, you could have a *Glossary* run-in paragraph pull a *Definition* paragraph after it.

  A run-in example is shown in Figure 3–4, in front of the last paragraph. The text within the run-in is *Ridebis*. Notice that there is an end of paragraph mark after this, and before the non-bold paragraph that follows.

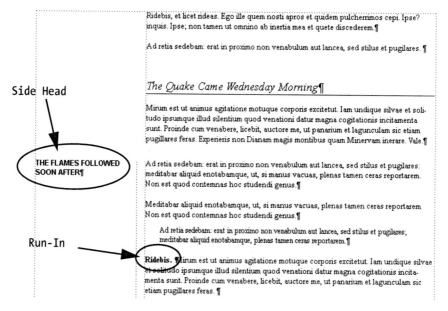

Figure 3–4.   This exhibits a document with special pagination format settings.

- *Side Head*   This setting can only be used if the page layout includes a side head area. If you have a side head page layout, setting paragraphs as *Side Head* allows them to jump into this special part of the page layout, as shown in Figure 3–4.

NOTE To add a side head area to your master pages, select a body page text frame while on the master pages . Choose *Format>Customize Layout>Customize Text Frame*. In the dialog that appears, you will see the *Room for Side Heads* option and can checkmark it, if desired.

- *Across All Columns* Paragraph formats with this setting will cause text to straddle across the page in multiple column layouts. This setting has no effect in a single column layout.

- *Across All Columns and Side Heads* Paragraph formats set to *Across All Columns and Side Heads* will cause text to straddle across the page and the side head area. This setting has no effect in layouts with no side head, nor in single column layouts.

The Paragraph Designer's Numbering properties sheet appears next. It is shown in Figure 3–5.

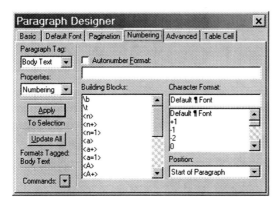

Figure 3–5. The Numbering properties sheet manages numbering formats.

Numbering in FrameMaker is very powerful. FrameMaker provides building blocks for creating as many levels of numbering as you would like. Numbering displays can be one of the following:

- bullets (round bullets, diamond bullets, and any other character that can be made by invoking a special font)

- alphabetic characters in lowercase (a, b, c, d, …) or uppercase (A, B, C, D, …)

- numbers (1, 2, 3, 5, …)

- roman numerals in lowercase (i, ii, iii, iv, …) or uppercase (I, II, III, IV, …)

- words (Note, Warning, Important …)

The numbering building blocks may seem difficult to understand at first. Basically,

- If the building block includes a plus symbol (+), then the numbering increments by one, allowing you to count from *1* to *2* to *3* and so on, from *A* to *B* to *C* and so on, or *i* to *ii* to *iii* and so on

- If the building block includes an equal sign (=) and a number, then the numbering display of that paragraph will equal that value. For example, if a paragraph is designed to use the numbering building block *<n=1>*, then the paragraph would have a *1* for its numbering. If instead the *<A=1>* is used, then the display would be an *A*. An example of the former is shown in Figure 3–6

To add special punctuation to your numbering:
\t = tab
\b = bullet
\m = em dash
\sn = en space
\sm = em space
\e = ellipse

NOTE   This numbering definition also includes a period that shows up after the number, and two \t tags. In the resulting display, FrameMaker puts in a tab in place of each \t.

Other building blocks within the numbering are <$chapnum> and <$volnum>, which allow you to set up numbering for books (sets of files). The building blocks are set up within the paragraph formats, and then additional settings are adjusted in the book window.

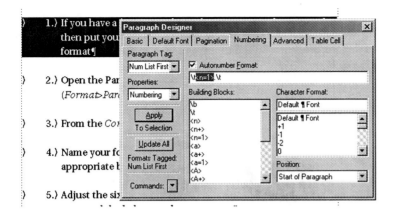

Figure 3–6.   *A paragraph using the* <n=1> *numbering building block.*

NOTE   Books are not covered in detail here, but are essential to publishing multi-chapter documents with tables of contents from all chapters. Refer to the FrameMaker online help for additional information.

The next properties sheet in the Paragraph Designer is the *Advanced* sheet, shown in Figure 3–7.

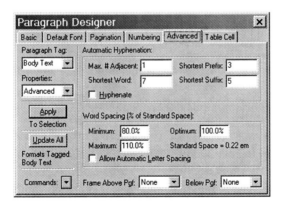

Figure 3–7.   *The Paragraph Designer's Advanced properties sheet.*

Advanced properties are fairly self descriptive. The exception may be the *Frame Above Pgf* and *Below Pgf* shown along the bottom edge. Each of these has a pop-up menu, from which the template designer can select a graphic. This is how *decorative* lines, images, and logos can consistently be placed above or below headings or other text.

Once attached to a paragraph format, the graphic will show up with every occurrence of that format.

NOTE   The images must be built into the template, too. The procedure for doing so is described in "Reference Pages" on page 57.

The Paragraph Designer's final properties sheet, Table Cell, is shown in Figure 3–8.

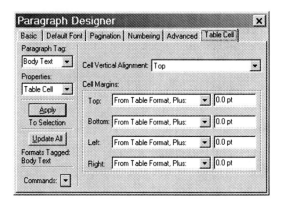

Figure 3–8.   The Paragraph Designer Table Cell properties sheet.

These properties kick in whenever text typed in a table uses the paragraph format. This is how you set text to align vertically within table cells, or to have more or less white space separating the text from the cell borders.

Also included in the Paragraph Designer are the *Apply* and *Update All* buttons. The button you click will depend on your scope— whether you want to affect a single paragraph, or all the paragraphs using a particular format.

The Apply button acts only on the paragraph in which you have your insertion point. The Apply button is used when:

- you want to change the format being used by the paragraph. Another word for this is *tagging,* as in "I am tagging this paragraph with the Heading1 format"

- you want to change settings for that single paragraph (which, by the way, produces an override)

NOTE When you adjust single paragraphs, they no longer match the property settings of other paragraphs with the same name. This is called an *override.* When output to XML, none of the override information is retained. Technically, no formatting information is retained. If you wish a paragraph to be different when XML is imported, it is best to create a special paragraph format *(with structure, especially, it is a best practice to give these different paragraphs their own style names and build their use into the structured template and EDD—for consistency of formatting).*

Obviously. But if I need to defend or justify this..

The other button—Update All—acts on all the paragraphs that use the format selected in the Paragraph Designer. This is also how you change settings of formats in the catalog. If you use the Paragraph Designer to modify the settings for a paragraph format called Heading1 and then click Update All, for example, every paragraph currently using the Heading1 style will change to match the new settings. Those settings are also used for any paragraph tagged with that format, from that point forward. Update All is used

- when you have adjusted the properties for a paragraph format and want to make sure that these changes are reflected in all paragraphs using that format

- when you want to rename a paragraph format

Now that you understand the Paragraph Designer and paragraph formats, you can follow the following directions to create a paragraph format:

1. If you have an existing paragraph format similar to the one you are about to make, press *Enter* to create an empty paragraph, place your insertion point in that paragraph, and tag it with the existing format.

2. Open the Paragraph Designer by selecting *Format>Paragraphs>Designer.*

3. Select *New Format* from the *Commands* menu.

4. Name your format in the Tag text box, and checkmark the appropriate boxes:

   Store in Catalog means that the paragraph format will be added to the list of available formats in the Paragraph Catalog and will be available to tag onto other paragraphs.

   Apply to Selection means that the paragraph format will be applied (tagged) to the paragraph in which your insertion point lies.

5. Click the *Create* button.

6. Adjust the six properties sheets as desired, clicking either *Apply* or *Update All* as you move from one sheet to the next (as long as you perform the next step, *Apply* is acceptable to use between sheets; however, the *best practice* would be to click *Update All* between sheets and avoid any chance of overrides).

7. Click *Update All* to lock in the paragraph's settings when finished.

To modify an existing format, you would follow similar steps.

1. Place your insertion point in a paragraph that is using the paragraph format you wish to modify.

2. Open the Paragraph Designer by selecting *Format>Paragraphs>Designer.*

3. Adjust the six properties sheets as desired, clicking either *Apply* or *Update All* as you move from one sheet to the next (as mentioned above, Update All is recommended).

4. Click *Update All* to lock in the paragraph's settings.

Deleting and renaming are also possible for paragraph formats. To delete, use the following process:

1. Open the Paragraph Designer by selecting *Format>Paragraphs>Designer*.

2. From the Commands menu, select *Delete Format*.

3. In the dialog box that appears, select the unwanted format and click *Delete*, and then *Done*.

NOTE   This removes the format from the catalog, but does not *untag* any text using the format. Your next step is to locate (Find) any paragraphs using the deleted format and tag them with another format.

To rename a format,

1. Place your insertion point in a paragraph that is using the paragraph format you wish to rename.

2. Open the Paragraph Designer by selecting *Format>Paragraphs>Designer*.

3. Delete the format's name in the Paragraph Tag box in the upper left corner, and type the new one.

4. Click *Update All.*

A dialog appears asking if you wish to rename the format from the old name to the new name.

5. Click *OK.*

Not only will the new format name appear in the catalog, but the old name will be removed. All paragraphs in the document that were using the format will be tagged with the new name.

Use the delete and rename options as often as you like when creating a template, but sparingly after you begin creating FrameMaker documents from your template. After you have a collection of documents, renaming or deleting causes cleanup issues.

Character Formats

Character formats, along with paragraph formats, are designed to adjust the look of your text. Character formats, however, are designed to affect small ranges of text instead of entire paragraphs. These formats can be layered on top of characters, words, or phrases within a paragraph.

Because character formats are designed for emphasizing small ranges of text, you can use them to do things like make a word bold, enlarge a character, or make a cross-reference link blue.

NOTE In a structured document, character formats can be associated with certain elements—such as a Term element—to automatically emphasize the content.

Character formats are created using the Character Designer. The Character Designer, which is used to create and modify character formats, is shown in Figure 3–9.

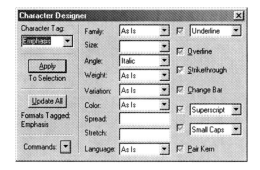

Figure 3–9.   The Character Designer controls character formatting.

While the Paragraph Designer is complex, with six properties sheets that affect everything from indents to fonts to table cell settings, the Character Designer is relatively simple. It has only one properties sheet. The single sheet of the Character Designer is an exact match to the Paragraph Designer's Default Font properties sheet.

NOTE In working with the Character Designer, it is important to understand that it has a second use. The Character Designer can also be used to verify text properties. Any time that you select text and have the Character Designer window open, it will display the settings of the selected text.

To create character formats, you can select text that you wish to tag, but this is not necessary. The following steps may be used to create a character format. To control what is adjusted, and avoid changing too much, these steps include the use of the *As Is* setting.

1. Open the Character Designer (*Format>Characters>Designer*)

2. From the Commands menu, select *Set Window to As Is*.

   This ensures that no text properties are set in the Designer.

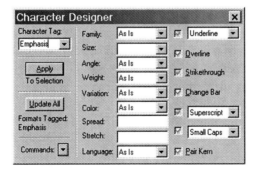

3. Adjust the settings as needed to create the character format, only changing what is neccessary and leaving everything else as is to avoid changing too much.

4. From the Commands menu, select *New Format*.

5. Name your format in the Tag text box, and checkmark the appropriate boxes.

    Store in Catalog means that the paragraph format will be added to the list of available formats (Paragraph Catalog) and will be available to tag onto other paragraphs.

    Apply to Selection means that the paragraph format will be applied (tagged) to the paragraph your insertion point is in.

6. Click the *Create* button.

The character format is now ready to use. You can apply it to text (using the Apply button or the Character Catalog). You can also access it anywhere that character formats are available through a dialog box. Character formats appear in the Paragraph Designer Numbering properties sheet, for example, and can be selected to automatically apply to numbering displays. Character formats also appear when you are creating cross-reference formats, variables, and many other parts of a template.

Master Page Layouts

As discussed in Chapter 2, you work on body pages when creating a FrameMaker document. Behind the body pages is a set of master pages. A master page (shown at left in Figure 3–10) is where you design and store the layout. The layout is made up of *background frames* (headers and footers), *body page text frames* (which you then fill on the body pages), and *graphics* (those that need to automatically appear on the page).

A body page that corresponds to a master page is shown in Figure 3-10. The background items (the text frames) that are visible on the master pages can only be edited on the master pages, therefore the frames are not visible on the body pages.

As you can see on the right in Figure 3-10, the body page only has the frame showing for the body page text frame. This is the area in which you can type when creating your documents. In a template, this area may be empty or filled with example text.

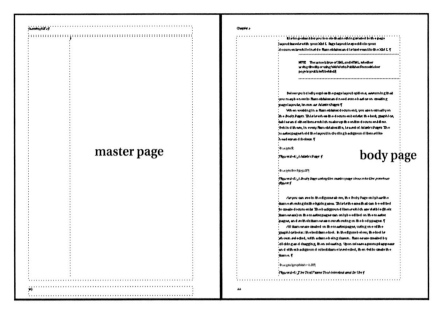

master page

body page

Figure 3–10.   A master page and corresponding body page are displayed.

NOTE   In a structured template, the body pages must be empty within the set of application files.

All background and text frames are created on the master pages using the Text Frame tool, which is one of the graphics tools. The tool is circled in Figure 3–11.

Frames are created by clicking and dragging, and then releasing. Upon release, a prompt appears, as shown in Figure 3–12.

Select either background or text frame, then click *Set* to create the frame.

Once frames are drawn on the master pages, content (your document) may be added on the body pages. The content will fit within the created frames. If you adjust the master page layout, all body pages will adjust and content will reflow.

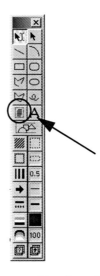

Figure 3–11. The Text Frame tool is selected.

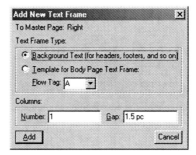

Figure 3–12. This is the prompt for frame type.

NOTE   If you create a layout on a master page with multiple body page text frames, note that these are connected automatically for you. This gives you the ability to have complex layouts.

These frames are connected in the order created, so create them in the order in which you want your text to flow.

You can have up to 100 master pages, but most likely you will only have a few. There are two default master pages: *Right* and *Left*. These should be used for your main layout, as they are the only two master pages that alternate automatically and give you a double-sided layout. Any other master pages that you want can be created with *Special>Add Master Pages*.

> **NOTE** You must be in the master page view for this menu option to be available.

You may create up to 99 custom master pages, for a total of 100 possible master pages (including Right and the optional Left). Once created, you may Apply these custom master pages using *Format > Page Layout > Master Page Usage*. In FrameMaker 7.0 (and later versions), you may set up a master page mapping table to tie the use of certain paragraphs or elements to page layouts.

> **NOTE** More information on master page mapping tables may be found in the FrameMaker online help for versions 7.0 and 7.1.

Reference Pages

Reference pages provide a place to store information to which you might want to refer from your document. They can also store setup data for FrameMaker. These include reference pages for:

- *Graphics* The reference pages hold graphics that you need to reuse. Adobe templates have default graphics, but you can add your own, such as corporate logos, lines, and icons. These graphics are then *placed* by attaching them to paragraphs in the Paragraph Designer's Advanced properties sheet's *Frame Above Pgf* and *Below Pgf* settings.

- *HTML mappings* These show up when you Save As XML, and in some Adobe templates they are there by default; they are not necessary for HTML via WebWorks Publisher.

- *XML mappings*   These only show up when you Save As XML. These mappings are not necessary for XML round trip or XML via WebWorks Publisher.

- *Comments*   These exist only if you create them. Reference pages are a good place to store comments about a template or document.

- *Generated List*   These are used by FrameMaker for tables of contents, lists of figures, and other lists.

- *Generated Index*   These are used by FrameMaker for the standard index, author index, and other index types.

- *FrameMath*   These exist only if you create them. FrameMath pages are used for custom equation characters.

- *Master Page Mapping Table*   These are only in documents when requested, and allow you to tie paragraphs and elements to master pages so that FrameMaker can adjust the page layout as you insert content (requires a manual start).

At minimum when creating a template, you will want to check your template to see what reference pages have been placed there by FrameMaker. Remove those that you do not need, such as the HTML Mapping Table pages. This will keep your template clean and easier to maintain.

One of the more common uses of reference pages is to store frequently used graphics. Reference page graphics can be lines, images, and logos (see Figure 3–13). These graphics can be consistently placed with headings or other text. Once attached to a paragraph format, the graphic will show up with every occurrence of that format.

In a new FrameMaker document (*New>Document>Portrait*), go to *View>Reference Pages* and you will see a page similar to that in Figure 3-13. It includes several graphic frames containing lines. These lines can be attached to paragraph formats so that lines appear automatically whenever a format is used. To attach one of the existing lines to a paragraph,

1. Notice the Single Line graphic if you are still on the reference pages.

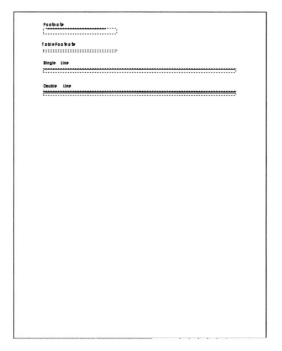

Figure 3–13.   A reference page is displayed with default graphics showing.

2. Return to the body page view by selecting *View>Body Pages.*

3. Place your insertion point in a paragraph that is using the format to which you want to attach the graphic; for example, Heading1.

4. Open the Paragraph Designer.

5. In the Advanced properties sheet, use the pop-ups next to *Frame Above Pgf* and *Below Pgf* to select the Single Line graphic.

6. Click *Update All.*

You should immediately see the graphic attached above and below paragraphs tagged with the Heading 1 paragraph format.

If you wish to create a new graphic,

1. Select *View>Reference Pages* and locate the page with graphics already on it (such as Single Line).

2. On the Tools palette, click the Graphic Frame tool.

3. Draw a frame on the reference page by clicking the left mouse button and holding it down as you drag to the desired frame size (avoid overlapping other items on the page).

NOTE   Do not worry about aligning the frame with other frames on the page. FrameMaker will align the graphic frame edge to the left edge of your body page text frame when attaching the graphic above/below paragraphs.

4. Release the left mouse button once your frame is the size you want it to be. Do not make it too large, as this will cause too much white space to appear in the document.

The Frame Name dialog box appears.

NOTE   You can use the *Graphics>Object Properties* settings to move graphics against the top/left edges of the frame, among other settings. This gives you more control over the white space around each graphic's edges.

5. Type a name for the frame in the text box, and click *Set*.

6. Put a graphic in the frame and, if necessary, adjust the frame's size and width.

7. (OPTIONAL) Using the Text Line tool in the Tools palette, type the frame's name above the frame.

Your graphic is now ready to attach to paragraph formats. To do this, use the instructions on page 59 for attaching the Single Line graphic to the Heading1 paragraph format.

Table Formats

FrameMaker allows you to have many tables in your documents. Tables can be small—just a single cell—or they can be very large and spread across many pages. Formatting for tables is controlled by table formats. Table formats are created using the third of our FrameMaker designers—the Table Designer. The Table Designer's Basic properties sheet is shown in Figure 3–14.

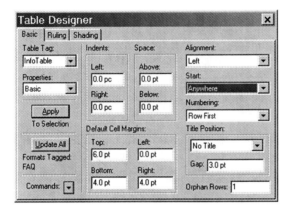

Figure 3–14.   The Table Designer Basic properties sheet is displayed.

The Ruling properties sheet is shown in Figure 3–15.
The Shading properties sheet is shown in Figure 3–16.

To create a table format,

1. Put your insertion point in your text frame, click *Table > Insert Table*, select one of the available formats, type values for the columns and rows, and then click *Insert* to insert a table.

2. Adjust the table to the size you would like.   how?

3. Open the Table Designer (*Table>Table Designer*).

4. Select *New Format* from the Commands menu.

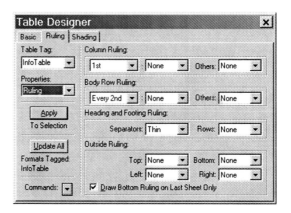

Figure 3–15. The Table Designer Ruling properties sheet is displayed.

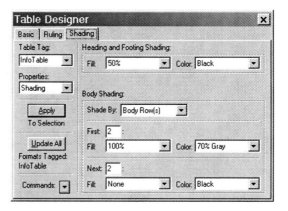

Figure 3–16. The Table Designer Shading properties sheet controls shading within tables.

5. Give your table a tag and check Apply to Selection (best practice).

6. Adjust the three properties sheets as needed.

7. Set up your sample table to look the way that you want and use the desired formatting. Setting up the example is important because FrameMaker picks up settings from the table in addition to the settings it has from the three properties sheets. These extra settings include the following:

• Different paragraph formats applied in each cell (including use of different formats between columns)

- Heading/Footing row paragraph formats (can be different between the heading and footing rows)

- Column widths of the individual columns

8. While still in the table, click *Update All* to lock in both the properties in the Table Designer and the properties of your sample table.

Variable Definitions

Variables are used to automate text displays and updates. There are two types of variables—system and user.

- *System variables* are managed by FrameMaker. Their definitions are a combination of FrameMaker building blocks and character formats.

- *User variables* are managed by template designers. Their definitions are strictly text plus character formats.

The best way to explain what each is, and what variables do, is with examples. All variables are defined and managed through the *Special>Variables* dialog box. This has buttons for *Edit Variable* to modify existing variables, and *Create Variable* to create user variables *(system variables cannot be created).*

Example 1: CompanyName User Variable

Your company's name needs to appear throughout your documents. You define a user variable and give it a name, such as *CompanyName*. You define it by typing in your company's name. Then, each time the company name is needed in the text, you insert the variable and the company's name appears.

Example 2: ProductName User Variable ~~Interesting Example~~

You want to include a product name in a text file that is going to be used as a text inset (one FrameMaker file imported *by reference* into another) for several product manuals. You want to have the product name change depending on into which manual you insert the text inset file. You set up a *ProductName* user variable in the template for use in creating each manual. Then, whenever the text inset file is used, the displayed name changes to whatever ProductName is defined to be in each manual. This allows you to write something once but use it multiple times. You don't have to change the text, because it changes on its own in each context.

Example 3: Current Date System Variable

You need the current date displayed on a letter transmitting a proposal. To be more precise, you want the date to update automatically each day. You insert the *CurrentDate* system variable and FrameMaker inserts the date. Each day FrameMaker updates it without you doing anything else.

Example 4: Running H/F System Variables

In your page layout, you want the heading (or footing) text to reflect the content on each page. So, you set up a system variable for a *running* (ever-updating) header. FrameMaker pulls content from each page—including text and attribute values—to produce each heading, and updates automatically if you change the document. FrameMaker also adjusts the header or footer as you move from one chapter to the next, or from section to section.

FrameMaker version 6.0 and later provides twelve Running H/F variables.

Cross-Reference Formats

FrameMaker cross-references are created through a dialog box. In any open document, you can select *Special>Cross-Reference* and FrameMaker will let you point to any part of a document. You can then create a link to it. The cross-reference text appears. It also updates as you edit the document, ensuring the correct reference text appears in your printed documents regardless of how many times you revise the document.

All cross-references become links when you output to HTML, PDF, and other formats. Cross-references also retain their linked information in XML as attributes.

Conditional Text Settings

FrameMaker's conditional text feature allows you to set up a document so that some content may be shown or hidden, allowing you to print multiple documents from a single file or book.

Conditions are not always needed in a template. The purpose of conditions is to allow you to produce multiple documents from a single file or book. To make this work, you mark text with named conditions. Then, when you want to view a document, you Show text that is needed and Hide text that is not. For example, a book might be published in US English and UK English. Because there are subtle changes in spelling, terms, and phrases, the content is almost the same between the two versions of the book. You could mark certain characters and words with conditions, then use the Show/Hide to view the document content in each language. The end result is one set of files that produces two books. The savings in terms of writing, comparing, and editing can be significant.

Conditions work to a certain degree in FrameMaker 7.0, but only in the structured FrameMaker document and not in the XML. FrameMaker 7.1, however, has the ability to retain conditions on export to XML through process instructions. *And Dita handles Conditional text in a nother way, thru the structure.*

Creating a Simple Template

In this section, you can follow the instructions to make a template for a cookbook—at least the important parts of one. Refer to earlier descriptions in this chapter if you are not sure what parts make up a template.

To begin this new template, use the following instructions to start a new document:

1. Click *File>New>Document.*

2. When the New dialog box appears, select *Portrait.*

3. Save this file as *mycookbook.fm* in any folder.

Now that you have the beginnings of a document, follow the instructions in the upcoming sections. They will help you to create a simple, custom template. When you finish the instructions provided here, your finished template will produce documents that look something like Figure 3–17.

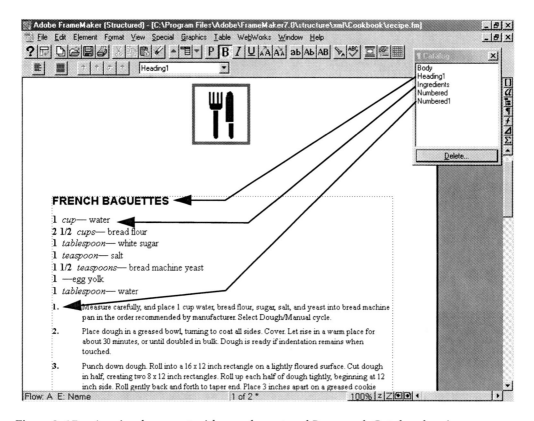

Figure 3–17. A recipe document with page layout and Paragraph Catalog showing.

Modifying, Creating, and Deleting Paragraph Formats

Several paragraph formats are required to create the recipes displayed in the sample documents. This section shows you how to define the look of four paragraph formats: Heading1, Numbered1, Numbered, and Body. It also walks you through the creation of an Ingredients paragraph format.

NOTE The additional paragraphs in the template are there to provide options for formatting other portions of the cookbook. The exercises focus on the formatting needed by the recipe.

When you build your own templates, do not create more formats than you need.

FrameMaker starts with a short list of paragraph formats in the document that we used. This list is shown in Figure 3–18.

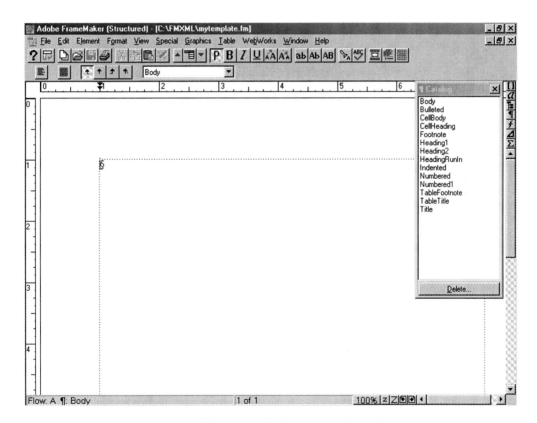

Figure 3–18. A new document exhibits its default Paragraph Catalog entries.

Before creating formats, you should delete any unwanted formats from the catalog. Leave the Body, Heading1, Numbered1, and Numbered paragraphs and delete the rest. To delete formats,

1. Open the paragraph catalog by clicking the *Paragraph Catalog* button (¶) in the upper right corner of your document window.

2. When the catalog opens, click the *Delete* button at the bottom.

   The following Delete Formats from Catalog dialog box appears.

3. Select the first tag that you want to delete (for example, Bulleted), and click *Delete*.

4. Repeat for all the tags except those you were instructed to keep. These four are shown in the following graphic.

5. After deleting the unwanted formats, click *Done.*

   The Paragraph Catalog now shows only the four necessary formats, as seen in the following graphic.

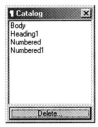

6. Save your template file.

Now that you have the Paragraph Catalog pared down, you need to add the new format called Ingredients. Before creating a new paragraph format, put your insertion point in a paragraph that has an appearance (definition) similar to what you want. This allows you to have those settings automatically used in the new format, which should save you time in redefining them.

In the document that you created, there is not yet any text. Type the word **Ingredients** as a placeholder on the first line and make sure that the text is tagged with the Body paragraph format. Since Body is similar to Ingredients, you can use Body as a starting point in creating your new paragraph format. To accomplish this, follow these steps:

1. Open the Paragraph Designer (*Format>Paragraphs>Designer*).

2. From the Commands menu, select *New Format.*

3. Type **Ingredients** in the Tag text box, and check Store in Catalog and Apply To Selection.

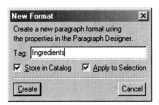

4. In the Paragraph Designer, go to the Default Font properties sheets and change the Weight to Bold.

5. Click *Update All* to make that change and lock in the Ingredients paragraph definition.

    That is the only change to be made in this example. Feel free to experiment with the properties and adjust the look and behavior of Ingredients.

You now have the minimum paragraph formats to proceed with your document. Using the paragraph tags you have created, type some sample recipe text similar to that shown in Figure 3–19. You need only enter the minimum text to test your paragraph formats.

Sample Heading1

Ingredients Format
1. Step using Numbered1.
2. Step using Numbered.
Total preparation time: XX minutes (Body format)

Figure 3–19.   Here is some sample text to type in your recipe template.

For now, leave these paragraphs looking the way that they do. Once you complete the exercises, you might go back and play with the paragraph formats a bit to make them look better and adjust spacing.

Creating Character Formats

Character formats are used to change ranges of text—making a word bold, for example. Follow the next set of steps to create a Bold character format using the Character Designer.

To make this format and apply it to the *Total preparation time* sample text in your template, select that sample text. This is not a requirement, but it will serve to give you an example with which to test your formatting. The format can be automatically applied (as demonstrated in the following steps) and your text range will change to bold text.

1. Open the Character Designer
   (*Format>Characters>Designer*).

2. From the Commands menu, select *Set Window to As Is.*

   Using As Is allows you to clear the value present in the Character Designer so that you can set just the bold attribute. Otherwise, you might create a format that would adjust more than you want it to adjust.

3. Click the *Weight* popup and select *Bold* (if Bold is not available, it could mean that the document is using a font that does not allow bolded text. Try changing the font family until Bold becomes available).

4. From the Commands menu, select *New Format.*

5. Name the format in the Tag text box, and check both boxes.

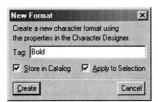

6. Click *Update All* to lock in the character format's settings.

You now have bolded text in your document using the Bold character format. It is now available in the Character Catalog and can be used on other text.

add to template as needed

✳ Creating Cross-Reference Formats

Anything that is tagged can be referenced within a FrameMaker document. In structured documents, any item you wish to refer to must have a special attribute.

Use the following steps to create a cross-reference from one step to another for more information. Using cross-references in FrameMaker is an important part of your online publishing because the cross-reference becomes a hyperlink when output for online delivery.

1. Select *Special > Cross Reference.*

    The Cross-Reference dialog box appears.

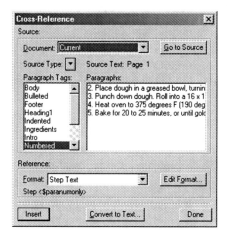

    In the Source portion of this dialog box, link to a specific source (the item to which you wish to refer).

    In the Reference portion, select and create formats.

2. To create a format, click *Edit Format.*

    The Edit Cross-Reference Format dialog box appears.

3. In the Name area, type a name for your cross-reference. For example, use Step Text.

4. In Definition, use building blocks, character formats, and punctuation to make example formats. For example, use

```
Step <$paranumonly>
```

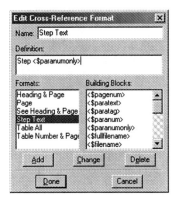

5. Click Add to add the format, and then Done to leave the dialog box.

6. Save your template.

Your cookbook template now has a cross reference format that you may use to refer to a procedure step.

Once the format is created, you can use it to create cross references within the document or to other documents. Any document that is open can be referred to, and documents must be open so that FrameMaker can add *link* information in the referenced paragraph.

There are a few other tips on working with cross-references:

- Use the non-breaking space \ (slash-space) instead of a regular space when defining your cross-references. This allows your cross references to wrap without awkward breaks—such as between pages and a following page number.

- Use \' and \' to produce curly quotes. Typing straight quotes in your cross-reference formats will produce straight quotes in your cross-references.

- Use bold, italic, and other formatting by creating character formats that you can include in the cross-reference formats.

- Begin all cross-reference format definitions with the *Default Para Font* building block. This makes it possible to copy/paste cross-references and avoid picking up extra text formatting, especially when copying and pasting into paragraphs of different font properties.

NOTE This same tip can be applied to variables. Starting definitions of user variables with Default Para Font makes it easy to copy/paste them for reuse. If you do not use this setting, then *pasted variables* may not match the text into which they are pasted.

Modifying and Adding Master Pages

With the text formats done, it is now time to create the master pages for your cookbook. To make adjustments, select *View>Master Pages* to go to the master pages.

Because this document started as a new portrait document, there is one master page—Right. The default for portrait documents is to be single sided. After you get the Right page set up, the instructions will explain how to change the document to be double sided.

On the Right master page, you can see a large frame taking up most of the page. This is a template for a body page text frame. When you are on the body pages of a document, this is the text frame in which you create your document.

If you place your insertion point inside this frame, you will see `Flow: A ¶ Body Text` along the status bar (lower left corner of your document window). The flow is all of the frames connected together. On the body pages, this allows you to have many pages of a document connected, allowing text to flow from one page to the next while you type. Most documents are just one flow, and Flow A is the default.

NOTE If you plan to export to XML, keep all of your content in one connected flow. The Save As XML command only sends out your primary flow, and content in other flows is ignored.

Move your insertion point into the thin frame near the top of the page. This is an area you can use for your page header. It is a background frame, designed to be editable only on the master pages. Whatever is typed in this frame will appear at the top of every body page that uses this master page.

With your insertion point still inside the header background frame, type *My Sample Cookbook*, followed by a space.

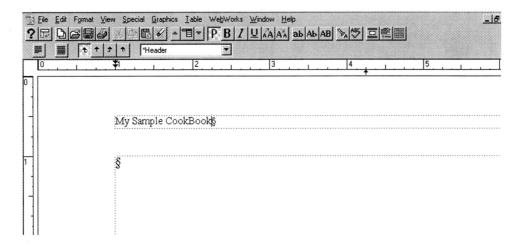

Figure 3–20.   This shows text being entered in the master page header.

By default, the text in the header frame is using a Header paragraph tag, although this format does not have a matching definition in the Paragraph Catalog (which is why an asterisk appears in front of its name). Select the text (leaving the space not selected) and apply the Bold character format. Your header text should now be bold.

NOTE   The purpose of leaving a space at the end of the paragraph is to have a cushion to keep the character format from running all the way to the end of paragraph mark. If a character tag is applied on an entire paragraph, it can sometimes cause an asterisk to appear—as if there is an override on the format. The space keeps the asterisk from appearing.

Hit the Tab key twice to move to the right edge of the frame. Type **Page** followed by a space. From the *Special>Variable* dialog box, insert the *Current Page Number* variable, followed by a space, the word *of*, and another space. Go to *Special>Variable* again and insert the Page Count variable. This will automatically display the page number and total page count in the header.

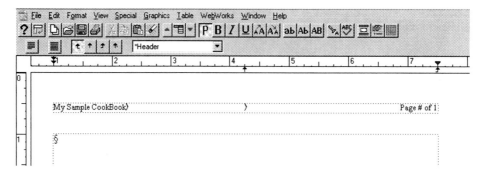

Figure 3–21.   A look at the finished header.

Open the graphics tools palette by clicking the 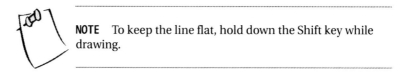 button along the right edge of your document window.

Select the Line tool, which is the second button down on the left side. Draw a line underneath the header background frame from edge to edge. To draw the line, click down at one edge of the frame and hold the mouse button down until it reaches the other edge. Then, release the mouse button to complete the line.

NOTE   To keep the line flat, hold down the Shift key while drawing.

Add the footer information in the small frame at the bottom of the Right master page using the following instructions:

1. Place your insertion point inside the text frame.

    Notice that the paragraph format is Footer on the status bar. It has an asterisk in front of its name because Footer is not in the Paragraph Catalog. Since it is only used on the master pages, it does not need to be listed in the catalog where those creating the document body might inadvertently use it.

2. Click *Tab* once to move to the center of the frame.

3. Type **Copyright 2003** in the frame.

4. Save your file.

Creating a Double-sided Document

To change your document to double sided, select *Format>Page Layout>Pagination.* The Pagination dialog box appears. This is shown in Figure 3–22.

Figure 3–22.   Use the Pagination dialog box to select double- or single-sided pages.

Select *Double Sided.* Leave the 1st Page Side set to *Right,* so that the first page in your file will be considered a right-hand page and the left/right will alternate from there. You might also set Before Saving & Printing to *Make Page Count Even.* This lets FrameMaker force a blank left page when it is needed to complete your double-sided document. It also allows FrameMaker to remove extra empty pages if you delete content.

Once you click the *Set* button, your document will become double sided. A Left master page will appear alongside the Right master page. Because you set up your Right master page in advance, the Left page should automatically come in with a layout that mirrors the Right page.

To make an additional master page for the first page of the chapter, follow these steps:

1. Select *Special > Add Master Page.*

2. For the Name, type **First**, then click Add

   Make sure that the Right page is selected for Copy from Master Page.

3. Once the page is created, delete the header.

4. Select the body page text frame (the typing area) by holding down *Control* and clicking over the frame.

   Small black handles should appear around the edge of the selected frame.

5. Resize the text frame using the top resize box, so that the frame top is at the 2.5" mark on the ruler.

6. From the *Symbols.fm* file in FrameMaker's clipart folder, select the fork and spoon image. Copy to place it on the clipboard.

7. Go to the First master page and paste the graphic, then position it. You may use *Graphics>Object Properties* and *Graphics>Align* to adjust or center it.

8. Click Save.

In the real world, you will probably make additional master pages for the front matter, index, and other special pages of your cookbook. In this example, however, the directions end with Right, Left, and First master pages.

NOTE The master page name *First* is used in this example specifically because Adobe uses this name in most of their sample templates—so you may easily import master pages from another sample template, if desired. The name *First* does not, however, have any special meaning and can easily be substituted for ChapterStart, RightNoHeader, or any other name. It is recommended that you use names that will make sense to you.

Adjusting Document Properties

Document properties such as the Zoom and View options should be set at the very end as you save your template. Determine what Zoom percentage should be the default each time your template is opened, and set the Zoom using the ‖160%‖z‖Z‖ buttons at the bottom of your document window.

View options can be set at the start of your template but should be checked at the end because items like Borders and Text Symbols will change if you adjust them while you work. In the View Options dialog box—opened by clicking *View>Options*—you set the measurement units that will be used by all the FrameMaker dialog boxes while you are in the template and any document using the template. This dialog box is shown in Figure 3–23.

The Display section at the bottom shows items like the Borders and Text Symbols that can be turned on or off. These can be set here, and can be adjusted directly on the View menu. The exception is Graphics, which is only available here and when working in a FrameMaker book.

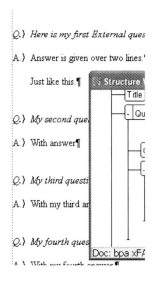

Figure 3–23.   The View Options dialog box allows measurement unit options to be set.

Additional document properties are adjusted through the *Format>Document* menu. Go into each item under the Document menu and set it as desired for your files. If you plan to create a cookbook, you should take the time to go into *Format>Document>Numbering* and set numbering for Chapter, Page, and Paragraph to their *Continue Numbering* choices. One page of the Numbering Properties dialog box is shown in Figure 3–24.   NO it isn't

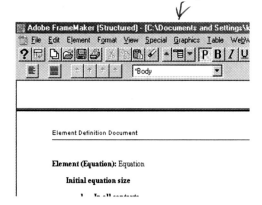

Figure 3–24.   The Numbering Properties dialog box is where numbering features are set.

Also lumped into document properties are things like custom markers. If you plan to create online help or HTML/XML with WebWorks Publisher, you might take a moment to create custom Filename markers, as shown in the following instructions:

1. Select *Special>Markers.*

   The Marker dialog box appears.

2. From the Marker Type pop-up menu, select *Edit* so that you can open the next dialog box to create a custom marker.

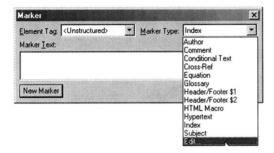

3. Remove the *CustomMarkerType* that appears and type **Filename** as the new marker type.

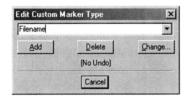

   Make sure that the "F" is capitalized. Like everything else in FrameMaker, marker names are case sensitive. To work seamlessly with WebWorks, use the capital letter and exact name.

4. Click *Add.*

5. Click *Done.*

The custom marker type is now a part of your document and you can close the Marker dialog box.

Save your template. It is now ready to use to create basic recipe documents.

Reviewing the Import Formats Feature

One of the strengths of FrameMaker is that it lets you create templates that have all the information needed to create your documents. You can then use this to create all new documents and everything will match. You are able to easily create consistent documents because the formats are predefined. This eliminates any *formatting on the fly* that might be done with word-processing tools.

Once you have a template, you can use it to adjust new documents or existing documents. You can also use it on documents that have been imported from other tools like MSWord and WordPerfect.

The following instructions step you through the process of importing formats from a template into a document:

1. Open the template that has the formats.

2. Open the document into which the formats need to be imported. Stay in this document.

3. Click *File>Import>Formats*.

   The Import Formats dialog box will appear.

4. At the top of the Import Formats dialog box, click the pop-up menu next to Import From Document and choose your template (only open documents are listed in the pop-up menu, so if your template was closed it cannot be selected).

NOTE Before importing a template into a document, it is a *best practice* to remove the existing formats from the document's catalog. This allows you to then repopulate the catalog with the template's formats. Otherwise, you may end up with formats in the catalog that are not in the template, causing confusion and possible tagging errors during layout.

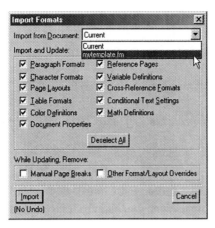

5. Choose the formats that you want to import.

6. If you want to remove manual page breaks and clean up formatting overrides, choose those options.

7. Once you have chosen the desired items, click the *Import* button at the bottom of the dialog box.

   The active document now has the formats imported from the template, and you can begin authoring or editing the document as needed.

8. Close your template without saving.

When an import is done, the formatting is imported and adjusted by name. Any formats in the document with the same name as in the template will be redefined as specified in the template. Formats that do not exist in the document, but are in the template, will be added to the document's catalog. Formats in the document but not in the template will not be touched. So, the import is more of an *adjust and add* for formats than a *match to template* sync of formats.

NOTE Any time you adjust your documents, return to the template to make the changes also. If you make changes here and there in different documents, you will lose consistency and your template will be less effective in controlling your formatting.

Importing formats can also be done on an entire FrameMaker book. The following steps are slightly modified from those for importing formats into a single document:

1. Open the template that has the formats.

2. Open the book file.

   The book window appears.

3. In the book window, use Control-click or Shift-click to select the files into which you want to import formats.

4. Click *File>Import>Formats*.

   The Import Formats dialog box appears.

5. At the top of the Import Formats dialog box, click the pop-up menu next to Import From Document and choose your template.

6. Choose the formats that you want to import.

   At the book level, take care when importing document properties. This can adversely affect the numbering setup for your book. Also take care with importing variables if you have adjusted variable definitions to be chapter/file specific.

7. If you want to remove manual page breaks and clean up formatting overrides, choose those options.

8. Once you have chosen the desired items, click the *Import* button at the bottom of the dialog box.

   The files you selected in the book now have the formats imported from the template and you can begin authoring or editing as needed.

9. Close the template without saving.

Anytime you modify your template, import the formats into your documents again. This can be done at any point to clean up a document.

NOTE You can also import formats and choose Current from the Import From Document pop-up menu. This forces a document to import into itself and is a quick way to clean up overrides or remove manual page breaks. Just choose those options and all of the formats.

Moving Forward (Creating Your Own Template)

Now that you have a rudimentary idea of what is in a template, you can begin planning your own template. You will need to create the minimum parts discussed so far in this chapter, and will likely need to adjust some of the other formats mentioned in "Reviewing a FrameMaker Document and Its Formats" on page 39.

Be sure to perform document analysis and determine in advance what you want your template to contain. That framework is necessary before you can sit down and begin creating your template. Skipping that step might also mean long rounds of editing once you begin using your template and noticing the holes in the design.

Before beginning a template, you need to know what you want to do with that template. Once you know what you want your document to look like, use the formatting capabilities in FrameMaker to make it happen.

In the real world, how do you turn your document plan into a FrameMaker template? Here are a few tips:

- Work with the big picture in mind

- Name your formats carefully

- Create your template efficiently

NOTE Because the space available in this book for formatting allowed for just enough information to get you started, it is recommended that you check out additional FrameMaker template resources (see Chapter 15). You might also refer to FrameMaker online help or the manual that you received with your FrameMaker software CD.

Summary

FrameMaker has very powerful formatting capabilities. You may adjust everything from page layout to text formatting to custom viewing to output settings.

With advance planning and an understanding of how FrameMaker works, you have the ability to perform round tripping of your XML plus produce documents in any printed and online format that you need.

CHAPTER 4

Reviewing the FrameMaker Connection to XML

IN THIS CHAPTER, we review the importing and exporting of XML—with and without an Application setup to automate your XML round trip. This should give you an understanding of the FrameMaker–XML dynamic.

Reviewing XML Round Trip in FrameMaker 7.0

A FrameMaker round-trip Application helps you ensure that the resulting XML files are valid. This section deals with valid XML and therefore uses structured documents. Saving a structured document as XML gives you elements with multi-level hierarchy and allows validation.

Technically, an unstructured FrameMaker document could produce valid XML if you had a DTD with a very flat hierarchical structure.

NOTE   This section describes behaviors specific to FrameMaker 7.0. For information on FrameMaker 7.1's process for round-trip XML, see "Reviewing XML Round Trip in FrameMaker 7.1" on page 94.

Working without an XML Application

It is important for you to know what FrameMaker does out-of-the-box, and then learn what additional set-up steps you might need to take to perform round tripping of your XML. In this section, you will examine what happens to XML when no Application is used to show what FrameMaker does initially.

To reiterate from the terminology section, an XML Application allows you to do exporting and importing (round trip) of XML. In FrameMaker, specifically, this is Save As XML (export) and Open XML (import).[1] The next two sections describe these actions.

Exporting XML

One part of the round trip is the XML export, accomplished using (*File>Save As>*choose *XML*). Save As XML may be done from regular, unstructured FrameMaker documents or from structured FrameMaker documents. The round trip only really works well for structured documents.

Take an example structured document such as the one shown in Figure 4–1, and *SaveAs XML*.

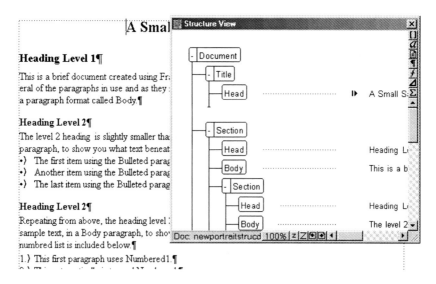

Figure 4–1. *This is a simple structured FrameMaker document with displayed Structure View.*

---

1. You can also perform *File>Import* of an XML fragment.

NOTE   In FrameMaker 7.0, if you *File>Save* the structured FrameMaker document created from the opened XML, it will save a FrameMaker file; however, in FrameMaker 7.1 the file is instead saved to XML. No FrameMaker-format file is saved unless you specifically perform a *File>Save As*.

What you are seeing in Figure 4–1 is the document view of a small FrameMaker document (on the left), with its corresponding Structure View (on the right).

Notice the Structure View and elements in the tree view of the structure (Document, Section, and so forth). The resulting XML has the same structure and content as the FrameMaker structured document. The XML document, however, has no formatting, as seen in Figure 4–2. This is normal, as XML does not include formatting! The structural element names (Document, Section, and so forth) match those of the original FrameMaker structured document.

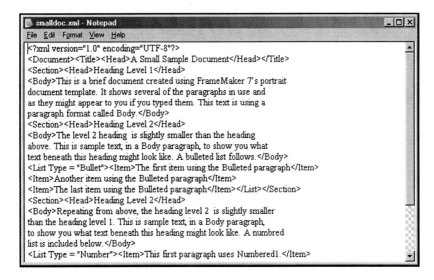

Figure 4–2.   XML document displayed in Notepad has no formatting.

Another way to look at this same document would be through a Web browser, such as Microsoft® Internet Explorer®, as shown in Figure 4-3. Viewed through Internet Explorer, you will see colored tags and collapse/expand controls. You see XML presented this way in Internet Explorer because of that browser's built-in style sheet.

```
<?xml version="1.0" encoding="UTF-8" ?>
<Document>
  <Title>
    <Head>A Small Sample Document</Head>
  </Title>
  <Section>
    <Head>Heading Level 1</Head>
    <Body>This is a brief document created using FrameMaker 7's portrait document
      template. It shows several of the paragraphs in use and as they might appear to
      you if you typed them. This text is using a paragraph format called Body.</Body>
    <Section>
      <Head>Heading Level 2</Head>
      <Body>The level 2 heading is slightly smaller than the heading above. This is
        sample text, in a Body paragraph, to show you what text beneath this
        heading might look like. A bulleted list follows.</Body>
      <List Type="Bullet">
        <Item>The first item using the Bulleted paragraph</Item>
        <Item>Another item using the Bulleted paragraph</Item>
        <Item>The last item using the Bulleted paragraph</Item>
      </List>
    </Section>
  </Section>
  <Section>
    <Head>Heading Level 2</Head>
    <Body>Repeating from above, the heading level 2 is slightly smaller than the
      heading level 1. This is sample text, in a Body paragraph, to show you what
      text beneath this heading might look like. A numbred list is included
      below.</Body>
```

Figure 4–3.   An XML document in Microsoft Internet Explorer displays familiar tags.

The XML in Figure 4–3 has no proprietary formatting added—FrameMaker outputs clean XML—and may easily be placed in an XML database or retrieval system. The XML may also be shared across your enterprise and opened in Notepad, GoLive®, and other XML-capable tools.

With no Application, no changes are made to the structure upon exporting. Therefore, for example, all elements with capitalized names have capitalized names in the XML. While not necessarily a problem, it may be desirable to remove the case or adjust element names or structure when sending content to XML. This is a change that may be built into an Application—specifically, in a Read/Write Rules file that is made part of the Application.

In the next section, you review XML moving in the other direction—importing it.

Importing XML

Part of working with XML and FrameMaker is importing XML into FrameMaker (*File>Open*). This creates a structured FrameMaker document—although if you do not use an Application, then the results may not be pretty. In the following example, we look at one resulting document.

An XML document instance may be opened by clicking *File>Open*, browsing to select the XML file, and opening it. Upon opening, several dialog boxes may appear, such as:

and then perhaps:

The first dialog box gives you an opportunity to select an Application. No Application is selected.

The second dialog box comes up because FrameMaker cannot associate a DTD with the XML file, as that is one of the things an Application could do. Selecting No Application means it cannot reach the DTD.

NOTE Although not covered in these steps, if you create XML and include a DOCTYPE, you may get it to access the DTD without an Application. We do not cover this here, as a best practice is to set up an Application. This is covered later in the book (see Chapter 14).

The tags (elements) used in the XML document are used by FrameMaker. To see the resulting document's structure, either open the Structure View window (by clicking the button at the document window's top-right edge) or turn on *Element Boundaries as Tags* from the View menu.

Once the XML file is opened in FrameMaker, you can move through it the same way that you would move through any structured FrameMaker document. Its structure is the same as the original structured document from which it was exported, which was shown previously in Figure 4–1. In Figure 4–4, you can see the unformatted FrameMaker document and corresponding Structure View.

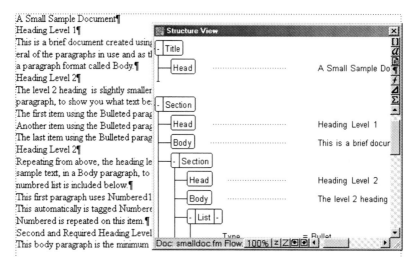

Figure 4–4. Structured FrameMaker documents created by the XML import contain the proper structure but no formatting.

Looking at the unformatted document, you might wonder how such a plain document might be useful. The truth is that it may not be useful without formatting. You wouldn't want to publish this to paper or PDF now, would you? Therefore, your round-trip Application should be set up and include a formatting component (that basically tells FrameMaker to access a template and apply its formatting to the content). If you do not do this, you will always get the plain version and need to import from the template to get files formatted—a process you must go through every time you open one of your XML documents in FrameMaker! Save yourself the trouble by using an Application.

In the section that follows, you will see how an Application improves the look of your XML by making it possible to return it to its original, fully-formatted state while still producing unformatted XML output.

Working with an Application (Round Trip)

As seen in "Importing XML" on page 90, the XML with no Application came into FrameMaker unformatted. Ugly, isn't it? To make the round trip work, you often need more than just XML and FrameMaker. You need a FrameMaker XML Application. This saves you from having to do hand-importing or accidentally distributing an unformatted document. Allow FrameMaker to help you put your best foot forward.

Exporting XML

When you use an XML Application to Save As XML (*File>Save As*>choose *XML*), then the XML will be written according to the structure and any adjustments made that are part of the Application (such as the Read/Write Rules adjustments mentioned earlier). Extra information, like a DOCTYPE or a style sheet reference, can also be added to the XML. In the *simpledoc* Application shown later, for example, a DTD is added to an Application and the XML file changes to include:

```
<!DOCTYPE document SYSTEM "sd.dtd">
```

The full filepath to the DTD can be included by FrameMaker.

Importing XML

Importing XML into FrameMaker (*File>Open*) using an Application allows you to access the template and have a formatted document right away. No formatting is lost in the transition.

There was no formatting in the sample document originally opened in Figure 4–4. If an Application is selected, as shown in Figure 4–5, then the resulting structured document will be formatted.

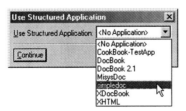

Figure 4–5.   Select simpledoc *as your structured Application.*

Once the XML Application is selected, the document should open and automatically be formatted by FrameMaker—following the instructions that the template designer placed in the Application. The simple document shown previously, therefore, would return to its original state, appearing as it did in Figure 4–1 (before being saved as XML).

How do you get from no Application to an Application? You build one. This is just one of the tools you prepare when you develop your FrameMaker structured template. You will read more about XML Applications in Chapter 11.

Reviewing XML Round Trip in FrameMaker 7.1

If you are working in structured FrameMaker 7.0 (*with* or *without* an Application) and save the XML file in FrameMaker, you will be prompted for an *.fm* filename and will save the file in FrameMaker format.

If, however, you are working in structured FrameMaker 7.1 (*with* or *without* an Application) it will Save As XML automatically—prompting you for the structured Application name immediately (unless the structured Application name has already been set for the file).

This behavior difference in FrameMaker 7.1 is because a file opened as an XML file in FrameMaker 7.1 is designed to save back into XML—no FrameMaker formatted file is saved. Take a look at the screen shot in Figure 4–6, which shows the *.xml* extension on the name, even though the file is open in FrameMaker and has been saved in FrameMaker.

 NOTE   The Save button on the QuickAccess bar continues to show that the file needs to be saved, even though it has been saved as XML. That is apparently by design.

If you do want to save a FrameMaker 7.1 file, you must perform a Save As and select **Document 7.0 (**.fm*)** or a similar **.fm* choice.

When Saving As a FrameMaker document, be sure to change the file extension from *.xml* to *.fm*—otherwise, you may get the error message shown in Figure 4–7.

Once you provide a filename with an extension other than *.xml*, FrameMaker 7.1 will allow you to save the file.

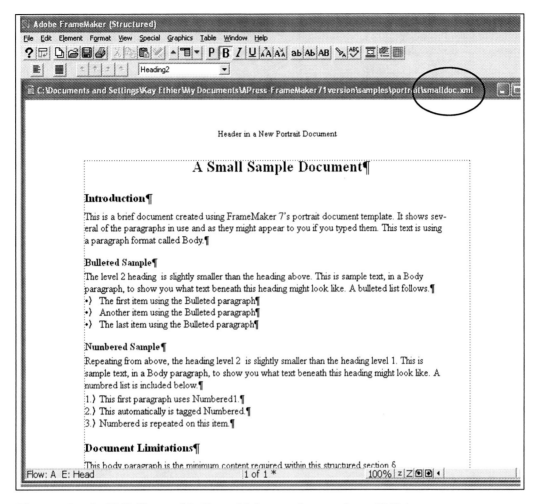

Figure 4–6. An XML file saved in FrameMaker continues to be an XML instance (smalldoc.xml).

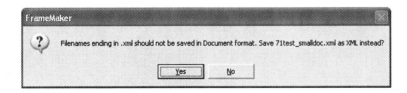

Figure 4–7. Saving As a FrameMaker document without changing the XML extension will result in this error message.

Summary

FrameMaker 7.x imports and exports XML. While the importing and exporting procedures are easy—and produce real, non-proprietary XML—adjustments and additional setup are sometimes needed to take full advantage of FrameMaker's powerful formatting capabilities.

Round-trip XML within FrameMaker 7.0 requires specific Save As operations, whereas this has been automated in FrameMaker 7.1 to Save As XML when Save is selected.

CHAPTER 5

Reviewing Multichannel Publishing Output Options

IN THIS CHAPTER, you will discover the potential outputs from your FrameMaker documents.

Using FrameMaker for Paper Document Publishing

FrameMaker was designed to be a publishing tool. It allows users to control text, graphics, and pages. To publish to paper, users may print directly from FrameMaker. Having documents with structure gives additional control that can help pages, and their content, be more consistent.

Printing Overview

Documents and books can be printed directly from FrameMaker. The following settings are for documents and books.

Printing from a Single Document

You can choose *File>Print* from any open document. You may then select the pages you wish to print. You can also choose special options, like registration marks, as shown in Figure 5–1.

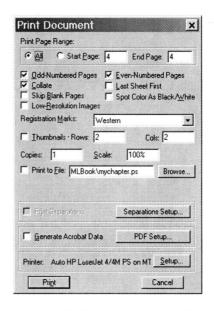

Figure 5–1.   *To print a single document, use the Print Document dialog box.*

Printing from a FrameMaker Book

You also have the ability to print all or some of the files from the book level. The Print Book dialog box includes a popup that, when printing to a PostScript file, lets you make a single file or many smaller files. The Print Book dialog box is shown in Figure 5–2.

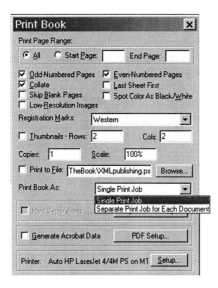

Figure 5–2. Printing files from a book requires the Print Book dialog box.

Outputting PDF from FrameMaker

There has been a rumor that one of the reasons for Adobe purchasing Frame Technology (the creators of FrameMaker) was because FrameMaker created very high-quality postscript files. Because Adobe was eying Acrobat as its vision of the future, Adobe wanted a tool that could produce great postscript files—later to become PDFs—so that Adobe could move into the electronic publishing realm. While this may or may not be true, the fact is that FrameMaker *does* create very high quality postscript and does a great job of creating interactive (dynamic) PDFs.

While you do not necessarily have to adjust your template to output to PDF, there is a PDF Setup menu that allows you to adjust PDF output. The PDF setup can be done at the book level on all files, or done as you go through the Print Document menu. The latter is shown in Figure 5–3.

Once you click the PDF Setup button, FrameMaker opens the PDF Setup dialog box, which contains four properties sheets. The first sheet, Settings, is shown in Figure 5–4.

The Settings include a PDF Job Options choice, which helps you control your PDF output quality. It comes with four choices: eBook,

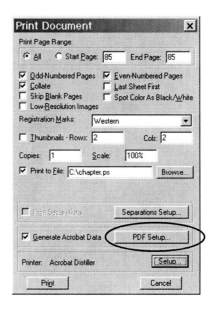

Figure 5–3.   PDF Setup is highlighted on FrameMaker's Print Document dialog box.

Print, Press, and Screen—these vary from one version of Acrobat to another. Select the choice with the name that best describes how the PDF will be used by the end user.

The next sheet (Bookmarks) which includes PDF Bookmark controls, is shown in Figure 5–5.

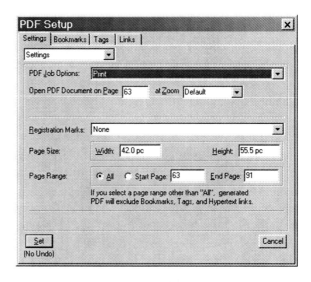

Figure 5–4.   The Settings sheet is the first sheet in PDF Setup.

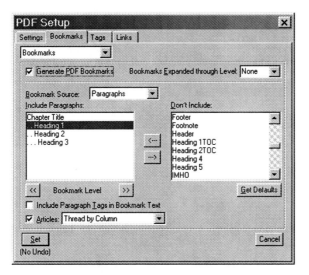

Figure 5–5.   The Bookmarks sheet is the second sheet.

FrameMaker gives more bookmark control than any other program. You can set bookmarks to appear for specific paragraphs or elements. You can also select nesting levels for the resulting bookmarks.

Article placement is also controlled here. Articles control how users experience PDFs by modifying how scrolling occurs. FrameMaker allows you to set articles for *down the page* (thread by text frame) scrolling or—if you have a multiple column layout—for *down each column in turn* (thread by column) scrolling.

NOTE   Including articles in your PDF will increase its file size. If you do not need the articles, then do not turn on this option.

Tags come next in the PDF Setup dialog box. The Tags sheet is shown in Figure 5–6.

Tags are only used for making accessible PDFs. If the documents do not need to comply with the government's Section 508 requirements for accessibility, do not choose Generate Tagged PDF. It will make the PDFs unnecessarily larger.

The final PDF Setup sheet is Links, which is shown in Figure 5–7.

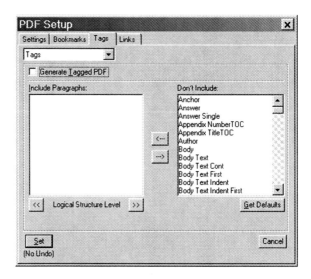

Figure 5–6.   The Tags sheet comes next in the PDF Setup dialog box.

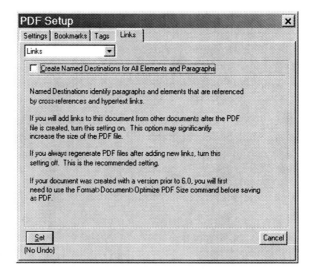

Figure 5–7.   The fourth properties sheet in the PDF Setup dialog box is the Links sheet.

Take a moment to read the text on the Links sheet—it is self-explanatory.

One other thing that you need to be aware of is that PDF settings can be set at the book level with the PDF Optimization Options. This menu is shown in Figure 5–8.

When printing to PDF, the printer driver is key. You need to select a quality printer driver to get quality PDF output. Only the Acrobat Distiller (postscript creation) process produces *dynamic* PDFs with working hypertext links. PDFWriter cannot create links, therefore its PDFs are *static*. The PDFWriter printing process is shown in Figure 5–9.

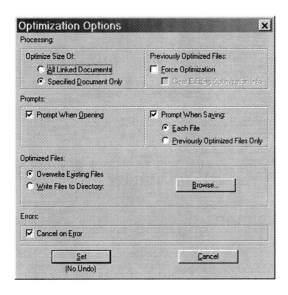

Figure 5–8. The Acrobat Distiller printer driver creates postscript, which is distilled by the Acrobat Distiller program.

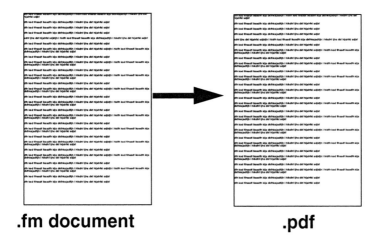

.fm document   **.pdf**

Figure 5–9.   PDFWriter creates PDFs.

While the Save As PDF option is available in FrameMaker 6 and 5.5, it was not properly configured to select the right printer driver. Save As PDF in Version 7 does make it easier to create PDFs using the right printer driver.

The PDF may look good with PDFWriter, but the links will not work at all. To keep the links active, print to Acrobat Distiller, or—if using FrameMaker 7.x—Save As PDF. The document will then go through the process shown in Figure 5–10 to create a PDF.

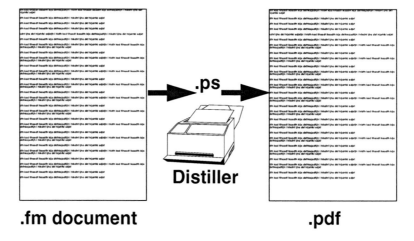

.fm document   .pdf

Figure 5–10.   PostScript printer drivers like Acrobat Distiller create postscript and distill to create PDFs.

In this method, Adobe Distiller acts as a *virtual printer* to turn the postscript file into a PDF-viewable format. All of the links in the files will be live links.

Outputting Well-formed XML Markup

In this section, you will review FrameMaker's capabilities in terms of marked-up output from regular, unstructured documents.

NOTE   You may output well-formed markup from structured documents as well, if you do not have a DTD or schema against which you validate.

An unstructured recipe document's output is shown in Figure 5–11 and Figure 5–12 as an example. The code shown was created by opening the unstructured document and choosing Save As XML and HTML.

Because the XML was created from an unstructured FrameMaker document, the XML elements were created on the fly. FrameMaker used the format names—as it had only the formatting to go by—which is why the element names are more about formatting than data.

Because no structure was presented to show the hierarchy, there isn't really a structure. Each heading has a beginning tag, content, and an end tag before the paragraph under that heading begins. In the ingredients list, for example, each ingredient stands alone, so reusing the entire ingredients list could be difficult to do with this XML.

```xml
<?xml version="1.0" encoding="UTF-8"?>
<?xml-stylesheet href="cookbook-unstruc-output.css" type="text/css" charset="UTF-8"?>
<XML>
<TITLE> French Baguettes</TITLE><DIV>
<Heading1>
<A ID="pgfId-998602"></A>
<DIV>
<IMAGE xml:link="simple" href="cookbook-unstruc-output-1.gif" show="embed" actuate="auto"/>
</DIV>
French Baguettes</Heading1>
<Ingredients>
<A ID="pgfId-998617"></A>
<Bold>
1</Bold>
<Emphasis>
  cup</Emphasis>
--<ItemName>
 water</ItemName>
</Ingredients>
<Ingredients>
<A ID="pgfId-998621"></A>
<Bold>
2 1/2</Bold>
<Emphasis>
  cups</Emphasis>
--<ItemName>
 bread flour </ItemName>
</Ingredients>

... REMAINDER OF CODE CROPPED
```

Figure 5–11.   This is XML from an unstructured FrameMaker recipe document.

```
<!DOCTYPE HTML PUBLIC "-//W3C//DTD HTML 4.0//EN"><HTML>
<HEAD>
<META HTTP-EQUIV="Content-Type" CONTENT="text/html; charset=ISO-8859-1">
<META HTTP-EQUIV="Content-Style-Type" CONTENT="text/css">
<META NAME="GENERATOR" CONTENT="Adobe FrameMaker 7.x/HTML Export Filter">
<LINK REL="STYLESHEET" HREF="cookbook-unstruc-output.css" CHARSET="ISO-8859-1" TYPE="text/css">
<TITLE> French Baguettes</TITLE>
</HEAD>
<BODY BGCOLOR="#ffffff">
<DIV>
<H2 CLASS="Heading1">
<A NAME="pgfId-998602"></A><DIV>
<IMG SRC="cookbook-unstruc-output-1.gif">
</DIV>
French Baguettes</H2>
<P CLASS="Ingredients">
<A NAME="pgfId-998617"></A><EM CLASS="Bold">
1</EM>
<EM CLASS="Emphasis">
  cup</EM>
--<EM CLASS="ItemName">
 water</EM>
</P>
<P CLASS="Ingredients">
<A NAME="pgfId-998621"></A><EM CLASS="Bold">
2 1/2</EM>
<EM CLASS="Emphasis">
  cups</EM>
--<EM CLASS="ItemName">
 bread flour </EM>
</P>

... REMAINDER OF CODE CROPPED
```

Figure 5–12.   The HTML from a unstructured FrameMaker recipe document is displayed.

You most likely could not validate this XML unless you took the time to create a DTD that used the format-named tags created by FrameMaker.

For HTML, this isn't so bad. Formatting can be applied easily by a browser with or without a style sheet (although a cascading style sheet is created during the Save As HTML process). This is usable HTML.

Outputting Valid XML Markup from Structured Documents

Moving back into structured documents, this section more closely examines the markup produced by FrameMaker. In this section you will see output from structured documents to XML and HTML.

Output from the structured recipe document is shown in Figure 5–13 and Figure 5–14 as an example (the structured recipe document is shown later in this book). The code shown was created by opening the unstructured document and choosing a Save As XML and HTML, respectively.

Because the XML was created from a structured FrameMaker document, the XML elements are created using the defined structure. FrameMaker uses the element names so the output will use naming that is more focused on data than formatting. This is the ideal output.

Because structure was present, the hierarchy is used and you can see the relationships (nesting) between elements. In the indents list, for example, each ingredient is wrapped between the <Ingredients> and </Ingredients> tags (the code is cropped before the end tag in the figure above), so reusing the entire ingredients list would be easy to do with this XML.

Validation can be done for this XML, as long as there is a DTD present against which to validate. Because you are working with structured documents, you will have an EDD that can easily be saved as a DTD. This, therefore, is the choice with the best—and in some cases *only*—possibility of validation.

The HTML from Figure 5–12 and Figure 5–14 are similar, except that the structured document uses more <DIV> and <SPAN> to imply the relationship between elements. You will want to check your HTML carefully to ensure FrameMaker has properly identified your heading levels as desired. This HTML will still be usable within a browser, or with the cascading style sheet created with it.

```
<?xml version="1.0" encoding="UTF-8"?>
<!DOCTYPE Recipe SYSTEM
"file:///C:/Program%20Files/Adobe/FrameMaker7.x/structure/xml/Cookbook/cookbook.DTD" [

<!-- Begin Document Specific Declarations -->


<!-- End Document Specific Declarations -->

]>
<Recipe Category = "Other"><Name>French Baguettes</Name>
<Ingredients><Item><Quantity>1</Quantity><Unit> cup</Unit><ItemName> water</ItemName></Item>
<Item><Quantity>2 1/2</Quantity><Unit> cups</Unit><ItemName> bread
flour </ItemName></Item>
```
… REMAINDER OF CODE CROPPED

Figure 5–13.   This is XML from a structured FrameMaker recipe.

```
<!DOCTYPE HTML PUBLIC "-//W3C//DTD HTML 4.0//EN"><HTML>
<HEAD>
<META HTTP-EQUIV="Content-Type" CONTENT="text/html; charset=ISO-8859-1">
<META HTTP-EQUIV="Content-Style-Type" CONTENT="text/css">
<META NAME="GENERATOR" CONTENT="Adobe FrameMaker 7.x/HTML Export Filter">
<LINK REL="STYLESHEET" HREF="recipe-output.css" CHARSET="ISO-8859-1" TYPE="text/css">
<TITLE> </TITLE>
</HEAD>
<BODY BGCOLOR="#ffffff">
<DIV CLASS="Recipe">
<A NAME="elementId-999501"></A><A NAME="pgfId-998767"></A><P CLASS="Name">
French Baguettes</P>
<DIV CLASS="Ingredients">
<A NAME="elementId-999510"></A><A NAME="pgfId-999511"></A><P CLASS="Item">
<SPAN CLASS="Quantity">
1</SPAN>
<SPAN CLASS="Unit">
  cup</SPAN>
<SPAN CLASS="ItemName">
-- water</SPAN>
</P>
<P CLASS="Item">
<A NAME="pgfId-999537"></A><SPAN CLASS="Quantity">
2 1/2</SPAN>
<SPAN CLASS="Unit">
  cups</SPAN>
<SPAN CLASS="ItemName">
-- bread flour </SPAN>
</P>
```
… REMAINDER OF CODE CROPPED

Figure 5–14.   This is HTML from a structured FrameMaker recipe.

Outputting Online Help

Another output option FrameMaker can create is online help. Online help can be created using XML and XSLT (to transform) or style sheets (to display). Therefore, you can output XML and produce online help. You can also do this in a more automated way using WebWorks Publisher, Professional Edition.

Unlike the Standard Edition that installs with FrameMaker, the Professional Edition—as well as the latest 2003 edition—allows you to create online help from FrameMaker books.

Summary

FrameMaker was designed to be a publishing tool. It allows control over how documents look and how the content moves together. FrameMaker gives power to author your documents for print and then output them to many other formats.

Adding structure and XML capabilities gives another level of control. This allows document production—and output—with better formatting and content consistency.

PART II

USING APPLICATIONS FOR
XML PUBLISHING

CHAPTER 6

Preparing to Perform the Exercises

THIS CHAPTER PROVIDES an overview of the setup for using this book's example files. You need to perform this setup if you wish to use the example files covered in this part of the book.

Preparing Your Desktop

Before you begin working with the concepts described in this section, you might want to install the sample files available for this book.

 NOTE The sample files are available at *www.apress.com/book/download.html*. They are in an EXE file and will need to be extracted.

Once you download the sample files from the Apress website, you will have all the sample documents and FrameMaker setup that you need to follow the book examples.

The downloaded file contains sample XML, FrameMaker templates and related files, and a *structapps.fm* file that you will need to setup in advance.

Extract the entire contents of the EXE to a folder on whatever drive has your FrameMaker installed. An FMXML folder will be created on your drive.

Finding the Sample Files

The FMXML folder should extract with the Samples subfolder. Inside the samples folder should be the following subfolders:

- catalog

- cookbook

- faq

- simpledoc

Keep the sample files where they are, but copy the subfolders. Then, browse to your FrameMaker install directory and paste the subfolders into FrameMaker's XML folder. If you did not specify another path when installing FrameMaker on Windows®, the XML folder's default location will be
c:\Program Files\Adobe\FrameMaker7.x\structure\xml

NOTE The x in the path should be replaced by whatever point-release digit your folder displays. For example, if you have FrameMaker 7.1 installed, the x will be replaced by a 1:

c:\Program Files\Adobe\FrameMaker7.1

Once you paste inside FrameMaker's XML folder, you should have four new subfolders with paths similar to
c:\Program Files\Adobe\FrameMaker7.1\structure\xml\catalog

Installing Sample XML Applications

Now that you have downloaded the sample files, a file now needs to be adjusted in FrameMaker so that you may access the sample XML round-trip files. You will adjust this file now, but a more detailed explanation of it and its uses comes later.

You need to adjust a file within FrameMaker that contains information on XML round-trip Applications. The file is called *structapps.fm*. There is a shortcut to open it and to force FrameMaker to read through it for revisions. These are included in the following steps:

1. Click *File>Structure Tools>Edit Application Definitions*.

   The *structapps.fm* file opens.

2. Maximize the *structapps.fm* file so that you can see its name and path clearly on the FrameMaker title bar.

3. Click *File>Open* and browse to the FMXML folder that you created when you unzipped the EXE file in the previous section.

4. In the FMXML folder, select the *structapps.fm* file provided.

5. Open your Structure View by clicking the *Structure View* button in the upper-right corner of the document window.

6. Scroll through the Structure View until you see an element called XMLApplication, with text across from it that says *catalog*.

7. Click once on the XMLApplication element bubble in the Structure View.

8. Scroll down the Structure View until you can see the XMLApplication element for *simpledoc* and Shift-click over that element bubble.

   All of the XML Applications for your sample documents should be highlighted in the Structure View and in the document.

9. Click *Edit>Copy*.

10. Close this file without saving it.

11. In the *structapps.fm* file that is still open, click just under one of its XMLApplication elements in the Structure View.

    The arrow depicting the insertion point should appear just to the right of the line that descends from the root StructuredSetup element bubble.

12. Click *Edit>Paste*.

    You should now have the pasted XMLApplication elements showing alongside those that were in the *structapps.fm* file to start.

13. Click *Save*.

14. Click *File>Structure Tools>Read Application Definitions* to force FrameMaker to notice the new elements.

15. Close this file, saving it if it prompts you again.

Your FrameMaker is now ready to use the sample applications and related files.

Installing Cell Phone Emulation Software

OpenWave has a cell phone emulation tool available—as of this writing—for free download. Their website is *www.openwave.com*. If you plan on using or creating WML, then you will want to download the OpenWave emulator and follow their installation instructions.

Once you have the emulator installed, you will be able to open WML and some XML outputs created from FrameMaker documents.

Checking Your Installation

In this section, you will need to open an XML file to test that your sample setup is working properly. More detailed explanation will be provided including the why and how of this setup in future chapters.

1. From the *..\FrameMaker7.x\structure\xml\simpledoc* folder, open *simpledoc.xml*.

2. When prompted, select the *simpledoc* structured application.

3. Click *Continue*.

4. When the file appears in FrameMaker, save it as *simpledoc.fm*.

If you do not have the simpledoc folder, refer to "Preparing Your Desktop" on page 113 for instructions on placing these sample files.

If at Step #2 in the preceding instructions your *simpledoc* structured application is not listed, go back through the instructions in "Installing Sample XML Applications" on page 115, making sure to perform the step to Read Structured Application (as done in Step 14 on page 116).

If the document is all left-justified plain text, then check your sample installation and try again.

If the document is still plain text, then double check the paths listed to the sample files. If you have placed the samples anywhere other than specified, you will need to edit the paths in the *structapps.fm* file (see Chapters 11 and 14 for more details).

If the document has formatted text, headers on the page, and a centered title, then your setup is working and you should be able to use the samples in the upcoming chapters.

Moving through the coming chapters, as each document sample is discussed, you might want to open the named file and browse through it.

[handwritten marginalia: Fixed paths Still Didn't work FM8 has Different paths but I copied exactly]

[handwritten marginalia: Frame 8's Sto temple nameshave changed. No thing is formatted]

NOTE   If you inadvertently save a file with unwanted changes, just return to the original extracted files. These should be in the *\FMXML\samples* folder on your main drive if you have not deleted or moved them.

CHAPTER 7

Exploring a Structured Document

THIS CHAPTER DESCRIBES structured documents and the procedures for maneuvering in structure. You will learn how the structure tools are used. You will be walked through editing documents to ensure you are comfortable with structure. You will also learn where the structure comes from. Understanding this will help you better understand how to produce your own structure later.

Navigating in Structure

Up to this point in the book, you have seen images of structure but have not taken a hard look at its details. In this section, you will walk through several sample structured documents. You'll take a close look at each document's elements and attributes, the relationships between them, and how the structure affects the documents. You will also learn about authoring and editing procedures.

Figure 7–1 shows a document with its Structure View and describes the different pieces. The pieces are labeled within the figure to help you locate each piece and match it to the description.

(A)

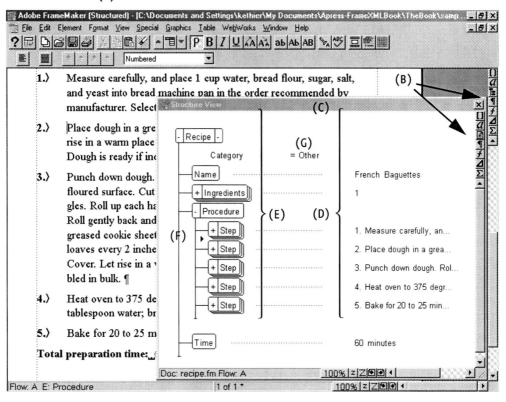

Figure 7–1. This view shows structured document detail.

(A) Document window

(B) Document window and *Structure View* buttons

(C) Structure View window

(D) Text snippets

(E) Element bubbles

(F) Insertion point

(G) Attributes

The buttons along the right edge require some additional explanation as well. On the left in Figure 7–2 are the Document Window buttons. On the right are the *Structure View* buttons.

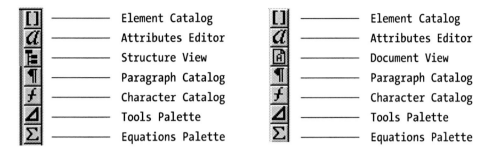

————	Element Catalog
————	Attributes Editor
————	Structure View
————	Paragraph Catalog
————	Character Catalog
————	Tools Palette
————	Equations Palette

————	Element Catalog
————	Attributes Editor
————	Document View
————	Paragraph Catalog
————	Character Catalog
————	Tools Palette
————	Equations Palette

Figure 7–2.   The buttons shown are on the Document window and Structure View window.

The only difference between the two is the third button down. In the Document window, you can click this button to display the Structure View. Clicking this button in the Structure View makes the Document window the active window.

Moving through structured documents differs from moving through unstructured documents. Your insertion point now has a position within the structure in addition to its position in the document. You can place your insertion point by clicking in the Document window as you normally would, or you can click in the Structure View window. The latter method is often the easiest way to position your cursor between elements.

When trying to insert elements—depending on where you put your insertion point—different elements will be shown as valid in the Element Catalog. Therefore, learning how to get a proper insertion point is critical.

The insertion point shows up in the Structure View as a small black triangle. If you click *Insert* when this triangle appears, the resulting element will appear at the location of the triangle.

Placing an Insertion Point between Elements

Clicking to the right of a line descending from an element gives you an insertion point just to the right of its vertical line. If you insert an element at that point, it will be a child of the original element.

Placing an Insertion Point inside an Element

Clicking to the right of an element gives you an insertion point inside that element. If there are no child elements, then the triangle appears next to the element. This is shown in Figure 7–3.

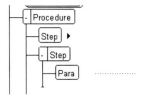

Figure 7–3.   This view shows an insertion point inside a Step element with no child elements.

If the element has child elements, the triangle drops beneath it and appears to the right of its vertical line. This is shown in Figure 7–4.

Figure 7–4.   This exhibits an insertion point inside a Step element with a Para child element.

Placing an Insertion Point in Element Content

When you are inside the content of an element—such as typing text within body or heading elements—your insertion point displays differently in the Structure View. Depending on whether you are inside the content or near a tag, the cursor looks like the different types of arrows shown in Table 7–1.

Table 7–1.   Cursor Position Arrows

POSITION	CURSOR DISPLAY
At the first character position in the element content (just inside the element beginning tag)	▯▸
At the last character position in the element content (just before the element end tag)	▸▯
Anywhere else in the content (not at the beginning nor at the end)	▷

Collapsing and Expanding Structure

As you go deeper into your structure, the multitude of vertical lines can become confusing. This is when collapsing and expanding can be helpful.

By collapsing or expanding, you can adjust what structure you see. In this way, the Structure View can be used as a kind of outline. This is an advantage you get with structured documents.

Collapsing and Expanding Elements

Elements that have child elements appear in the Structure View with symbols next to their names on their element bubbles. These symbols are plus (+) and minus (–).

In Figure 7–5, the Recipe element is an example. In front of Recipe on its element bubble, you can see a minus.

To collapse the Recipe element, click on the minus. Once it is collapsed, you will not be able to see any of its child elements and the minus will turn into a plus. This is shown in Figure 7–6.

Clicking on the plus in front of Recipe expands the child elements again, and you get a view like that in Figure 7–5 again.

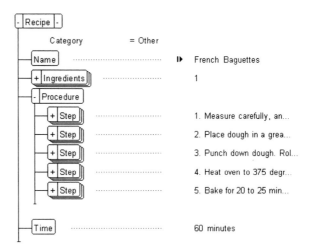

Figure 7–5.   Plus and minus symbols within a Structure View indicate child elements.

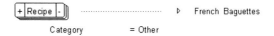

Figure 7–6.   The Structure View shows the collapsed recipe.

NOTE   You can also collapse or expand all sibling elements within a parent by holding down the Shift key while you click on the plus/minus. This enables you, for example, to collapse the structure to view all the main headings within a document.

In this way, you can determine what you see in the Structure View. Although the document window view does not change, you should still find navigation made easier by collapsing and expanding elements because the two views are linked together.

Collapsing and Expanding Attributes

In the Structure View, attributes appear under their elements. This can be seen in the Recipe element of Figure 7–6. The Category attribute and its Other value are shown below the Recipe element.

Collapsing and expanding these attributes is helpful for navigation and also for editing of attributes. The attributes collapse and expand using the plus and minus symbols that appear to the right of the element name. Therefore, in the Recipe example, the minus to the right of Recipe is for collapsing/expanding the Category attribute.

Clicking on the minus to the right of the element name hides the attributes for that element, and the minus turns into a plus. Clicking on this plus symbol brings attributes into view. Depending on what attributes you have, and if any are optional and have no value, you might have to click the plus twice to see all of the attributes. Once you have clicked the plus as necessary, the plus should turn into a minus.

Attribute view options are set under *View>Attribute Display Options.* If you want to see all attributes for all elements, adjusting with this dialog box is an easy way to expand all attributes. This dialog box is shown in Figure 7–7.

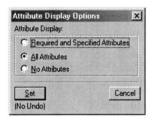

Figure 7–7.   The Attribute Display Options dialog box allows for adjustments to attributes.

In the recipe example, the Recipe element has just one attribute. The number of attributes can be substantially more depending on how complex your EDD is. Longer attribute lists can be more *intrusive* in your view. An example of an element with many attributes showing is provided in Figure 7–8. This is the *XDocBook* sample FrameMaker file.

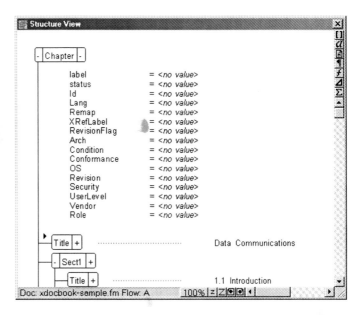

Figure 7–8. An element is shown expanded to display its many attributes.

Reviewing a Sample Document

DTD=a set of definitions of elements and attributes, and rules for using them (to create valid markup documents).

The first document example uses a portion of the XML XDocBook DTD. Some preliminary information will help you understand this XML version of DocBook.

DocBook is a DTD that has been around since the days of SGML. DocBook and the XML version, *XDocBook*, were designed for creating computer hardware and software books (or papers), although this DTD can be used for other types of documents.

XDocBook version 4.1.2 installs with FrameMaker 7.0 and 7.1. This installed XDocBook provides elements for making many different parts of a document or book. Inside FrameMaker, the elements are set up within an EDD and formatting is related to the elements. The *xdocbook-sample.fm* example file used here is a brief chapter. The following screen shots walk through *xdocbook-sample.fm* from the beginning. The file starts with the text *Chapter 1* and a root element called Chapter. This is shown in Figure 7–9.

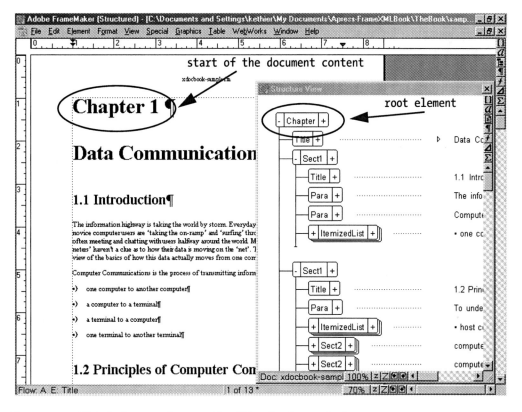

Figure 7–9.   This is the root element of an XDocBook sample document.

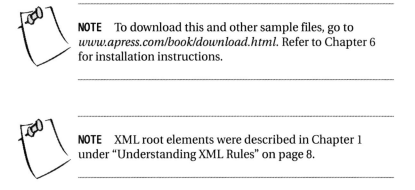

NOTE   To download this and other sample files, go to *www.apress.com/book/download.html*. Refer to Chapter 6 for installation instructions.

NOTE   XML root elements were described in Chapter 1 under "Understanding XML Rules" on page 8.

If you select *View>Element Boundaries (as Tags)* in FrameMaker, you can see view the same document with its elements showing as beginning and end tags, rather than the tree structure seen in Figure 7–9. This alternative *tag view* is shown in Figure 7–10. This is just another representation of the same XDocBook structure.

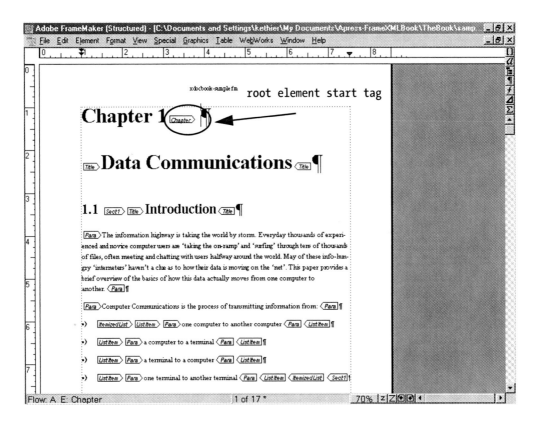

Figure 7–10.   An alternate view of the XDocBook sample document is the Element Boundaries as Tags view.

NOTE   As you move forward into your own projects, you will have to decide which way of viewing structure works best for you.

NOTE   In this figure, the Chapter 1 text appears to be outside the element's beginning tag. This is the way FrameMaker displays the numbering, which appears as background text in front of the paragraph start.

In Figure 7–10, the Chapter element end tag is not shown. It is at the very end of the document. Remember that, in XML, the root element wraps around all the other tags in the document structure. This is true within our structured FrameMaker documents that are designed to go out to XML.

Nested inside the Chapter element are multiple levels of sections. Each is numbered, making it clear as you move through the document what level section you are in. For example, Sect1 is the element used for sections inside the Chapter element. These would be your first level sections (1.1, 1.2, etc.) in the sample document. Inside Sect1 elements can be Sect2 elements (1.1.1, 1.1.2, etc.). Some of this section nesting is visible back in Figure 7–9, although it is shown in the hierarchical tree view.

Within the section elements, then, are many lower level elements. Some can contain text, while others hold other elements, form tables, hold graphics, or create special objects like markers or index terms. Examples of many of these are shown in the figures that follow.

Figure 7–11 shows one Sect1 element's content. This is just one of the possible sets of child elements inside a Sect1 element. XDocBook is a very detailed DTD/EDD, and many combinations are possible. While Para and ItemizedList elements are inside this Sect1 element, there are other types of elements allowed within it. These will be listed in the Element Catalog—your guide throughout the authoring process—which displays the available elements.

Take a closer look at the Sect1 descendents shown in Figure 7–11. If you place your insertion point inside the Sect1 parent, between two sibling Para elements, the Element Catalog will list the elements that are valid at this point (see Figure 7–12).

NOTE   If you see more or fewer elements than are expected (based on the screen shots here), it may be that you have a different setting selected for *Element>Set Available Elements*. This setting and its options are described in "Inserting Elements" on page 140.

You will be able to insert any of the elements that are shown in Figure 7–12. Because there are so many options in this particular EDD (XDocBook), the available elements list is so long that all

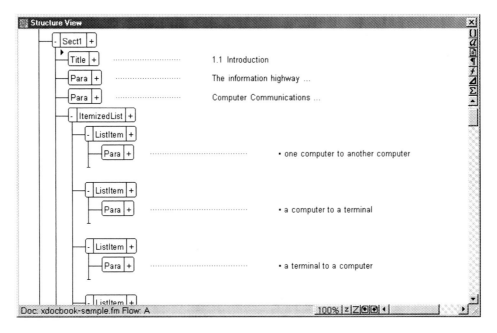

Figure 7–11. *This details the contents of a* Sect1 *element.*

available elements cannot be shown within the Element Catalog screen capture.

A little further down in this *Chapter* sample file, locate the elements for a *Figure*. This begins with a Figure element that contains two child elements: Title and Graphic.

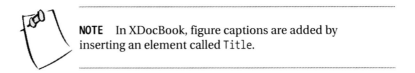

NOTE In XDocBook, figure captions are added by inserting an element called Title.

Instead of just inserting a graphic, a Graphic element is placed inside a parent element, Figure in this structure. By then giving Figure structure rules governing its siblings, you can control whether or not a Caption element needs to be inserted with the Graphic element, thereby becoming its sibling. You can also control whether authors can place a caption above or below the graphic, helping you enforce any corporate style guide rules about caption placement. This is something that is not possible in unstructured documents. The Figure structure is shown in Figure 7–13.

Figure 7–12.   The Element Catalog shows elements available for insertion.

Notice the shape of the Figure and Title elements. Most of your elements will look like this. This shape is given to all elements that can contain text or other elements.

Now notice the shape of the Graphic element. Because it is an object-type element, it does not have rounded edges like most of the other elements. There are object-type elements like the Graphic element in the structure shown in Figure 7–13. The object-type elements are Marker, CrossReference, Equation, and Graphic.

The element type is set by the element designer as each element is created in the EDD.

NOTE   The element type is not the same as the element name. Do not be confused by the element named Graphic in Figure 7-13 that is also of the graphic *type*. The element type in that case matches the element's name. Types are used to identify special objects within FrameMaker, such as a marker. For details regarding element types and how they are assigned, refer to Chapter 12.

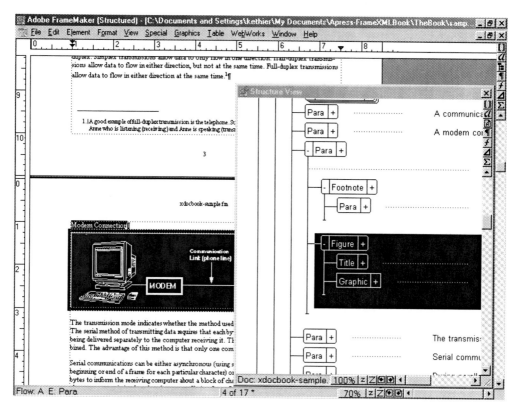

Figure 7–13.   This shows Figure structure in the XDocBook example.

The other elements that hold text or other elements (and show up in the Structure View with rounded edges) are: Container, Footnote, Table, TableTitle, TableHeading, TableBody, TableFooting, TableRow, and TableCell. There are also Rubi and RubiGroup type elements. The Rubi characters are small characters that appears above a word to show its pronunciation. The RubiGroup is used in structure to hold both the Rubi text and the text above which it appears (the Oyamoji text).

The next piece of structure examined here (and shown in Figure 7–14) is the structure of a list. In the figure, the list is highlighted to show you where a bulleted list appears in the document window and in the Structure View.

You should note that the ItemizedList parent element in the list structure contains child elements that make up the actual items in the list.

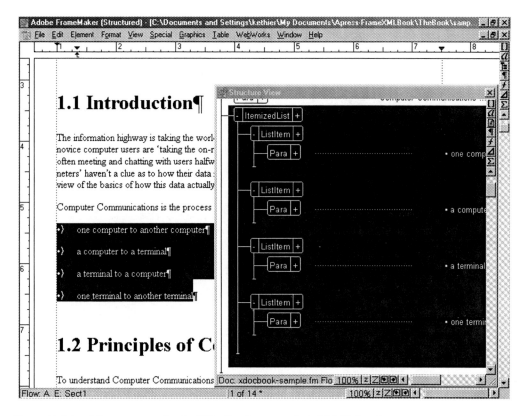

Figure 7–14.   List structure in the XDocBook example is highlighted.

NOTE   In XDocBook, the ListItem elements contain Para elements that then hold the content (text). A simpler structure might just have ListItem (or Item, or whatever you want to call them) elements in which text can be entered. This is up to you when you create your own structure.

Another part of the structure worth taking a closer look at is the table structure. In Figure 7–15, you can see the complex structure of the table. While the table is only about two inches in height on the page, the structure needed to create its columns and rows is much longer. In fact, the view percentage of the Structure View in the screen shot had to be lowered to 70 percent to fit it in the screen shot. Many elements are needed to make up the table, including some that FrameMaker requires that XML does not.

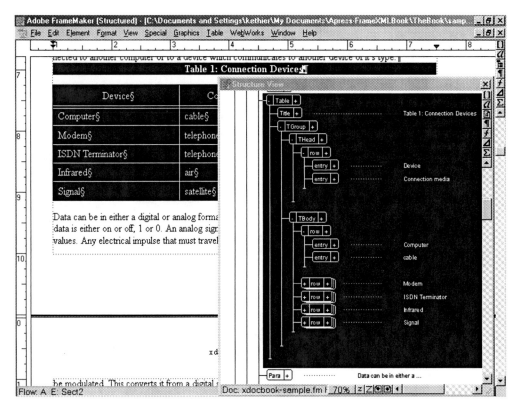

Figure 7–15. Table Structure in an XDocBook Example.

For example, notice that the rows are all wrapped inside elements called TBody and THead. These names refer to two of the three types of rows you can add to a FrameMaker table—Table Body rows and Table Heading rows. Of course, the third is Table Footing rows, but it isn't shown because this table does not have a footing row.

NOTE FrameMaker tables have heading rows and footing rows that redisplay (the entire row does) on each page of multipage tables. The table body rows do not repeat, and are used for the table content.

These extra elements are necessary around the table rows inside FrameMaker. An XML table, however, would not require these and could just have rows within a table element—a simpler structure.

This is important to understand, because from this you can start to see that FrameMaker's formatting could potentially drive changes in your XML structure.

For now, that is all to be examined in the XDocBook structure. Hopefully it gives you an idea of what can be done with XDocBook.

Reviewing a Cookbook Sample Document

In this section, you will review another sample document. This document was created using a structured cookbook template.

Within the *recipe.fm* file is a recipe. As shown in Figure 7–16, Recipe is the root element. Its child elements are: Name, Ingredients, Procedure, and Time.

Drilling down in the structure to the Ingredients element, you have Item elements. Each Item element's content is broken down into detailed pieces.

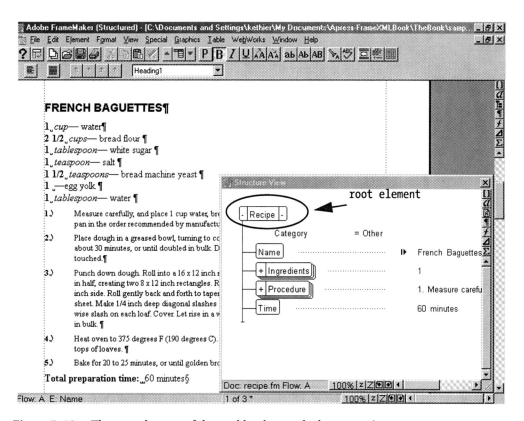

Figure 7–16.   The root element of the cookbook sample document is Recipe.

NOTE Take a moment and think about online searches. Can you imagine someone searching for recipes and wanting the information broken down by these details? How about sorting ingredients to make a shopping list? This is just one of the potential benefits of using XML. So, in this case, the structure is designed more for its eventual purpose than for a need within the layout or formatting.

The Ingredient element is shown expanded in the Structure View in Figure 7–17. The Quantity, Unit, and ItemName child elements together make up each Item.

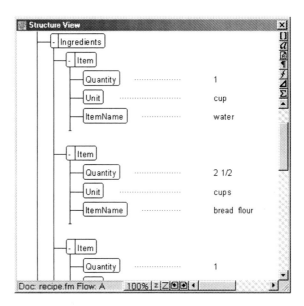

Figure 7–17. The Structure View shows Recipe ingredients as elements and child elements.

In the print version of the cookbook, the structure can be checked to ensure that all the necessary pieces are included within the document. Without structure, it would be solely up to the writer or editor to keep content consistent and ensure all pieces are present and in the same order.

With structure, FrameMaker can validate to ensure:

- Proper formatting

- Content completeness

- Content order

- Frequency

In "Editing Structure" on page 139, you will see more information on the authoring process and how Item elements are added, along with their child elements.

Editing a Structured Document

Now that you understand what is going on in these structured documents, it is time to look at how the documents can be adjusted. You edit structured documents in a different way than you edit unstructured documents. There are ways to edit content, and ways to edit the structure (elements, attributes). You'll be using the document view, plus the Structure View and the Element Catalog. The Element Catalog will serve as your guide, showing you the elements you can use at different points in the document.

Editing Content (Text)

In this section, you will learn how to add and delete text in structured documents.

Adding Text

To add text, place your insertion point inside an element that is allowed to contain text. Knowing which elements may contain text usually comes from being familiar with a structure, so do not be frustrated if it takes you a few clicks to find an element that allows text. If your insertion point is in an element that may contain text, then the Element Catalog will show a choice such as <TEXT>. When this is shown in the catalog, you can begin typing and will immediately see your typed text appear. It will show up in the Document window (as content) as well as in the Structure View (as a text snippet). An example Element Catalog with <TEXT> available is shown in Figure 7–18.

NOTE If <TEXT> does not appear in the Element Catalog, then you will need to move your insertion point. When <TEXT> is not shown in the Element Catalog, FrameMaker will beep as you type and no text will appear.

Once you are inside an element, typing text is the same with structure as without it.

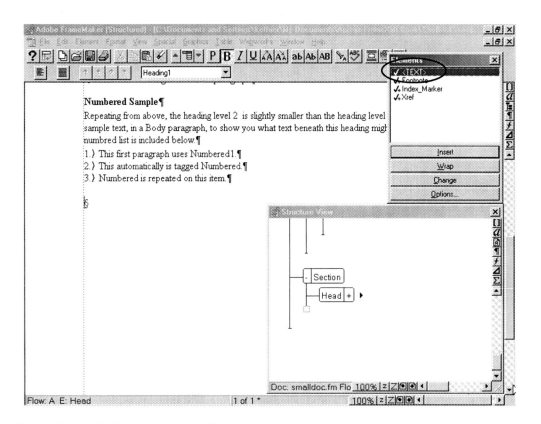

Figure 7–18. An insertion point is shown inside an element that can contain text.

Deleting Text

Deleting text is the same if you are within a element. As long as you do not cross the boundary of an element, all is the same.

You can select with the mouse, double-click to select words, and use your click/Shift-click to select ranges and then delete the selection. You can also double-click the text snippet in the Structure View to highlight the element's content, and then delete it.

Crossing any element boundary forces that element to select. If you drag across multiple element boundaries, then all the elements involved will select. This is true even if the tags are showing and you only drag across a beginning or end tag—FrameMaker automatically selects the beginning and end tags together along with the content. If you need to delete information within two or more elements, the pieces will need to be done separately.

Editing Structure

The Element Catalog allows you to easily insert, change, or wrap elements. As seen in Figure 7–19, there are buttons for each of these actions at the bottom of the Element Catalog.

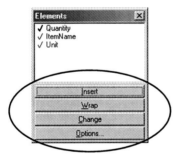

Figure 7–19.   The Element Catalog buttons are circled.

Also at the bottom of the Element Catalog, is an Options button. Selecting this brings up the Set Available Elements options as shown in Figure 7–20 (the other three choices are important to understand and are described later in this chapter).

Each of these Set Available Elements options adjusts the list of elements that you see in the Element Catalog. The settings guide you as you build valid documents. The choices are explained in Table 7–2.

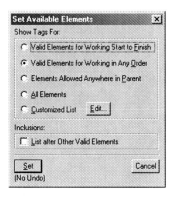

Figure 7–20.   One Element option is Set Available Elements.

Inserting Elements

Inserting is how you add structure as you write. When you insert an element, three things happen:

1. The inserted element appears in the Structure View.

2. In the Document window, the cursor moves into the new element. If you have Element Boundaries on, you will see around the cursor.

3. The Element Catalog adjusts to show the child elements available inside that element.

When you are inserting elements, the elements listed in the Element Catalog often have symbols next to them. These symbols require some explanation.

- *Bold Checkmark*   This indicates that the element is valid at the current insertion point. These are the ideal elements to insert.

- *Bold Checkmark with plus symbol*   This indicates that the element is an inclusion. Inclusions are problematic in XML, because there is no equivalent in XML and documents may be valid in FrameMaker but invalid when output to XML. These are not a good idea to use.

NOTE   Inclusions are inherited from SGML, so they are provided in FrameMaker to be used in SGML Applications.

- *Light Checkmark*   This indicates that the element is valid at the insertion point but will need another element to complete a valid structure. You will need to insert another element after this one to make sure your document remains valid. These are fine to use.

- *Bold Question Mark*   This indicates that the element can replace the selected element (or after the insertion point). These can make the surrounding structure invalid if you are not careful.

- *No Symbol*   This means that the element is not valid at the current insertion point. If you insert this element, be prepared to correct the surrounding elements to make the document valid again. Avoid elements with no symbol.

Also important with the Element Catalog are the options that you set for available elements. Figure 7–20 showed the Options dialog box. Depending on which option you select, different elements appear in the Element Catalog (refer to Table 7–2).

The entry (authoring) process looks something like this: First, a new item is begun by clicking along the line of descent from the Recipe element. This insertion point allows new items to attach as siblings to the other items in the recipe.

To insert the Item element, select *Item* in the Element Catalog. Click the *Insert* button at the bottom of the Element Catalog. This is shown happening in Figure 7–21, in the upper right corner of the screen.

The element inserts, and the Item element bubble appears in the Structure View. You now have an insertion point in the document but cannot type. The child elements that are allowed inside Item then show in the Element Catalog and can be inserted.

When you insert elements, new choices show in the Element Catalog.

In the next section, you will get more involved in these sample documents and perform some editing tasks.

Table 7–2.   Set Available Elements Options

OPTION	ELEMENTS DISPLAYED	PURPOSE
Valid Elements for Working Start to finish	Bold checkmark Question mark	Writing a document from the top down.
Valid Elements for Working in Any Order	Bold checkmark Light checkmark Question mark	Editing out of order but want to keep the document valid.
Elements Allowed Anywhere in Parent	All elements allowed within the current parent element	Editing the structure of the parent element.
All Elements	All elements defined in the document's EDD	Editing and not worried about validity. Or, wrapping unstructured content and need access to all elements as you go.
Customized List	Elements you specify	When you want to control what elements are used, and the order in which they appear.

NOTE   If you make your own structure, you can make it as flexible or restrictive as you want. In the Recipe example, the structure is very strict and few elements are listed as valid (bold checkmark) in the Element Catalog. The XDocBook example, on the other hand, is flexible and many elements are often listed in the Element Catalog as valid.

Wrap

Wrapping allows you to wrap elements around existing content or existing elements. You must first select the content or elements that need to be wrapped. When you select the *wrapper* element and click *Wrap*, the wrapper element's beginning tag goes above the start of

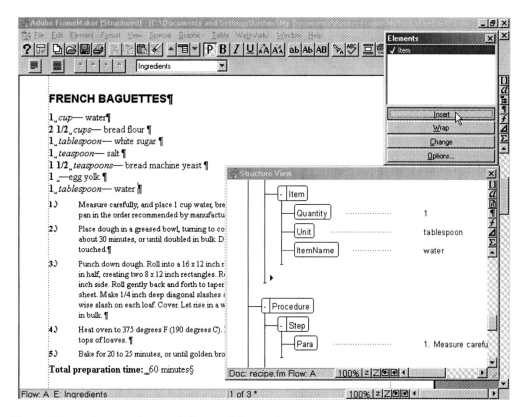

Figure 7–21.   An Item *element is inserted in a recipe.*

Figure 7–22.   The Element Catalog shows elements allowed inside the Item *element.*

your selection, and the end tag goes below the end of your selection. Each of these is best clarified with an example.

An example of wrapping content is a Para that contains terminology. The EDD includes a GlossaryTerm element that is supposed to be used for terms. Therefore, you would highlight the text in the Para element that is the term you want, select GlossaryTerm from the Element Catalog, and click *Wrap*.

An example of wrapping elements is a Para element that needs to be placed inside a Note. Click to highlight the Para element that you want in the Structure View, select Note from the Element Catalog, and click *Wrap*.

NOTE   There is also an Unwrap on the Element menu. If you select an element, all of its descendents are highlighted. Selecting *Unwrap* removes the element and leaves all of the descendents.

Change

If you insert an element and then need to change it, you can use Change to turn the element into another element.

For example, if you have a Para element that you wish to turn into a Note, select the Para element bubble in the Structure View, highlight Note in the Element Catalog, and click *Change*. In the Structure View, you will see the Para element change into a Note element. Formatting may also adjust in the Document window.

Move (Drag or Nudge)

In addition to the items available on the Element Catalog, you have the option to move items by dragging and nudging.

With *dragging*, you can choose to adjust the formatting automatically if the context of the element changes. In this case, formatting would be set up in advance in the EDD. View the bulleted list in Figure 7–23. The items in the list use the *Bulleted* paragraph format. Each item's text is inside a Para element (the elements can be seen in the Structure View). If a Para element is dragged out of its current location inside a ListItem element, and that Para element is then dropped into another part of the structure, the text within the Para element will reformat according to its new context—the element it is now inside.

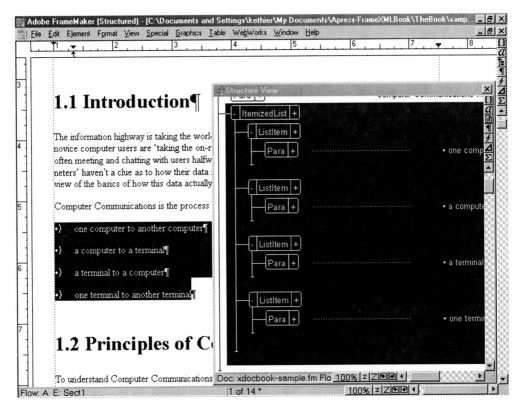

Figure 7–23.   A bulleted list in a structured document will look like this.

Nudging provides you with the ability to promote or demote elements in the structure. This means that you can make a parent a child, or a child a parent.

To nudge and change a child element into a parent element, click on the element that you want to promote. Move your hand slightly to the left—very slightly! The cursor will turn into a fat, black arrow. When you see this arrow, release the mouse button and the element will be promoted in the structure. You should see its movement in the Structure View. You may see formatting changes in the document caused by its change of location in the hierarchy.

To nudge and change a parent element into the child of another element, click down on the element that you want to demote. Move your hand slightly to the right—very slightly! The cursor will turn into a fat, black arrow. When you see the arrow, release the mouse button and the element will be demoted. You should see its movement in the Structure View. You may see formatting changes in the document caused by its change of location in the hierarchy.

NOTE Nudging can cause validation errors, so watch for red indicators. If any red shows in the Structure View, you may need to move or nudge the element until it is in a valid location.

Merge and Split

Finally, you can merge and split elements. Because you cannot necessarily backspace or enter in structure, merging and splitting are important for combining or breaking apart elements.

To split, place your insertion point in your text where you want an element to break and click *Element>Split*.

To merge, select two sibling elements that you wish to combine and click *Element>Merge*.

Understanding from Where Structure Comes

In this section, you get to the heart of the structure—the EDD. The EDD is from where your structure comes. If you are the structure designer, you will create an EDD and enter your elements, their attributes, and your content rules into it.

Figure 7–24 shows part of an EDD for a structured recipe document.

There are certain syntax rules that you need to know in order to understand the EDD in Figure 7–24 and other EDDs you may work with. Referring to this figure may help you see some of this syntax in context.

When an element is created, that element is given a rule regarding its structure. In FrameMaker, this is shown in the EDD as the *General Rule*. You can see this with the element named Recipe, which is shown in Figure 7–24.

The child elements (or text) that may be included inside the element being defined are named in the General Rule. The syntax symbols are used, along with the child element names, to signify the order and frequency of those elements. The frequency symbols are described in Table 7–3.

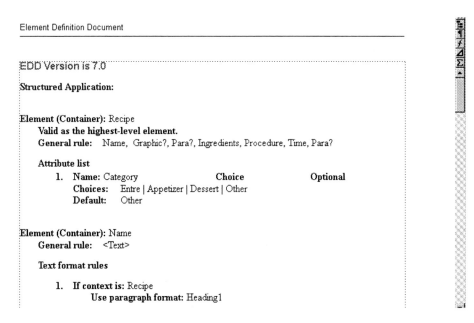

Figure 7–24.   This structure is part of an EDD.

Table 7–3.   Symbols Indicating Frequency

SYMBOL	EXAMPLE	REQUIRED OR OPTIONAL	MEANING (HOW MANY)
(No Symbol)	Para	The element is required for the structure to be valid.	Only one can be inserted at the specified location.
Question Mark	Para?	The element is optional and can be used or omitted.	Only one can be inserted at the specific location, or you can have none since it is optional.
Plus	Para+	The element is required for the structure to be valid.	As many as you want can be inserted at the specific location, but you are required to have at least one.
Asterisk	Para*	The element is optional and can be used or omitted.	As many as you want can be inserted at the specific location, or you can have none since it is optional.

In addition to the symbols for frequency, there are symbols for the order of occurrence of child elements (see Table 7–4). These are used in the General Rule between element names.

Table 7–4. Connector Symbols

SYMBOL	EXAMPLES	MEANING
comma: ,	Head, Para Head, Para+, Graphic?	The elements must occur in the order given. The symbols mentioned in Table X-X do not lose their meaning.
pipe: |	Para | List Para | List | Table | Graphic	One of the elements may occur. Thinking of this as an OR, as in "this element OR that element" may be helpful.
ampersand: &	Para & List Para & List & Table & Graphic	All of the elements may occur in any order. Thinking of this as an AND, as in "this element AND that element" may also be helpful. With the ampersand, the elements can occur in any order but all must occur (unless an asterisk or question mark appears with it).
parenthese: ( )	Head, (Para | List) Head, Para, (Para | List | Table)+	Parenthesis may be used to group elements. This can allow you to hone the rule so that child elements are controlled the way you want.

NOTE   Authored documents that follow the General Rules for all elements in the EDD are considered to be valid documents.

These symbols are explored more thoroughly in the next section, using the Recipe example.

Reviewing the Cookbook EDD

In this section, portions of the cookbook DTD will be examined. This will give you an understanding of the structure within the *recipe.fm* sample document.

First, look at the Structure View of your example recipe, shown in Figure 7–25.

In this particular screenshot, the elements are collapsed so that you can see all of the child elements inside Recipe.

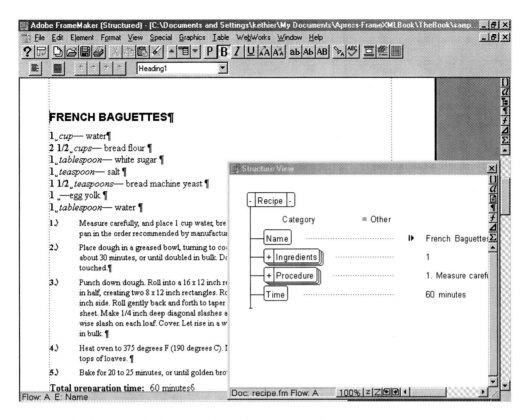

Figure 7–25.   View the Recipe example in the Structure View.

This recipe has a structure that includes a Name element inside the Recipe element. The Name element uses a Heading1 paragraph format. The structure and formatting come from the EDD.

Now take a look at the EDD portion relating to Recipe and Name. In Figure 7–26, you will see the Cookbook EDD portion that requires Name to be inside Recipe.

Also in the EDD are the settings for the Name element. As you can see, the Name element is designed to contain text rather than other elements. You can insert a Name element and then type directly into it.

The Name element also contains formatting information that tells FrameMaker to automatically tag its content with a paragraph format called Heading1 if the Name element is inside a Recipe element. That is why the paragraph format automatically appears when you insert the Name element.

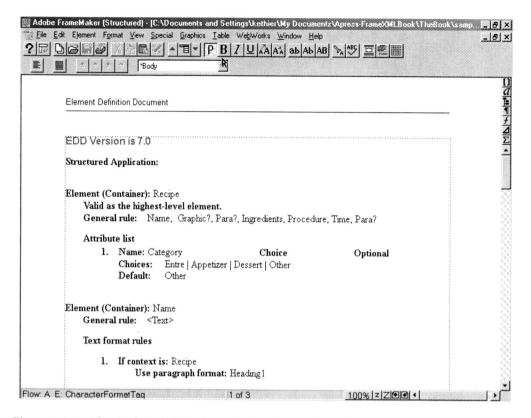

Figure 7–26.   The CookBook EDD shows the Recipe *and* Name *elements.*

Summary

In this section, structure was put under a microscope for several sample documents. You saw what structure looks like, how it can be adjusted, and where it comes from (the EDD).

The EDD contains information on elements and attributes, along with formatting information. As elements are inserted, moved, or otherwise adjusted, the formatting may adjust with them.

NOTE   EDDs are explored further in Chapters 10 and 12. Chapter 10 also describes how a FrameMaker EDD fits with a DTD for XML round tripping.

CHAPTER 8

Importing XML to Create Structured FrameMaker Documents

THIS CHAPTER DESCRIBES how XML becomes a FrameMaker structured document and some of the controls behind the scenes. The results are explored in this chapter.

Using an XML Instance

There are different ways to use an XML instance. Some use—or reuse—involves complex repository systems or proprietary tools. The methods of use described here, however, involve simple file management.

The sections below take a closer look at the XML-to-FrameMaker process and Import and Open options. In this chapter, you will find information on both of these options and what happens to your XML during each procedure. Common error messages encountered will also be explained.

XML instance = XML document

Importing an XML File

FrameMaker's *File>Import>File* is one method of getting XML into FrameMaker. This import provides you with the following two options for using your XML:

1. *Import of an XML instance (FILE>IMPORT>FILE) with IMPORT BY REFERENCE* This process provides some of XML's extensibility and reuse capabilities to FrameMaker documents—and takes advantage of FrameMaker's linking (text inset) capability. Often used to reuse XML in another document, the Import by Reference function holds the XML in the FrameMaker document as a text inset (text insets are described in the next section).

2. *Import of an XML instance (FILE>IMPORT>FILE) with COPY INTO DOCUMENT* This is a good shortcut to structured documents if you do not have a FrameMaker structured Application set up. It provides access to the template that *File>Open* does not provide in the absence of a structured Application. It is usually used when importing into an *empty* FrameMaker file (actually, the document has to have at least one element—an existing structure—before the import). If this empty file is created from your template, it allows its formatting to be in place for use on the imported XML.

Importing by Reference (Text Insets)

The source in an unstructured document may be a FrameMaker file, or may be of any file type that FrameMaker has a filter to import. The import filters include Word, WordPerfect, Interleaf, and many more.

A text inset is created when one file (the source) is imported by reference (thereby linked) into a FrameMaker file (the destination). To edit the inset (the source), you return to that source file. When the source changes, the inset in the destination file reflects these changes. Figure 8–1 clarifies the relationship between an inset and its destination (this figure is applicable to both FrameMaker *and* structured FrameMaker documents).

To clarify the relationship in an XML round-trip environment, Figure 8–2 shows the same relationship but with XML as the source.

Reviewing how a recipe XML document can be opened directly in FrameMaker, you will find that structure is created automatically as the import is done. FrameMaker uses the XML elements (tags) to produce the structure.

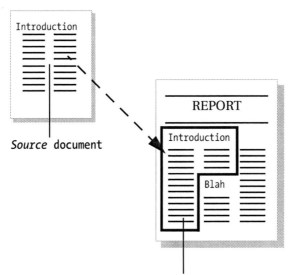

Figure 8–1.   Text inset linking is clarified.

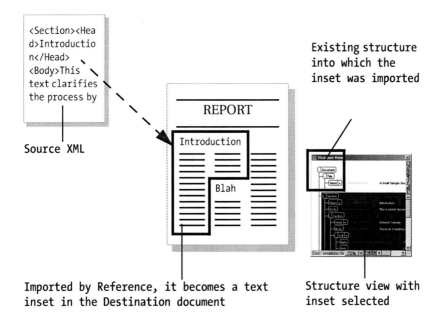

Figure 8–2.   An XML source creates a text inset.

In FrameMaker, assume for example purposes that you have a FrameMaker structured document and some XML to reuse. The XML is the source file that will be inset into the FrameMaker destination document.

If you wish to use the Import by Reference option and create a text inset, the process will work something like this:

1. Create the XML document (source).

    Because you will bring this in as a part of a larger document (or at least inside an existing structure with a root element), you will want to omit the DOCTYPE and any *internal DTD* information.

2. Open your structured document (destination).

    Your structured document cannot be completely empty. It must have at least one element so that FrameMaker *sees* it as a structured document. Importing the element definitions is not enough, so make sure that you insert an initial element— even if it means removing it after your XML is imported.

NOTE   In the real world, you will design your XML structure to allow certain elements to be the *root* element in the insets. Other elements would be designed to wrap around them at the document level.

3. Click in the structured document, putting your insertion point where you want the XML placed. Be sure to consider your structure.

4. Click *File>Import>File*.

    The Import dialog box appears, as shown in Figure 8–3.

5. Browse and click on the inset XML document filename.

6. At the bottom of the dialog box, select *Import by Reference,* if it is not already selected (this selection is what creates the inset).

   This is also shown in Figure 8–3.

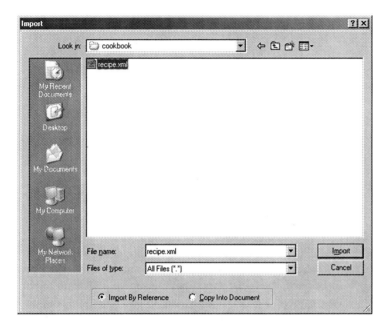

Figure 8–3.   The Import dialog box appears.

7. Click *Import.*

   Because you have selected a non-FrameMaker file, the *Unknown File Type* dialog box appears. The XML file type should be selected in the listing (as shown).

NOTE If XML is not selected, double-check the file you are importing. You may have a non-XML file or inadvertently grabbed the wrong file.

8. Click *Convert.*

9. When the Import Structured Text by Reference dialog box appears, select either Automatic or Manual updating.

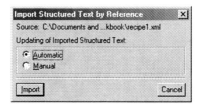

Automatic means that each time your destination document is opened, the latest version of the source will be pulled in. If you choose *Manual* instead, the source will not update unless you deliberately update it.

10. Click *Import.*

11. In the next dialog box—Use Structured Application—select the Application appropriate for the structure being used in the source and destination documents.

12. Click *Continue.*

The XML should now be structured FrameMaker content and visible in your document.

NOTE   It is recommended that you validate your document at this point to ensure the imported elements are in a proper location and that no required elements are missing.

13. *Save* your file.

You now have a single structured document, with your XML source linked—and inset—within the FrameMaker destination file. You can open the Structure View and peruse the structure created from the XML elements.

Anytime that the XML source changes, the change can be reflected within the FrameMaker file. To test this,

1. Modify the source XML and *Save* it.

2. Double-click the corresponding inset in the destination document.

3. In the dialog box that appears, select the structured Application as before.

4. Click *Continue*.

The inset will now reflect the modified XML text.

Errors during Inset Creation

If you see an error log instead of structured FrameMaker content, then your XML document may require some adjustments. One common error is caused by the presence of a DOCTYPE declaration. You may need to remove this from your XML source and try again. An example of the DOCTYPE error log is shown in Figure 8–4.

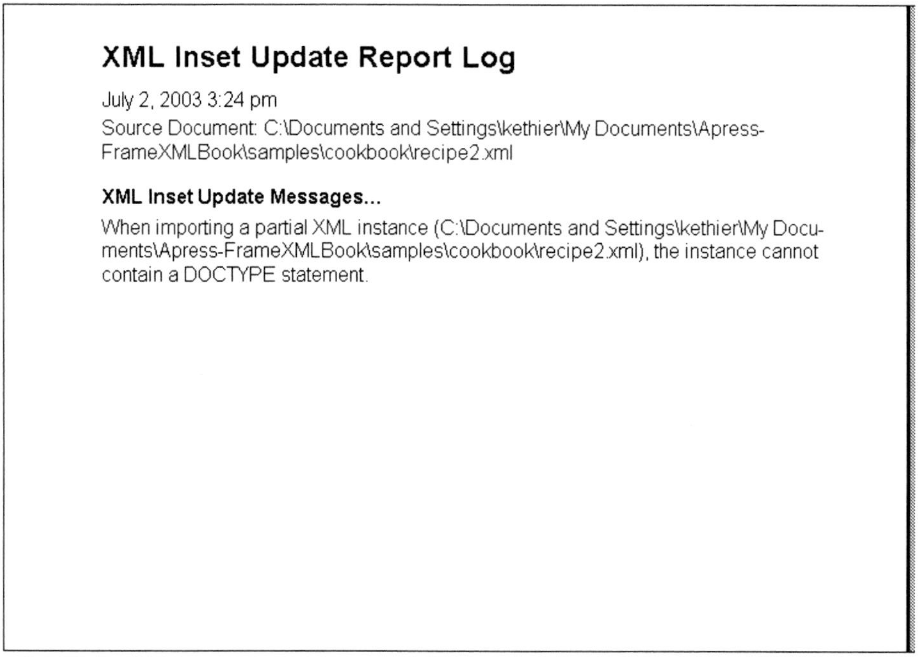

Figure 8–4.   An error can occur when importing XML with a DOCTYPE.

Importing by Copy Into Document

If you want to use the Import function, but do not want to create an inset, the process would work pretty much the same as when creating an inset. The differences are:

- At Step 6 on page 157, you would select *Copy Into Document* instead of *Import By Reference*

- Your imported XML would become structured content within the file and be directly editable. There would be no link, and updating could be done directly in the created FrameMaker document

Opening an XML File

In addition to being able to import an XML document into FrameMaker, you can open XML and create one—or many—structured documents (and saved) automatically.

A single structured FrameMaker document being created from an XML file was shown in Chapter 4. A separate example here creates multiple structured FrameMaker documents (a FrameMaker book and related files) by opening one XML file that contains external entities.

Review of Multi-file Book Creation

If the goal of working with XML includes creation of FrameMaker structured books, then some of your XML instances will be designed to create entire books.

When opening an XML instance (*File>Open*) to create a structured FrameMaker book, the XML will need to cite entities, use process instructions, and so forth, for the XML to create the book and all the files within the book.

To accomplish this, your XML instance must contain special constructs. XML has something called an *external* [text] *entity*. Using these external entities breaks large files down into separate XML documents. In FrameMaker, they can form FrameMaker books, providing users with access to all of FrameMaker's book-level features: numbering, pagination, and generated file creation.

The process for opening an XML document and creating a book goes something like this.

1. Create the XML document that will create the book. An example XML instance is shown in Figure 8–5.

2. Click *File>Open* and select the XML.

3. Click *Open*.

Entities are a kind of *replaceable* that you reference in your XML and then pull from elsewhere. Mathematically, it may be thought of as "let X = Y" where an entity is named X and when you type &X; in your XML then Y is displayed. External entities allow you to pull in separate XML documents, as is being done in Figure 8–5.

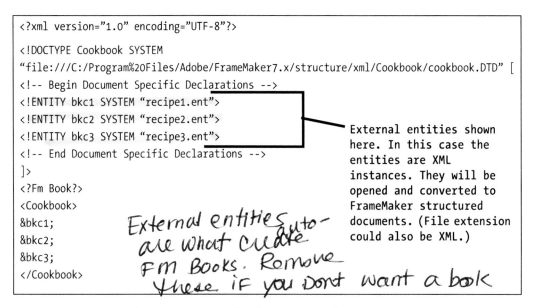

```
<?xml version="1.0" encoding="UTF-8"?>

<!DOCTYPE Cookbook SYSTEM
"file:///C:/Program%20Files/Adobe/FrameMaker7.x/structure/xml/Cookbook/cookbook.DTD" [
<!-- Begin Document Specific Declarations -->
<!ENTITY bkc1 SYSTEM "recipe1.ent">
<!ENTITY bkc2 SYSTEM "recipe2.ent">
<!ENTITY bkc3 SYSTEM "recipe3.ent">
<!-- End Document Specific Declarations -->
]>
<?Fm Book?>
<Cookbook>
&bkc1;
&bkc2;
&bkc3;
</Cookbook>
```

External entities shown here. In this case the entities are XML instances. They will be opened and converted to FrameMaker structured documents. (File extension could also be XML.)

External entities are what auto-create FM Books. Remove these if you Dont want a book

Figure 8–5.   An XML document creates a book in FrameMaker.

ERROR   An error regarding *DTD not found* may appear if your XML document has a DOCTYPE specified but the DTD is not in the listed path.

4. In the next dialog box—Use Structured Application—select the structured Application appropriate for the document being opened.

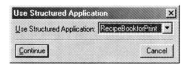

5. Click *Continue.*

6. When the Save Book dialog box appears, give your book a name (typing the extension is optional).

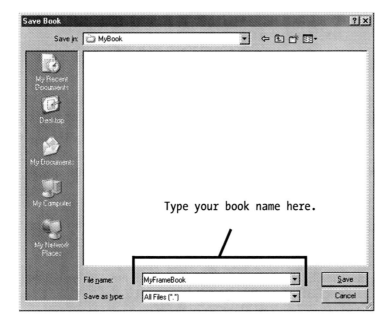

7. Click *Save.*

FrameMaker opens the book and saves it, then creates all the
files within the book from the entities (and element content
if any) and saves them. You can see these actions being
performed as they appear on the book's status bar (lower left-
hand corner of the book).

When FrameMaker finishes, you will have a book containing
multiple FrameMaker files ready for editing and updating.

ERROR   You may get an *Entities not found* error message
if any of the entities are not where expected, or if they
have filenames that do not match the entity listing.

There are several functions that—working together or separately—help you create FrameMaker books from XML. These are
processing instructions, XML external entities, and FrameMaker
Read/Write rules.

- *Processing Instructions (PIs)*   These can be placed within your
  XML. They tell FrameMaker when to perform certain tasks,

such as creating a book or creating a document with a specific name. For example:

```
<?FM book?>
<?FM document "recipe1"?>
```

- *Entities*   Similar to the example of Figure 8–5, the upcoming entity example shows a *name.ent* filename of that can be grabbed and used to create a FrameMaker file. The second line in a real document would appear further down, indicating where the FrameMaker file appears in the book.

```
<!ENTITY name SYTEM "name.ent">
&name;
```

- *Read/Write Rules*   Read/Write rules can be used to do many things. One of these is to take a particular element (and all descendents) and place into a file as named. For example:

```
reader generate book {
    put element "recipe1" in file "recipe1.fm";
}
```

More on Read/Write rules is available in Chapter 13 and in Adobe's *Structure Developer's Guide* found in the FrameMaker installation folder under OnlineManuals.

More on: Frame R-W Rules

Examining the Created Structure

The cookbook example structure imported in previous sections is shown partly collapsed in Figure 8–6. The root element in this structure is Recipe. This has an Category attribute, for which the value is *Other* (remember all attributes in XML have a name/value pair).

Nested inside Recipe are four child elements. The structure rules actually allow for more, and those rules will be examined shortly. The four child elements showing are Name, Ingredients, Procedure, and Time.

In the XML document in Figure 8–7, we see the same structure. You can see Recipe with the name/value pair of the attribute. You can also see the four child elements, shown in bold for easier viewing.

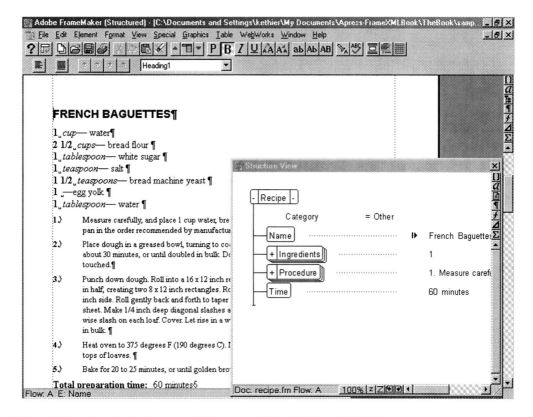

Figure 8–6. A recipe is shown with Structure View (collapsed view).

Reviewing the EDD and DTD Relationship

In the structured document explored in an earlier section, you saw elements with names like Recipe, Ingredients, and Time. To work within the FrameMaker structure, these elements were defined first. They were given names, assigned child elements or content, and given formatting instructions. These tasks happened within two documents: the DTD and the EDD. Both documents are explored here.

NOTE These documents were called into action in Step 4 on page 162 when the structured Application was selected.

```
<?xml version="1.0" encoding="UTF-8"?> <!DOCTYPE Recipe SYSTEM
"file:///C:/Program%20Files/Adobe/FrameMaker7.1/structure/xml/CookBook/Cookbook.DTD" [
<!-- Begin Document Specific Declarations -->
 <!-- End Document Specific Declarations -->
]> <Recipe Category="Other"><Name>French Baguettes</Name>
<Ingredients><Item><Quantity>1</Quantity><Unit> cup</Unit><ItemName>
water</ItemName></Item> <Item><Quantity>2 1/2</Quantity><Unit> cups</Unit><ItemName> bread
flour </ItemName></Item> <Item><Quantity>1</Quantity><Unit> tablespoon</Unit><ItemName>
white sugar </ItemName></Item> <Item><Quantity>1</Quantity><Unit> teaspoon</Unit><ItemName>
salt </ItemName></Item> <Item><Quantity>1 1/2</Quantity><Unit> teaspoons</Unit><ItemName>
bread machine yeast </ItemName></Item> <Item><Quantity>1 </Quantity><Unit></Unit><ItemName>
egg yolk </ItemName></Item> <Item><Quantity>1</Quantity><Unit> tablespoon</Unit><ItemName>
water </ItemName></Item></Ingredients><Procedure><Step><Para>Measure carefully, and place 1
cup water, bread flour, sugar, salt, and yeast into bread machine pan in the order recommended
by manufacturer. Select Dough/Manual cycle.</Para></Step> <Step><Para>Place dough in a
greased bowl, turning to coat all sides. Cover. Let rise in a warm place for about 30 minutes,
or until doubled in bulk. Dough is ready if indentation remains when touched.</Para></Step>
<Step><Para>Punch down dough. Roll into a 16 x 12 inch rectangle on a lightly floured surface.
Cut dough in half, creating two 8 x 12 inch rectangles. Roll up each half of dough tightly,
beginning at 12 inch side. Roll gently back and forth to taper end. Place 3 inches apart on
a greased cookie sheet. Make 1/4 inch deep diagonal slashes across loaves every 2 inches, or
make one lengthwise slash on each loaf. Cover. Let rise in a warm place for 30 to 40 minutes,
or until doubled in bulk. </Para></Step> <Step><Para>Heat oven to 375 degrees F (190 degrees
C). Mix egg yolk with 1 tablespoon water; brush over tops of loaves. </Para></Step>
<Step><Para>Bake for 20 to 25 minutes, or until golden
brown.</Para></Step></Procedure><Time>60 minutes</Time></Recipe>
```

Figure 8–7.   The recipe is shown in XML.

Viewing a DTD

DTDs contain lists of elements and related items that make up your structure. A DTD may contain

- Element names and corresponding content models (rules regarding what each element can contain)

- Attributes for defined elements

- Entity information

DTDs can be made independent of FrameMaker. You can make a DTD with Microsoft Notepad, TIBCO TurboXML, Altova XML SPY, and many other tools.

NOTE If desired, you may also create a DTD by exporting from a FrameMaker EDD.

XML also has schema, which define the elements and other parts of structure; however, FrameMaker does not currently support schema use (as of version 7.1). XML schema are written in XML, whereas DTDs are not.

Explaining an EDD

EDDs contain element and attribute information, which makes them similar to DTDs. In addition to structure information, EDDs allow you to set up *hooks* that reach into FrameMaker to invoke formatting and access features. Therefore, EDDs contain:

- Element names and corresponding content models (rules regarding what they can contain)

- Attributes for defined elements

- Formatting for your elements

On this last point, recall "Reviewing a Cookbook Sample Document" on page 135, when you looked at an example of a Heading1 paragraph format being applied to the Name element within our recipe.

In the DTD, there is a Name element with no formatting information. In the corresponding template, there is a Heading1 paragraph format. In the EDD, then, is a Name element with text formatting rules that state that Name, inside the parent Recipe, should be typed with the paragraph format Heading1.

The result is that when a Name element is inserted, the paragraph format automatically applies.

NOTE FrameMaker automatically applies its formatting when you insert, change, drag, import, paste, or wrap an element inside a structured document. FrameMaker also automatically applies its formatting when you reimport the element definitions from an EDD or other structured document.

EDDs and their creation are explained further in Chapter 12.

Summary

You can bring XML into FrameMaker through either the *File>Import* or the *File>Open* functions. When XML is brought into FrameMaker, document structure is created automatically using the XML elements.

The EDD provides you with element and attribute information that is similar to a DTD, plus the EDD includes formatting data. This allows you to apply formatting as XML is brought in, rather than having to do all the formatting by hand.

CHAPTER 9

Using Style Sheets and Namespaces in XML

IF YOU PLAN TO USE cascading style sheets (CSS) or Extensible Stylesheet Language (XSL) to format XML produced from FrameMaker documents, then you may find it helpful to have FrameMaker provide a starting point on your style sheets. The options available with FrameMaker and with Quadralay WebWorks Publisher are described in this chapter. XML namespace support in FrameMaker is also discussed in this chapter.

Understanding Style Sheets

When an XML instance is opened in a browser like Internet Explorer, the XML displays the way that the browser's own style sheets tell it to display. The browser settings control how the XML displays as well as your options for navigating the document. If you prefer to control the XML display, then you may choose to use CSS or XSL style sheets or other XML display options[1] for displaying your XML in a browser.

---

1. Another option is to use XSLT, a subset of XSL, to turn XML into other types of markups such as HTML. XSLT is not covered in this book, but it is a technology worth learning more about. Check out Michael D. Thomas' book, *Oracle XSQL*, for a great hidden tutorial on XSLT.

If you view one of the sample recipe XML files in the Internet Explorer browser, you may see something similar to the XML display in Figure 9–1.

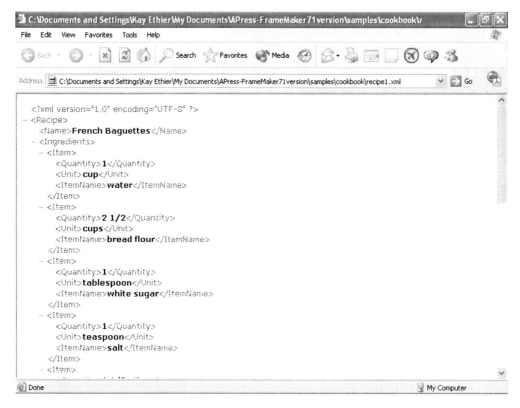

Figure 9–1.   An XML instance is viewed in Internet Explorer with default browser formatting.

Note the display of the beginning and end tags along with the content. Although you cannot see this in the screen shot, the angle brackets and end slashes show up in blue and the tags show up in red.

You should also note that in front of the beginning tags of elements with child elements (such as Ingredients near the top), a minus appears. Clicking this minus collapses the element's child elements. The minus then turns into a plus. Expand the child elements again by clicking the plus, which again displays as a minus. This is very similar to the way the FrameMaker Structure View allows you to collapse and expand your view.

If you want your XML to appear differently—to be easier to read or to look like a Web page—then you may use a CSS. The style sheet needs to be created, and then a pointer to it added in the XML file.

This causes the style sheet to be *called into action* when the XML file is opened in the browser. Figure 9–2 shows an XML document's top lines, with the CSS declaration in place.

```
<?xml version="1.0" encoding="UTF-8"?>
<!DOCTYPE Recipe SYSTEM "cookbook.dtd" [

<!-- Begin Document Specific Declarations -->


<!-- End Document Specific Declarations -->

]>
<?xml-stylesheet href="recipe_css.css" type="text/css"?>

<Recipe><Name>French Baguettes</Name>
<Ingredients><Item><Quantity>1</Quantity><Unit> cup</Unit><ItemName>
water</ItemName></Item>
<Item><Quantity>2 1/2</Quantity><Unit> cups</Unit><ItemName> bread
flour </ItemName></Item>

[remainder of XML instance cropped to save space]
```

Figure 9–2.   An XML instance is shown with CSS.

In this case, the CSS declaration is

```
<?xml-stylesheet href="recipe_css.css" type="text/css"?>
```

If the XML file in Figure 9–2 is opened in Internet Explorer, the CSS will be used to format it rather than the browser's default settings. An example XML instance with CSS in Internet Explorer is shown in Figure 9–3. This file uses the default CSS created by FrameMaker when the Save As XML operation is performed.

This looks quite different than the way it looked in Figure 9–1, does it not? If you wanted to adjust the way it looks, you could modify the CSS and refresh the view in the browser.

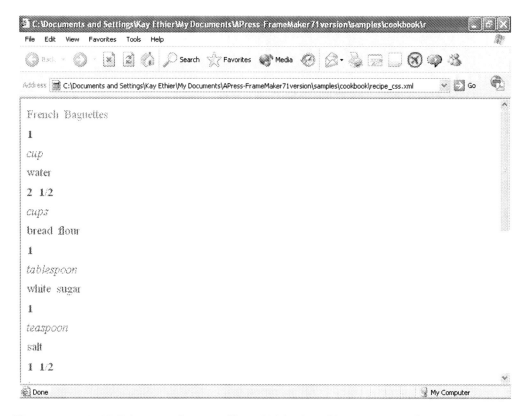

Figure 9–3.   An XML instance formatted by a CSS is viewed in Internet Explorer.

Reviewing Options for XML (XSL and CSS)

Once you have FrameMaker structured documents that look the way that you want them to look, FrameMaker can generate a corresponding style sheet. You may also use the style sheets that install with Quadralay WebWorks Publisher.

Using the FrameMaker CSS creation utility allows you to take the formatting from your template and essentially *convert* it into a style sheet for use with exported XML. The results may not be perfect, but at least you can use the FrameMaker-generated style sheet as a starting point.

The WebWorks Publisher Standard Edition (and the Professional Edition) also provides CSS and XSL within their installations.

CSS with FrameMaker

FrameMaker has a utility for generating CSS—specifically CSS2—from the structure that you create for your files. Using its CSS creation utility (*File>Structure Tools>Generate CSS2*), FrameMaker produces a CSS if you are in one of the following types of files:

- An EDD

- A structured template

- A structured document

CSS2 is short for cascading style sheet language, level 2. More information on the CSS specifications may be found at w3c.org.

Figure 9–4 shows the example recipe that you have seen in other parts of this book. This particular file, called *recipe1.xml,* is open in structured FrameMaker and has been formatted using a structured template, *Template2.fm.*

NOTE   Both of these files are available in the cookbook sample files available from the book's website. Instructions for accessing the samples are in Chapter 6.

The CSS created from this example recipe document is shown in Figure 9–5. To create this CSS from the same XML file, perform the following steps.

1. Open the recipe structured document.

2. From the menu, choose *File>Structure Tools>Generate CSS2.*

3. Next, when the Save dialog box appears, provide a file name for the CSS file, and Save.

4. A prompt will appear for an Application name, but because this is not needed for creating the CSS, select *<No Application>* and click the *Continue* button.

The CSS settings for the text are coming from the settings within the structured document. Colors and other text settings are picked up

FRENCH BAGUETTES¶

1 *cup*— water¶
2 1/2 *cups*— bread flour ¶
1 *tablespoon*— white sugar ¶
1 *teaspoon*— salt ¶
1 1/2 *teaspoons*— bread machine yeast ¶
1 — egg yolk ¶
1 *tablespoon*— water ¶

1.) Measure carefully, and place 1 cup water, bread flour, sugar, salt, and yeast into bread machine pan in the order recommended by manufacturer. Select Dough/Manual cycle.¶

2.) Place dough in a greased bowl, turning to coat all sides. Cover. Let rise in a warm place for about 30 minutes, or until doubled in bulk. Dough is ready if indentation remains when touched.¶

3.) Punch down dough. Roll into a 16 x 12 inch rectangle on a lightly floured surface. Cut dough in half, creating two 8 x 12 inch rectangles. Roll up each half of dough tightly, beginning at 12 inch side. Roll gently back and forth to taper end. Place 3 inches apart on a greased cookie sheet. Make 1/4 inch deep diagonal slashes across loaves every 2 inches, or make one lengthwise slash on each loaf.

Figure 9–4.   An example recipe is formatted using a FrameMaker structured template.

by FrameMaker from each element's paragraph and character format settings. These text settings are then written into the CSS.

Once you have the CSS, you may use it as it is or edit it. The CSS is a text file and may be edited in a text editor such as Notepad, or in website management tools such as Dreamweaver or GoLive.

The CSS style sheet in Figure 9–5 is shown in Figure 9–6 as opened in GoLive.

If you are not happy with the CSS that is generated by FrameMaker, your other option is to make a CSS of your own, using whatever tools you wish. If you do make your own style sheet, you will want to add a CSS declaration to your XML. You may also wish to automate the addition of the CSS declaration for future XML, and stop FrameMaker from creating a CSS for you. Each of these is discussed later in this chapter.

```
@charset "UTF-8";
/* Generated by FM Edd2Css */
/* Element: ParaIndent */
ParaIndent
{display: block;
font-family: Times New Roman;
font-weight: 400;
font-style: normal;
font-size: 10.0pt;
font-stretch: normal ;
color: #000000;
text-align: justify;
line-height: 120.0%%;
word-spacing: 0.25em;
margin-left: 0.5in;
text-indent: 0.0in;
margin-right: 0.0in;
margin-top: 0.0pt;
}
/* Element's context props */
/* TextFmt Rules Start */
ParaIndent
{
font-family: Times New Roman;
font-weight: 400;
font-style: normal;
font-size: 10.0pt;
font-stretch: normal ;
color: #000000;
text-align: justify;
line-height: 120.0%%;
word-spacing: 0.25em;
margin-left: 0.5in;
text-indent: 0.0in;
margin-right: 0.0in;
margin-top: 0.0pt;
}
/* TextFmt Rules End */
/* End Element: ParaIndent */
/* Element: Cookbook */
Cookbook
{display: block;
font-family: Times New Roman;
font-weight: 400;
font-style: normal;
font-size: 14.0pt;
font-stretch: normal ;
color: #ff0000;
text-align: left;
line-height: 121.43%%;
word-spacing: 0.25em;
margin-left: 0.0in;
text-indent: 0.0in;
margin-right: 0.0in;
margin-top: 0.0pt;
margin-bottom: 7.0pt;
}
/* Element's context props */
Cookbook > Recipe
{
margin-left: 0;
margin-right: 0;
text-indent: 0;
}
/* End Element: Cookbook */
/* Element: Recipe */
Recipe
{display: block;
font-family: Times New Roman;
font-weight: 400;
font-style: normal;
font-size: 14.0pt;
font-stretch: normal ;
color: #ff0000;
text-align: left;
line-height: 121.43%%;
```

```
word-spacing: 0.25em;
margin-left: 0.0in;
text-indent: 0.0in;
margin-right: 0.0in;
margin-top: 0.0pt;
margin-bottom: 7.0pt;
}
/* Element's context props */
Recipe > Name, Recipe > Graphic,
Recipe > Para, Recipe >
Ingredients, Recipe > Procedure,
Recipe > Time
{
margin-left: 0;
margin-right: 0;
text-indent: 0;
}
/* End Element: Recipe */
/* Element: Name */
Name
{display: block;
word-spacing: 0.25em;
margin-left: 0.0in;
text-indent: 0.0in;
margin-right: 0.0in;
margin-top: 0.0pt;
margin-bottom: 7.0pt;
}
/* Element's context props */
/* TextFmt Rules Start */
Recipe > Name
{
font-family: Arial;
font-weight: 700;
font-style: normal;
font-size: 16.0pt;
text-transform: uppercase ;
font-stretch: normal ;
color: #ff0000;
text-align: center;
line-height: 112.5%%;
word-spacing: 0.25em;
margin-left: 0.0in;
text-indent: 0.0in;
margin-right: 0.0in;
margin-top: 68.0pt;
margin-bottom: 6.0pt;
}
/* TextFmt Rules End */
/* End Element: Name */
/* Element: Graphic */
Graphic
{display: block;
word-spacing: 0.25em;
margin-left: 0.0in;
text-indent: 0.0in;
margin-right: 0.0in;
margin-top: 0.0pt;
margin-bottom: 7.0pt;
}
/* Element's context props */
/* End Element: Graphic */
/* Element: Ingredients */
Ingredients
{display: block;
word-spacing: 0.25em;
margin-left: 0.0in;
text-indent: 0.0in;
margin-right: 0.0in;
margin-top: 0.0pt;
margin-bottom: 7.0pt;
}
/* Element's context props */
Ingredients > Item
{
margin-left: 0;
```

```
margin-right: 0;
text-indent: 0;
}
/* End Element: Ingredients */
/* Element: Procedure */
Procedure
{display: block;
word-spacing: 0.25em;
margin-left: 0.0in;
text-indent: 0.0in;
margin-right: 0.0in;
margin-top: 0.0pt;
margin-bottom: 7.0pt;
}
/* Element's context props */
Procedure > Step
{
margin-left: 0;
margin-right: 0;
text-indent: 0;
}
/* End Element: Procedure */
/* Element: Time */
Time
{display: block;
font-family: Times New Roman;
font-weight: 400;
font-style: normal;
font-size: 14.0pt;
font-stretch: normal ;
color: #ff0000;
text-align: left;
line-height: 121.43%%;
word-spacing: 0.25em;
margin-left: 0.0in;
text-indent: 0.0in;
margin-right: 0.0in;
margin-top: 0.0pt;
margin-bottom: 7.0pt;
}
/* Element's context props */
/* Prefix Rules Start */
Time:before
{
content: "Total preparation
time:";
}
Time:before
{
font-weight: 700;
text-transform: none ;
letter-spacing: normal;
font-stretch: normal ;
color: #000000;
}
Time:before *, * Time:before,
Time:before
{
vertical-align: baseline ;
display: inline;text-decoration:
none ;
}
/* Prefix Rules End */
/* TextFmt Rules Start */
Time
{
font-family: Times New Roman;
font-weight: 400;
font-style: normal;
font-size: 14.0pt;
font-stretch: normal ;
color: #ff0000;
text-align: left;
line-height: 121.43%%;
word-spacing: 0.25em;
margin-left: 0.0in;
```

```
text-indent: 0.0in;
margin-right: 0.0in;
margin-top: 0.0pt;
margin-bottom: 7.0pt;
}
/* TextFmt Rules End */
/* End Element: Time */
/* Element: Item */
Item
{display: block;
font-family: Times New Roman;
font-weight: 400;
font-style: normal;
font-size: 14.0pt;
font-stretch: normal ;
color: #0000ff;
text-align: justify;
line-height: 121.43%%;
word-spacing: 0.25em;
margin-left: 0.0in;
text-indent: 0.0in;
margin-right: 0.0in;
margin-top: 0.0pt;
}
/* Element's context props */
/* TextFmt Rules Start */
Item
{
font-family: Times New Roman;
font-weight: 400;
font-style: normal;
font-size: 14.0pt;
font-stretch: normal ;
color: #0000ff;
text-align: justify;
line-height: 121.43%%;
word-spacing: 0.25em;
margin-left: 0.0in;
text-indent: 0.0in;
margin-right: 0.0in;
margin-top: 0.0pt;
}
/* TextFmt Rules End */
Item > Quantity, Item > Unit, Item
> ItemName
{
margin-left: 0;
margin-right: 0;
text-indent: 0;
}
/* End Element: Item */
/* Element: Quantity */
Quantity
{display: block;
word-spacing: 0.25em;
margin-left: 0.0in;
text-indent: 0.0in;
margin-right: 0.0in;
margin-top: 0.0pt;
margin-bottom: 7.0pt;
}
/* Element's context props */
/* TextFmt Rules Start */
Quantity
{
font-weight: 700;
}
/* TextFmt Rules End */
/* End Element: Quantity */
```

[remainder of CSS
cropped to fit]

Figure 9–5. An auto-generated cascading style sheet (CSS) is shown as text.

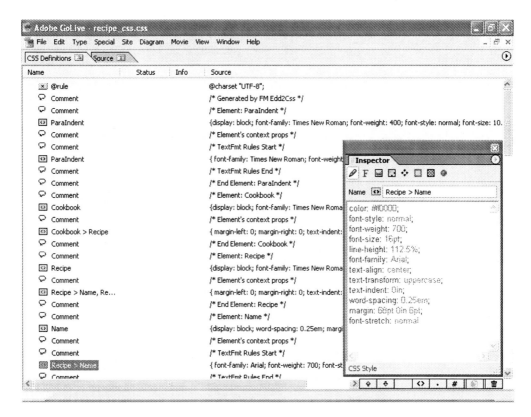

Figure 9–6. An auto-generated CSS is shown in the GoLive editing interface.

CSS with WebWorks Publisher

WebWorks Publisher Standard Edition is included on the FrameMaker installation CD and may be installed with FrameMaker.

WebWorks Publisher is designed to extract content from your FrameMaker documents and add markup around your content, making it easy for you to turn FrameMaker documents into HTML, XML, handheld device format, or even online help.

NOTE Online help templates are only installed with the WebWorks Publisher Professional Edition, not the Standard Edition that comes with FrameMaker.

The difference between the FrameMaker-generated style sheet and the WebWorks Publisher style sheet is that the WebWorks Publisher CSS is predefined. The style sheet *document.css* is installed with WebWorks Publisher and does not come from your document settings. See Figure 9–7 for the CSS as installed.

This style sheet is located in the WebWorks Publisher installation's Templates folder. Within each of the XML templates, you can navigate to a subfolder called Support. Within the Support folder is the *document.css* file.

If you use WebWorks Publisher to create XML with a CSS, then you will probably want to adjust the CSS file to get the look that you really want. You can adjust this file as needed, then use WebWorks to output your content with references to the style sheet. Your resulting XML output would use the style sheet when opened in a browser, as long as that browser supports CSS.

XSL with FrameMaker

FrameMaker, unfortunately, cannot generate an XSL style sheet. To use an XSL style sheet with FrameMaker, you will need to create an XSL style sheet with another tool and then add the reference to our XML documents (this is explained later in this chapter).

XSL with WebWorks Publisher

As with the WebWorks Publisher CSS, the XSL style sheet within WebWorks is predefined. The default XSL style sheet, *document.xsl*, is shown in Figure 9–8.

This XSL style sheet is located in the WebWorks Publisher installation's Templates folder. Within each of the XML templates, you can navigate to a subfolder called Support. Within the Support folder is the *document.xsl* file.

NOTE   Technically, the XSL style sheet of Figure 9–8 is CSS code with a few lines of XSL at the top. XSL style sheets used outside of WebWorks may appear quite different.

```
/* Document Defaults */

        a:active  { color: #0000CC}
        a:hover  { color: #CC0033}
        a:link    { color: #3366CC}
        a:visited { color: #9999CC}

        { font-family: Verdana, Arial, Helvetica, sans-serif; }
        .Body
        { color: #000000;
            font-size: 12px; font-style: normal; font-weight: normal;
            margin-left: 0em; margin-top: 0.5em; margin-bottom: 0.5em;
            text-align: left; text-indent: 0em; text-decoration: none;
            white-space: normal }
        .CellBody
        { color: #000000;
            font-size: 12px; font-style: normal; font-weight: normal;
            margin-left: 0em; margin-top: 0em; margin-bottom: 0em;
            text-align: left; text-indent: 0em; text-decoration: none;
            white-space: normal }
        .CellHeading
        { color: #003366;
            font-size: 12px; font-style: normal; font-weight: bold;
            margin-left: 0em; margin-top: 0em; margin-bottom: 0em;
            text-align: center; text-indent: 0em; text-decoration: none;
            white-space: normal }
        .GroupTitlesIX
        { color: #003366;
            font-size: 22px; font-style: normal; font-weight: bold;
            margin-left: 0em; margin-top: 0.5em; margin-bottom: 0.5em;
            text-align: left; text-indent: 0em; text-decoration: none;
            white-space: normal }
        .Heading1
        { color: #003366;
            font-size: 25px; font-style: normal; font-weight: bold;
            margin-left: 0em; margin-top: 0.5em; margin-bottom: 0.5em;
            text-align: left; text-indent: 0em; text-decoration: none;
            white-space: normal }
        .Heading2
        { color: #003366;
            font-size: 20px; font-style: normal; font-weight: normal;
            margin-left: 0em; margin-top: 0.5em; margin-bottom: 0.5em;
            text-align: left; text-indent: 0em; text-decoration: none;
            white-space: normal }
        .Heading3
        { color: #003366;
            font-size: 16px; font-style: normal; font-weight: bold;
            margin-left: 0em; margin-top: 0.5em; margin-bottom: 0.5em;
            text-align: left; text-indent: 0em; text-decoration: none;
            white-space: normal }
        .Heading4
        { color: #003366;
            font-size: 13px; font-style: italic; font-weight: bold;
            margin-left: 0em; margin-top: 0.5em; margin-bottom: 0.5em;
            text-align: left; text-indent: 0em; text-decoration: none;
            white-space: normal }
        .Indented1
        { color: #000000;
            font-size: 12px; font-style: normal; font-weight: normal;
            margin-left: 2.5em; margin-top: 0.5em; margin-bottom: 0.5em;
            text-align: left; text-indent: 0em; text-decoration: none;
            white-space: normal }
        .Indented2
        { color: #000000;
            font-size: 12px; font-style: normal; font-weight: normal;
            margin-left: 5em; margin-top: 0.5em; margin-bottom: 0.5em;
            text-align: left; text-indent: 0em; text-decoration: none;
            white-space: normal }
        .Indented3
        { color: #000000;
            font-size: 12px; font-style: normal; font-weight: normal;
            margin-left: 7.5em; margin-top: 0.5em; margin-bottom: 0.5em;
            text-align: left; text-indent: 0em; text-decoration: none;
            white-space: normal }
        .Indented4
        { color: #000000;
            font-size: 12px; font-style: normal; font-weight: normal;
            margin-left: 10em; margin-top: 0.5em; margin-bottom: 0.5em;
            text-align: left; text-indent: 0em; text-decoration: none;
            white-space: normal }
        .Indented5
        { color: #000000;
            font-size: 12px; font-style: normal; font-weight: normal;
            margin-left: 12.5em; margin-top: 0.5em; margin-bottom: 0.5em;
            text-align: left; text-indent: 0em; text-decoration: none;
            white-space: normal }
        .Level1IX
        { color: #000000;
            font-size: 12px; font-style: normal; font-weight: normal;
            margin-left: 2.5em; margin-top: 0em; margin-bottom: 0em;
            text-align: left; text-indent: 0em; text-decoration: none;
            white-space: normal }
        .Level2IX
        { color: #000000;
            font-size: 12px; font-style: normal; font-weight: normal;
            margin-left: 5em; margin-top: 0em; margin-bottom: 0em;
            text-align: left; text-indent: 0em; text-decoration: none;
            white-space: normal }
        .Level3IX
        { color: #000000;
            font-size: 12px; font-style: normal; font-weight: normal;
            margin-left: 7.5em; margin-top: 0em; margin-bottom: 0em;
            text-align: left; text-indent: 0em; text-decoration: none;
            white-space: normal }
        .Level4IX
        { color: #000000;
            font-size: 12px; font-style: normal; font-weight: normal;
            margin-left: 10em; margin-top: 0em; margin-bottom: 0em;
            text-align: left; text-indent: 0em; text-decoration: none;
            white-space: normal }
        .Level5IX
        { color: #000000;
            font-size: 12px; font-style: normal; font-weight: normal;
            margin-left: 12.5em; margin-top: 0em; margin-bottom: 0em;
            text-align: left; text-indent: 0em; text-decoration: none;
            white-space: normal }
        .NewXMLPage
        { color: #003366;
            font-size: 24px; font-style: normal; font-weight: bold;
            margin-left: 0em; margin-top: 0.5em; margin-bottom: 0.5em;
            text-align: center; text-indent: 0em; text-decoration: none;
            white-space: normal }
        .Preformatted
        { color: #000000;
            font-family: monospace;
            font-size: 12px; font-style: normal; font-weight: normal;
            margin-left: 0em; margin-top: 0em; margin-bottom: 0em;
            text-align: left; text-indent: 0em; text-decoration: none;
            white-space: pre }
        .SmartList1
        { color: #000000;
            font-size: 12px; font-style: normal; font-weight: normal;
            margin-left: 0em; margin-top: 0.25em; margin-bottom: 0.25em;
            text-align: left; text-indent: 0em; text-decoration: none;
            white-space: normal }
        .SmartList1After
        { margin-left: 0em; }
        .SmartList2
        { color: #000000;
            font-size: 12px; font-style: normal; font-weight: normal;
            margin-left: 2.5em; margin-top: 0.25em; margin-bottom: 0.25em;
            text-align: left; text-indent: 0em; text-decoration: none;
            white-space: normal }
        .SmartList2After
        { margin-left: 0em; }
```

[remainder of CSS cropped to fit]

Figure 9–7. This is a WebWorks Publisher Standard Edition CSS.

```
<?xml version="1.0"?>
<xsl:stylesheet xmlns:xsl="http://www.w3.org/TR/WD-xsl">

<!-- Page Rules -->

  <xsl:template match="/">
    <HTML>
      <HEAD>
        <xsl:apply-templates select="/wp:Document/wp:Title" />
      </HEAD>

      <STYLE>
        a:active  { color: #0000CC }
        a:hover   { color: #CC0033}
        a:link    { color: #3366CC}
        a:visited { color: #9999CC}


          { font-family: Verdana, Arial, Helvetica, sans-serif; }
        .Body
          { color: #000000;
            font-size: 12px; font-style: normal; font-weight: normal;
            margin-left: 0em; margin-top: 0.5em; margin-bottom: 0.5em;
            text-align: left; text-indent: 0em; text-decoration: none;
            white-space: normal }
        .CellBody
          { color: #000000;
            font-size: 12px; font-style: normal; font-weight: normal;
            margin-left: 0em; margin-top: 0em; margin-bottom: 0em;
            text-align: left; text-indent: 0em; text-decoration: none;
            white-space: normal }
        .CellHeading
          { color: #003366;
            font-size: 12px; font-style: normal; font-weight: bold;
            margin-left: 0em; margin-top: 0em; margin-bottom: 0em;
            text-align: center; text-indent: 0em; text-decoration: none;
            white-space: normal }
        .GroupTitlesIX
          { color: #003366;
            font-size: 22px; font-style: normal; font-weight: bold;
            margin-left: 0em; margin-top: 0.5em; margin-bottom: 0.5em;
            text-align: left; text-indent: 0em; text-decoration: none;
            white-space: normal }
        .Heading1
          { color: #003366;
            font-size: 25px; font-style: normal; font-weight: bold;
            margin-left: 0em; margin-top: 0.5em; margin-bottom: 0.5em;
            text-align: left; text-indent: 0em; text-decoration: none;
            white-space: normal }
        .Heading2
          { color: #003366;
            font-size: 20px; font-style: normal; font-weight: normal;
            margin-left: 0em; margin-top: 0.5em; margin-bottom: 0.5em;
            text-align: left; text-indent: 0em; text-decoration: none;
            white-space: normal }
        .Heading3
          { color: #003366;
            font-size: 16px; font-style: normal; font-weight: bold;
            margin-left: 0em; margin-top: 0.5em; margin-bottom: 0.5em;
            text-align: left; text-indent: 0em; text-decoration: none;
            white-space: normal }
        .Heading4
          { color: #003366;
            font-size: 13px; font-style: italic; font-weight: bold;
            margin-left: 0em; margin-top: 0.5em; margin-bottom: 0.5em;
            text-align: left; text-indent: 0em; text-decoration: none;
            white-space: normal }
        .Indented1
          { color: #000000;
            font-size: 12px; font-style: normal; font-weight: normal;
            margin-left: 2.5em; margin-top: 0.5em; margin-bottom: 0.5em;
            text-align: left; text-indent: 0em; text-decoration: none;
            white-space: normal }
        .Indented2
          { color: #000000;
            font-size: 12px; font-style: normal; font-weight: normal;
            margin-left: 5em; margin-top: 0.5em; margin-bottom: 0.5em;
                                text-align: left; text-indent: 0em; text-decoration: none;
            white-space: normal }
        .Indented3
          { color: #000000;
            font-size: 12px; font-style: normal; font-weight: normal;
            margin-left: 7.5em; margin-top: 0.5em; margin-bottom: 0.5em;
            text-align: left; text-indent: 0em; text-decoration: none;
            white-space: normal }
        .Indented4
          { color: #000000;
            font-size: 12px; font-style: normal; font-weight: normal;
            margin-left: 10em; margin-top: 0.5em; margin-bottom: 0.5em;
            text-align: left; text-indent: 0em; text-decoration: none;
            white-space: normal }
        .Indented5
          { color: #000000;
            font-size: 12px; font-style: normal; font-weight: normal;
            margin-left: 12.5em; margin-top: 0.5em; margin-bottom: 0.5em;
            text-align: left; text-indent: 0em; text-decoration: none;
            white-space: normal }
        .Level1IX
          { color: #000000;
            font-size: 12px; font-style: normal; font-weight: normal;
            margin-left: 2.5em; margin-top: 0em; margin-bottom: 0em;
            text-align: left; text-indent: 0em; text-decoration: none;
            white-space: normal }
        .Level2IX
          { color: #000000;
            font-size: 12px; font-style: normal; font-weight: normal;
            margin-left: 5em; margin-top: 0em; margin-bottom: 0em;
            text-align: left; text-indent: 0em; text-decoration: none;
            white-space: normal }
        .Level3IX
          { color: #000000;
            font-size: 12px; font-style: normal; font-weight: normal;
            margin-left: 7.5em; margin-top: 0em; margin-bottom: 0em;
            text-align: left; text-indent: 0em; text-decoration: none;
            white-space: normal }
        .Level4IX
          { color: #000000;
            font-size: 12px; font-style: normal; font-weight: normal;
            margin-left: 10em; margin-top: 0em; margin-bottom: 0em;
            text-align: left; text-indent: 0em; text-decoration: none;
            white-space: normal }
        .Level5IX
          { color: #000000;
            font-size: 12px; font-style: normal; font-weight: normal;
            margin-left: 12.5em; margin-top: 0em; margin-bottom: 0em;
            text-align: left; text-indent: 0em; text-decoration: none;
            white-space: normal }
        .Preformatted
          { color: #000000;
            font-family: monospace;
            font-size: 12px; font-style: normal; font-weight: normal;
            margin-left: 0em; margin-top: 0em; margin-bottom: 0em;
            text-align: left; text-indent: 0em; text-decoration: none;
            white-space: pre }
        .SmartList1
          { color: #000000;
            font-size: 12px; font-style: normal; font-weight: normal;
            margin-left: 0em; margin-top: 0.25em; margin-bottom: 0.25em;
            text-align: left; text-indent: 0em; text-decoration: none;
            white-space: normal }
        .SmartList2
          { color: #000000;
            font-size: 12px; font-style: normal; font-weight: normal;
            margin-left: 2.5em; margin-top: 0.25em; margin-bottom: 0.25em;
            text-align: left; text-indent: 0em; text-decoration: none;
            white-space: normal }
```

[remainder of XSL cropped to fit]

Figure 9–8.   XSL avalable within WebWorks Publisher Standard Edition.

If you use WebWorks Publisher to create XML with an XSL style sheet, then you will probably want to adjust the XSL file to get the look that you really want. You can adjust this file as needed, then use Web-Works to output your content with references to the style sheet. Your resulting XML output will use the style sheet when opened in a browser, as long as that browser supports XSL.

Including Style Sheet Settings in Your FrameMaker Structured Application

The creation of a CSS may be built into your structured Application. In version 7.0 and later, you can specify CSS creation as part of a structured Application.

Figure 9–9 shows the style sheet options available within the FrameMaker Structured Application file. As you will see in Chapter 11, you may set up an Application to automate certain actions upon XML export. Inclusion of a style sheet reference within the XML is one option.

The Application options include the ability to reference CSS and XSL files you already have (external to FrameMaker), or to generate a CSS based on your structured document's element definitions. In Figure 9-9, you see the Application with its corresponding Structure View.

In the Structure View, you can see the Stylesheets element that is part of the visible Application definition. The Stylesheets element includes several child elements: CssPreferences, AddFmCSSAttrToXML, RetainStylesheetPIs, and XmlStylesheet.

Under the CssPreferences element, there are two child elements you may wish to include in your XML Application to automate style sheet declarations in your XML. The first is the GenerateCSS2 element. If you insert this in your Application, then you will want to include with it an Enable child element (generates the CSS upon export to XML) or a Disable child element (does not generate a CSS).

The second child element under the CssPreferences element is the AddFmCSSAttrToXML element. If you insert this child element and give it a nested Enable child, the CSS reference will be added to the XML files as you create XML. An example of a CSS declaration is

```
<?xml-stylesheet href="recipe_css.css" type="text/css"?>
```

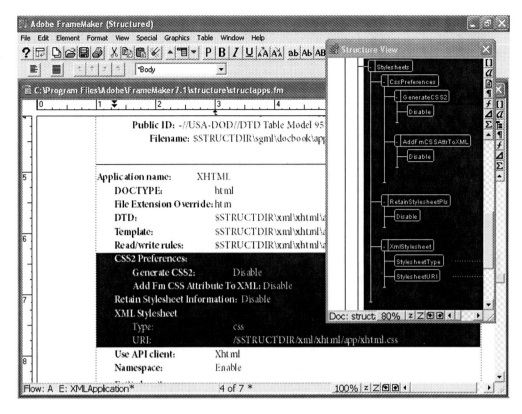

Figure 9–9. An example application shows style sheet settings.

Using the RetainStylesheetPIs element and setting it to Enable or Disable (by inserting one of these child elements) determines whether FrameMaker retains the style sheet declaration during a round trip of XML. If enabled, FrameMaker stores the style sheet process instruction as a marker as XML is imported. Then, when the XML is exported, it inserts the marker text into the XML.

Within the XMLStylesheet element, you may set StylesheetType and StylesheetURI elements. For the style sheet type, the content will be text that you enter—either *CSS* or *XSL* may be specified (although FrameMaker cannot generate an XSL style sheet, even if you specify the latter). The last part of this setup, the StylesheetURI element, allows you to specify the Uniform Resource Identifier (URI) for your style sheet. This element is also set up so that you can type the URI as text.

URI=Uniform Resource Identifiers. Information on URIs and URLs (Uniform Resource Locators) may be found at *w3c.org*.

Reviewing Namespace Support

XML documents may include namespaces. A namespace is a set of element and attribute names that may be used when XML documents are being reused by multiple software applications. Namespaces are a way of differentiating two elements that have the same name, but are each part of a different element set. This allows you to *mix* XML content from different element lists.

In XML, namespaces appear as a prefix followed by a colon, with the element name after the colon. The XML file includes a URI. An example is shown in Figure 9–10.

In Figure 9-10, the namespace URI is

```
<Document xmlns:html="http://www.w3.org/TR/REC-html40">
```

The prefix is the *html* in front of the colons. An example would be the <html:tr> beginning tag in the table row.

FrameMaker supports namespaces by preserving them when you import an XML document that includes namespaces. In the Structure View, elements that are using namespaces appear with an asterisk next to their names on the element bubble.

In addition to importing XML that includes namespaces, you may add or edit namespaces within FrameMaker structured documents. This allows you to export XML with namespaces.

For more information on enabling namespaces, check out the *Structure Application Developer's Guide* PDF located in the FrameMaker7.x/OnlineManuals folder.

```
<?xml version="1.0" encoding="ISO-8859-1"?>
<?xml-stylesheet href="document.css" type="text/css"?>
<!--
     Generated using Quadralay WebWorks Publisher 2003 for FrameMaker 8.0.0.1194 from template XML+CSS.
     Last updated on 12/11/03 11:32:28.
-->

<Document xmlns:html="http://www.w3.org/TR/REC-html40">
  <html:title>Impact Assessment Study Process  </html:title>

  <html:body>

     <html:table width="220" border="0" align="right" cellpadding="0" cellspacing="0">
        <html:tr>
           <html:td>
<html:a href="TOC.xml"><html:img src="images/toc.gif" border="0" alt="Table of Contents" /></html:a><html:a href="tundra.xml"><html:img
src="images/prev.gif" border="0" alt="Previous" /></html:a><html:a href="TestXHTML-3-1.xml"><html:img src="images/next.gif" border="0"
alt="Next" /></html:a><html:a href="IX.xml"><html:img src="images/index.gif" border="0" alt="Index" /></html:a>
           </html:td>
        </html:tr>
     </html:table>

     <html:p>
        <html:img src="images/logo.gif" width="174" height="46" alt="Put your logo here!" />
     </html:p>
     <html:hr align="left" />

     <html:blockquote>
<Chapter class="Heading1" style="display:block">
     <html:a name="183452"> </html:a>
     2   Impact Assessment Study Process
   </Chapter>
   <Body class="Body" style="display:block">
     <html:a name="183464"> </html:a>
     <wp class="Default" style="color: #ff0000;  font-style: normal; font-weight: normal; text-decoration: none; text-transform: none; vertical-
align: baseline">T</wp>he symposium on Biological Evaluation of Environmental Impact, was organized by the President's Council on Environmental
Quality (CEQ) and hosted by the Ecological Society American Institute of Biological Sciences in June 1976 at Tulane University.
   </Body>
   <Body class="Body" style="display:block">
     <html:a name="183460"> </html:a>
     The symposium on Biological Evaluation of Environmental Impact, was organized by the President's Council on Environmental Quality (CEQ).
   </Body>
   <Pullquote class="Default" style="display: block; color: #ff0000;  font-style: italic; font-weight: bold; margin-bottom: 6pt; margin-left:
14pt; margin-right: 7pt; margin-top: 0pt; text-align: center; text-decoration: none; text-indent: 0pt; text-transform: none; vertical-align:
baseline">
     <html:a name="183450"> </html:a>
     Critical attention was directed at new trends in techniques.
   </Pullquote>
   <Section class="Heading2" style="display:block">
     <html:a name="183469"> </html:a>
     2.1Ecologists Voice Views
   </Section>
   <Body class="Body" style="display:block">
     <html:a name="183470"> </html:a>
     This symposium focused on how the biological significance of environmental impacts can be both evaluated by ecologists and described to
decision-makers in the environmental<Emphasis class="Default" style="color: #000000;  font-style: italic; font-weight: normal; text-decoration:
none; text-transform: none; vertical-align: baseline"> </Emphasis>impact assessment process.
   </Body>
   <Bullet class="Default" style="display: block; color: #000000;  font-style: normal; font-weight: normal; margin-bottom: 3pt; margin-left:
18pt; margin-right: 0pt; margin-top: 3pt; text-align: left; text-decoration: none; text-indent: -18pt; text-transform: none; vertical-align:
baseline">
     <html:a name="183471"> </html:a>
     &#8226;Perhaps the two most difficult questions that biologists repeatedly face in assessing environmental impact are also the two most
important:
   </Bullet>
```
[remainder of code cropped to fit]

Figure 9–10.   XML is shown with namespaces.

Summary

Producing XML from FrameMaker may not provide you with all that you need. You may also need to use or produce style sheets, which will allow your XML instances to be viewed in browsers.

Both WebWorks and FrameMaker provide CSS-output capabilities. Only WebWorks has the ability to output XSL. If desired, you can create your own CSS and XSL files using other available tools, and then use them with XML from FrameMaker.

Namespace support is also included in FrameMaker so that you may use namespaces within FrameMaker or import XML that includes namespaces.

CHAPTER 10

Working with EDDs and Structured Documents

THIS CHAPTER EXPLORES the structure of FrameMaker documents, walking you through a structured document and its corresponding Element Definition Document (EDD).

Reviewing the Connection between EDDs and DTDs

As you begin considering FrameMaker for your XML publishing needs, the question may arise as to why you need to have an EDD *and* a DTD. This can especially be an issue if your organization has already defined a DTD and wants to minimize additional development time.

Without an EDD, you cannot easily publish XML using FrameMaker. The EDD is what lies between your DTD and the FrameMaker interface, allowing you to access FrameMaker's functions and formatting options.

About DTDs

A DTD is a set of element definitions, attribute definitions, and the rules for how elements and attributes can be used (the content models). A DTD can be used with an XML document. A parser may validate the document, using the DTD to establish the rules.

DTD = Document Type Definition

An example of a DTD for the cookbook sample files is shown in Figure 10–1 (empty lines have been removed to save space).

As you can see in this example DTD, the DTD defines the elements. For example, the first lines define the Recipe element and what it may contain.

```
<!ELEMENT Recipe (Name, Graphic?, Para?, Ingredients, Procedure,
                 Time, Para?) >
```

After the name of the element is the content model, which is the equivalent of the General Rule in an EDD. The content model specifies whether an element may have content and, if so, whether it may contain child elements or text. Any attributes (ATTLIST) that belong with the elements are also defined in the DTD. For example, the ATTLIST for the Recipe element includes one attribute called Category. Category is set up as a choice type attribute (or an *enumeration*, in XML terminology) and the choices are specified after the attribute's name.

```
<!ATTLIST Recipe Category (Entre|Appetizer|Dessert|Other) "Other" >
```

After the choices, is the Other, which denotes the default choice to be made if a document creator does not select a value for the attribute.

The DTD may be used by FrameMaker when XML files are opened. That is, if you declare the DTD within your XML file, then FrameMaker is able to validate against it as the file is opened. A *link* is not made, though, and once the file is open, FrameMaker stops using the DTD (see Chapter 11 for more information).

As can be seen in the sample DTD shown in Figure 10–1, a DTD contains no formatting information. Just as XML is designed to be free of formatting, the DTD is free of formatting. This makes DTDs more flexible, as they may be used by a variety of users and software tools with formatting applied at the user's discretion.

About EDDs

EDD=Element
Definition Document

Similar to a DTD, an EDD is also a set of definitions of elements, attributes, and the rules for how elements and attributes may be validly used (the General Rules).

An EDD may have the same elements and attributes that your DTD has; or it may not. In some publishing environments, the DTD

```
<!ELEMENT Recipe      (Name, Graphic?, Para?, Ingredients, Procedure,
                            Time, Para?) >
<!ATTLIST Recipe      Category (Entre|Appetizer|Dessert|Other)  "Other" >
<!ELEMENT Name        (#PCDATA) >
<!ELEMENT Graphic     EMPTY >
<!ELEMENT Ingredients
                      (Item, Item+) >
<!ELEMENT Item        (Quantity, Unit?, ItemName) >
<!ELEMENT Quantity    (#PCDATA) >
<!ELEMENT Unit        (#PCDATA) >
<!ELEMENT ItemName    (#PCDATA) >
<!ELEMENT Procedure   (Step, Step+) >
<!ELEMENT Step        (Para, ParaIndent?) >
<!ELEMENT Para        (#PCDATA) >
<!ELEMENT ParaIndent  (#PCDATA) >
<!ELEMENT Time        (#PCDATA) >
<!ELEMENT Cookbook    (FrontMatter, TOC, Recipe, Recipe+, IX) >
<!ELEMENT FrontMatter
                      (Title, Copyright) >
<!ELEMENT Title       (#PCDATA) >
<!ELEMENT Copyright   (#PCDATA) >
<!ELEMENT TOC         (#PCDATA) >
<!ELEMENT IX          (#PCDATA) >
```

Figure 10–1.   Element and attribute definitions are shown in an example DTD.

and EDD share some elements and attributes but have additional elements and attributes that are not in common.

The EDD resides in FrameMaker and is a FrameMaker structured document. The EDD allows its elements and attributes to have FrameMaker formatting associated with them, unlike the DTD.

The formatting and rules that you set up within the EDD may tell FrameMaker to apply a format tag, open a FrameMaker dialog box, or invoke a FrameMaker function. Most of FrameMaker's functions are available via the EDD setup. This is discussed in further detail in Chapter 12.

Authoring a Document With Structure

Building on the structure editing information in Chapter 7, this chapter provides information on how you may author a new structured document.

Before beginning work in structured authoring, check a few of your FrameMaker settings. Setting these in advance will ensure that the upcoming steps match what is displayed on your screen. The settings in question are discussed next.

NOTE   Many of these settings can be set in the template and saved within it, so they do not need to be set on individual files. Setting these in the template can save you time in adjusting your files later.

- From the menu, choose *Element > Set Available Element* and choose *Valid for Working from Start to Finish*

  This setting gives you control over the elements shown in the Element Catalog when you have an insertion point. With the suggested setting of Valid for Working from Start to Finish, the Element Catalog will only show elements valid at the current insertion point (those with bold checkmarks). If you are authoring new documents, then this setting is preferable to the other options (see Figure 10–2), such as All Elements. The All Elements setting allows the Element Catalog to show all elements in the structure whether they are valid or not.

NOTE   The *Show Tags For* options in this dialog box were described in "Inserting Elements" on page 140.

- Choose *View > Attribute Display Options* and *No Attributes* from the menu

Figure 10–2.   The Set Available Elements dialog box is shown.

You may or may not want to have the attributes showing in the Structure View. Especially in a structure with many attributes, having all elements showing their attributes can make the structure long and hard to navigate. To prevent attributes from showing in the Structure View, change the Attribute Display Options to display *No Attributes* (see Figure 10–3). You will still be able to expand any element's attributes as you want to see them, but they will not be in your way otherwise.

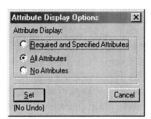

Figure 10–3.   The Attribute Display Options dialog box is displayed.

- Choose *Element > New Element Options* and select *Prompt for Required Attribute Values*; also checkmark *Allow Automatic Insertion of Children*

As new elements are inserted in your documents, you may be prompted to give the element's attribute values. To minimize this *interruption*, you set it to only ask you to fill in attributes that—according to your structure—are required to have a value. This saves you time in clicking past the Attributes dialog box each time you insert elements that have attributes and do not require values (such as elements with UniqueID type attributes, that probably will not need values until you refer to them).

The other part of this *New Element Options* set up is the *Allow Automatic Insertion of Children*. This refers to FrameMaker's ability to drop in child elements when parent elements are inserted. This can be a great time saver for authors, as it allows them to have multiple elements come in together so that they don't have to insert element after element for common structures (see Figure 10–4).

Figure 10–4.   The New Element Options dialog box is displayed.

NOTE   For the automatic insertion of child elements to work, the child elements must be specified as *Autoinsertions* in the EDD. If you are designing the EDD, you will want to specify Autoinsertions for all the common parent/child pairs within your structure. This feature can save authors a great deal of time in constructing structured documents.

Creating a Structured Document

Now that you have your settings adjusted as recommended, follow the instructions in this section to author a simple, structured document. You will use the *cookbook* sample files that you installed following the instructions in Chapter 6.

1. Open TEMPLATE1.FM from the *cookbook* folder.

2. Save As *myrecipe.fm* to create a new file and avoid overwriting the original.

3. Open your Structure View and Element Catalog, if these are not already open.

4. You may also wish to Zoom the document to 100 percent or higher for easier viewing.

5. With *myrecipe.fm* active, place your insertion point inside its empty, body text frame.

6. From the Element Catalog, select the Recipe element and click *Insert*.

   The Attribute dialog box appear since the Recipe element has a required attribute—Category.

7. Click the small triangle on the right side of the dialog box (see Figure 10–5), and then choose *Other* from the choices that pop up. Then, click the *Set Value* button to set the Category attribute's value to Other.

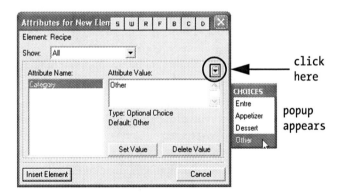

Figure 10–5. Attributes dialog box is shown for the new Recipe element.

8. Choose *Insert Element*.

   This starts your structured document. You will immediately see the Recipe element bubble appear in your Structure View.

The Element Catalog also changes, because your insertion point automatically moves into the element you just inserted.

9. Next, select the Name element in the Element Catalog with your insertion point inside the Recipe element, and click *Insert.*

   The Name element bubble appears in the Structure View. The Element Catalog changes and displays <TEXT> as a valid option, meaning that you may type content into this element.

10. Type a name for your recipe, such as *Toffee Bars* or *French Baguettes* or something similar.[1]

    Notice that the *Heading1* FrameMaker paragraph format was automatically applied to the contents of the Name element. In FrameMaker structured documents, the formatting is automatically applied so you can focus on elements and need not do any formatting.

11. Next, place your insertion point inside the Recipe element within the Structure View, but below its Name child element, by clicking just to the right of the vertical line below Name.

    A small black triangle should appear, showing your insertion point and denoting where an element will be attached if you insert one. In this case, any inserted element will be a child of Recipe and a sibling of Name.

12. Now, insert an Ingredients element and then immediately insert an Item child element.

    You will not need to move your insertion point before inserting Item, as your insertion point will automatically be inside Ingredients (see Figure 10–6) and this is where Item needs to be inserted in the structure.

    The element inserts, and the Item element bubble appears in the Structure View with a Quantity child element (if

---

1. Entering content into elements like Name is dealt with in the section, "Adding Text" on page 195.

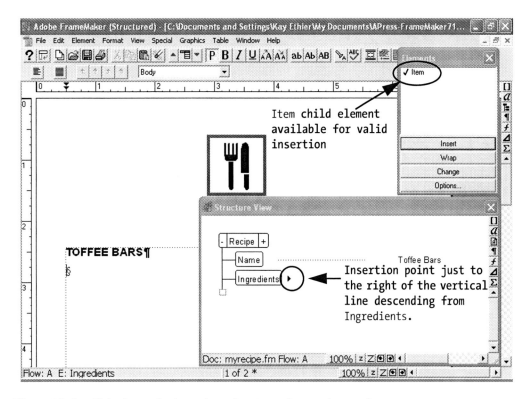

Figure 10–6.   This shows the insertion of an Item *element in a recipe.*

> *Autoinsertions* are turned on). In the document window, you will have an insertion point and can type inside the Quantity element.

Once you have the Item element and Quantity, you need to insert Unit, and ItemName. You will perform these steps in the next section.

Adding Text

In Step 10 in the preceding list, you typed text—your recipe's name—into the Name element. Typing text in elements is the same as typing text in an unstructured document—once you have your insertion point inside the element, that is.

An element must be inserted in your document, and your insertion point must be inside that element, before you can type. The element rule must also allow for text to be typed within it.

NOTE   If an element is allowed to contain text, then the <TEXT> indicator will appear at the top of the Element Catalog as it did in the previous section's exercises. You do not need to select or insert this, but can begin typing immediately when it is in the Element Catalog.

Continue with the document that you started in the previous section.

1. If not already in the document, insert a Quantity child element inside the Item element.

2. Once you have Quantity inserted, the Element Catalog shows that <TEXT> is an option and you may type a value. For example, type the number 1.

3. Next, insert the Unit element inside Item below the Quantity element (you will need to move your insertion point to the right of the line descending from Item to insert this child element).

   The Unit element bubble will appear in the Structure View and the Element Catalog will again display <TEXT>. You are now positioned to type text within Unit.

4. Type **each**.

5. Click to the right of the line descending from Item, and insert ItemName inside the Item element, just below Unit.

6. Without moving your insertion point, type *egg*.

7. To insert another Item element as a sibling to the first, place your insertion point on the line descending from Ingredients and below the Item just created.

8. Choose the Item element in the Element Catalog and click *Insert*.

9. Save your file.

NOTE Since this structure is very restrictive, and only one element is available at a time within the Item, once you have the Quantity element inserted, you can actually hit *Return* to automatically insert Unit, then hit *Return* again when you want to insert ItemName. Try this out by inserting another Item element on the line descending from the Ingredients element.

As you can see, the trick is getting your elements in and having a proper insertion point. Once you have elements in the document that allow text to be typed in them, you can type as you normally would within FrameMaker.

Adding a Graphic (Anchored Frame) Element

Within the example recipe structure, the structure is very tight and few elements will show up as valid in the Element Catalog. To be allowed to place a graphic in the document, you will need to be just under the recipe's Name element.

Follow these instructions to add an image to your document:

1. In your *myrecipe.fm* file, in the Structure View, place your insertion point on the line descending from the Recipe element, just below the Name element.

    The Element Catalog will show a Graphic element as available (valid) at the current location. The catalog will appear similar to the one shown in Figure 10–7.

2. Choose the Graphic element and click *Insert*.

    The Graphic bubble will show up in the Structure View and FrameMaker's anchored frame dialog box will open.

3. Insert the anchored frame (using the default settings will be fine).

    Now that you are in the FrameMaker anchored frame dialog box, you can adjust the settings just as you would for a

Figure 10–7.   The Element Catalog shows valid elements.

FrameMaker document without structure; the settings
behave the same in structured and unstructured
FrameMaker documents.

4. If you would like to place an image in the anchored frame,
    then either import, paste, or draw an image into your
    anchored frame.

5. Save your file.

Hopefully, creating the beginnings of this new document has
provided you with an understanding of how structured authoring is
performed. Feel free to continue editing the document and experi-
menting with the elements available in this structure.

If you take a look at how authoring works within a more complex
structure like XDocBook, you will see that there are many more elements listed as valid within the Element Catalog. If you start a
document based on XDocBook, you can place a Para element once
you insert a Chapter element and a Sect1 element. Once you have a
Para, there are many sibling elements listed in the Element Catalog.
You can insert any from this long list. This is not a very restrictive
EDD. The sample recipe, by comparison, is an extremely limited and
restrictive EDD.

Reviewing an Element Definition Document

In this section, a sample EDD named *cookbook.edd* is reviewed. This file should be in the FrameMaker install directory under *structure\xml\Cookbook*. That folder is where you were directed to place the sample folders in the instructions of Chapter 6.

Reviewing the Structure

Remember the cookbook sample document and its Name element? Remember the way that the Heading1 paragraph format was automatically applied? The EDD portion of this is shown in Figure 10–8. You can see the Name element at the bottom.

EDD Version is 7.0

Structured Application:

Element (Container): Cookbook
      General rule: Recipe, Recipe+
      Valid as the highest-level element.

Element (Container): Recipe
      Valid as the highest-level element.
      General rule: Name, Graphic?, Para?, Ingredients, Procedure,
                        Time, Para?

      Attribute list
          1.   **Name:** Category   **Choice**   **Optional**
               Choices: Entree | Appetizer | Dessert | Other
               Default: Other

Element (Container): Name
      General rule: <TEXT>

      Text format rules

          1.   **If context is:** Recipe
               Use paragraph format: Heading1

Figure 10–8.   The top portion of cookbook.edd looks like this.

The General Rule for name is <TEXT>, which is why you were able to type directly in this element during the previous exercises.

You should also note that the General Rule for the Recipe element is:

```
Name, Graphic?, Para?, Ingredients, Procedure, Time, Para?
```

Because commas are used to separate the child elements named in the General Rule, the elements must appear in the document in the order given when this EDD is used to create structured documents. If these child elements are not in this order within Recipe, the structured document will not be valid. Several of these child elements have a question mark after them, which means that they are optional within the structure (and may be omitted when documents are created).

NOTE If you wish to learn more about the syntax for General Rules, refer to "General Rule Syntax" on page 217 in this chapter. Chapter 12 also provides details on building an EDD that covers General Rule writing.

The next section of the cookbook EDD shows the Ingredients element and its child element, Item. This is shown in Figure 10–9.

Think back for a moment to the document-building steps you performed earlier in this chapter. It is because the Ingredients element is designed to hold Item elements (**General Rule:** Item, Item+) that the Element Catalog showed Item as available when you had your insertion point inside the Ingredients element.

Element (Container): Ingredients
    General rule: Item, Item+

Element (Container): Item
    General rule: Quantity, Unit?, ItemName

    Automatic insertions
        Automatically insert child: Quantity

    Text format rules

        1.   **In all contexts.**
                Use paragraph format: Ingredients

Figure 10–9.   The ingredients section of cookbook.edd is displayed.

Next in the EDD are the Item element's three child elements: Quantity, Unit, and ItemName. These are shown in Figure 10–10.

Quantity, Unit, and ItemName are all set up with a General Rule of <TEXT>. That is why you were able to type in them during the previous exercises.

The Recipe structure also includes a Procedure element and its descendants. The EDD elements for Procedure, Step, Para, and ParaIndent are shown in Figure 10–11.

Element (Container): Quantity
    General rule: <TEXT>

   Text format rules

       1.   **In all contexts.**
               Text range.
               Use character format: QuanBold

Element (Container): Unit
    General rule: <TEXT>

   Text format rules

       1.   **In all contexts.**
               Text range.
               Use character format: UnitItalic

   Prefix rules

       1.   **In all contexts.**
               Prefix:

Element (Container): ItemName
    General rule: <TEXT>

   Text format rules

       1.   **In all contexts.**
               Text range.
               Use character format: ItemName

   Prefix rules

       1.   **In all contexts.**
               Prefix: —

Figure 10–10.   Item's child elements from the cookbook.edd are detailed.

Element (Container): Procedure
    General rule: Step, Step+

    Automatic insertions
        Automatically insert child: Step

Element (Container): Step
    General rule: Para, ParaIndent?

    Automatic insertions
        Automatically insert child: Para

    Text format rules

        1.   **If context is:** {first} < Procedure
            Use paragraph format: Numbered1
            Else, if context is: {notfirst} < Procedure
            Use paragraph format: Numbered
          Else
            Use paragraph format: Body

Element (Container): Para
    General rule: <TEXT>

Element (Container): ParaIndent
    General rule: <TEXT>

    Text format rules

        1.   **In all contexts.**
            Use paragraph format: Indented

Figure 10–11.   This is the procedures section of cookbook.edd

The recipe structure does not contain table elements. For a table example, consider how tables are handled in the XDocBook EDD. The portion of the EDD pertaining to tables is shown in Figure 10–12.

NOTE   The Attribute lists have been removed to save space.

Another example that may help clarify for you how the EDD is really reaching into FrameMaker functions would be the behavior of graphics in structure. If you add a graphic type element in a sample

```
Element (Table): TGroup
      General rule:          THead?, TBody, TFoot?


Element (Table Heading): THead
      General rule:          row+


Element (Table Footing): TFoot
      General rule:          row+


Element (Table Body): TBody
      General rule:          row+


Element (Table Row): row
      General rule:          entry+


Element (Table Cell): entry
```

Figure 10–12.   Table type element TGroup *from XDocBook.EDD and related elements*

XDocBook document, you have attribute choices of *pasted* and *imported*. This modifies the behavior when a graphic type element is inserted:

1. If you choose *pasted*, you are saying, "this image is going to be pasted in from the clipboard." With that as the selected value on the attribute, inserting a Graphic element inside the Figure will open the anchored frame dialog box.

2. If instead you choose the *imported* attribute value, then inserting the Graphic element inside Figure would cause the *File>Import>File* dialog box to open instead.

   Pretty cool, eh?

Using Structure to Create Structure

An EDD is a structured document. Its structure is designed to help you create elements. Following its structure, you create elements, their attributes, and related rules. The EDD you create is then used to create your structured documents.

You author in an EDD in much the same way that you author in any structured document. Your structured content in an EDD creates another document's structure.

In Figure 10–13 is the top-portion of an example EDD. This EDD has a few elements at the start of its structure, and then many Element elements. These can be seen along the right-side of the figure, in the Structure View window.

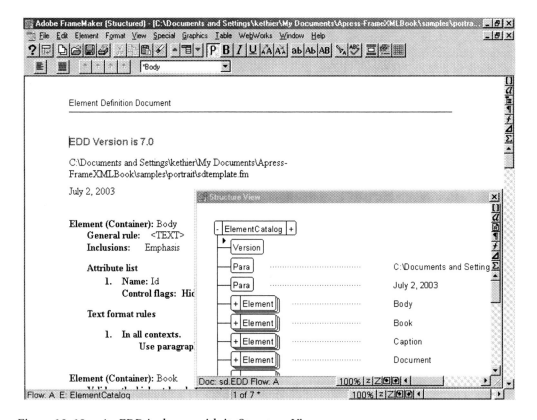

Figure 10–13.   An EDD is shown with its Structure View.

Part of the EDD showing on the left in Figure 10–12 includes the element information along with descriptive words and prefixes (such as *General Rule:*) to make the EDD easier to understand.

Element with a capital E in the structure signifies that you are creating an Element element. The Element element is what you use to make each element in your structure. The Head element, for example, would be created as an Element element and given the Head tag in the EDD.

Once an element has a tag, you can specify the element's settings, such as behavior and formatting, using the EDD's various elements. The structure elements within an EDD that allow you to create elements include

- a few preliminary EDD elements

- Element elements (for defining structure)

- elements for setting rules

- formatting-related elements

Setting Element Types

When reviewing the structure of a sample document in Chapter 7, it was pointed out that some elements appear with different-shaped element bubbles in the Structure View. In this section, we examine the different *types of elements* that you might find in an EDD and how they appear in the Structure View.

Element types are specific to FrameMaker's EDDs and are not used in related DTDs. The type allows FrameMaker to differentiate special constructs used in publishing, such as graphics, cross references, markers, and containers.

In Figure 10–14, you can see an element being created. The Element element is in place along with the Tag (name) element mentioned previously. The insertion point is in place for adding the Type element, and the different types are shown listed in the corresponding Element Catalog.

The element types are: Container, Footnote, Table, TableTitle, TableHeading, TableBody, TableFooting, TableRow, TableCell, Marker, CrossReference, Equation, Graphic, Rubi, and RubiGroup. Descriptions of each of these element types follow.

Container Elements

Container elements are the main element type—the type you will probably use most often. Container elements can contain text and

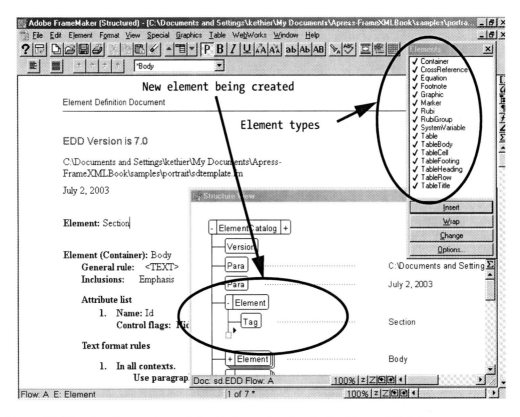

Figure 10–14.   An element is created with types showing in the Element Catalog.

other elements. All of your main elements for paragraphs, headings, and so forth will be Container elements.

When you select the Container element type, the Container element automatically comes in with a child General Rule element. The General Rule is where you define what is allowed to be inserted inside the element when using it in your documents. So, for example, you might create a BodyText element and make its General Rule <TEXT> so that you can type in the BodyText element when creating documents. Another example may be that you define a Recipe element, and define the General Rule:

```
Name, Ingredients, Procedure
```

The General Rule lists the child elements that Recipe can contain, with indicators for the order in which the child elements must occur. General Rule syntax is discussed later in this chapter.

Footnote Elements

Although XML is not concerned with page layout, elements that produce FrameMaker footnotes—that appear at the bottom of the page—need to be handled as a special type in the FrameMaker EDD. No related special information appears in the DTD.

Footnotes in FrameMaker are inserted using special Footnote-type elements that you create in your EDD. Outside of FrameMaker, they just become regular XML elements.

Table Elements

Within the EDD, there are multiple elements that produce specific table parts. The specific types are:

- Table

- TableTitle

- TableHeading

- TableBody

- TableFooting

- TableRow

- TableCell

Used together, these elements allow formation of tables inside the FrameMaker formatting engine. FrameMaker's rules of table structure must be considered, including specific constructs examined in the next section.

If you are new to FrameMaker, it may be worth pointing out to you some of the FrameMaker rules of table structure.

- If a table has a title, it must be the first child of the table-starting element

- Rows are of three types: heading rows, body rows, and footing rows

- A table must have at least one body row

- Any row must contain at least one cell

- Only table titles and table cells can contain text

When creating your EDD, you do need to create all the different elements of a table before you can create a proper, valid table in your structured documents.

NOTE If you try to insert a table using the Table menu, and you do not have the appropriate parts set up in the structure, the table will come in with default element names. Validation errors will show up in the Structure View, including invalid element name errors (red element bubbles).

Similar to the way that Container elements have a General Rule, the Table elements have a General Rule. The same syntax and connectors apply, but with an additional caveat—the rules cannot force table parts to break the rules of FrameMaker table structure mentioned at the start of this section.

Object Elements

Several of the element types are designed to provide access to special FrameMaker features. These include markers, cross references, anchored frames, and more. Each of the types is covered in this section, along with information about the behavior resulting from the use of each type's use.

NOTE When used in structured documents, all object elements appear as square-edged rectangles in the Structure View.

Marker Element

Elements defined as a Marker type will form FrameMaker markers when used when authoring structured documents. When inserting an element of this type, the Marker dialog box appears. The Marker Type box will show Index, Subject, or whatever selection was made in the EDD. You can use this selection or adjust it. You then type your marker content in the text box provided and click *New Marker*. This inserts your element.

Figure 10–15 shows the creation of a Marker element. You can see the Element element and its child elements in the Structure View at right.

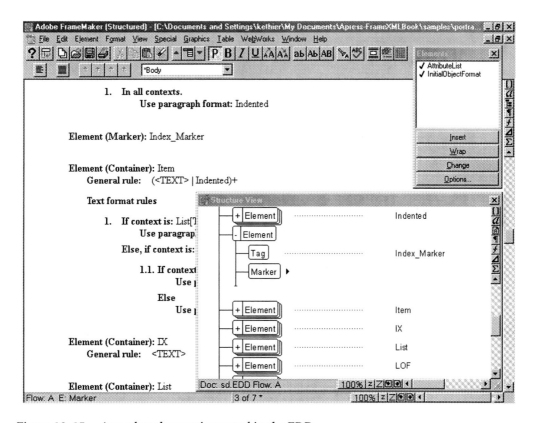

Figure 10–15. A marker element is created in the EDD.

Figure 10–16 shows this same Marker element being used in a structured document.

You can see the rectangular Index_Marker element bubble in the Structure View to the right of the page.

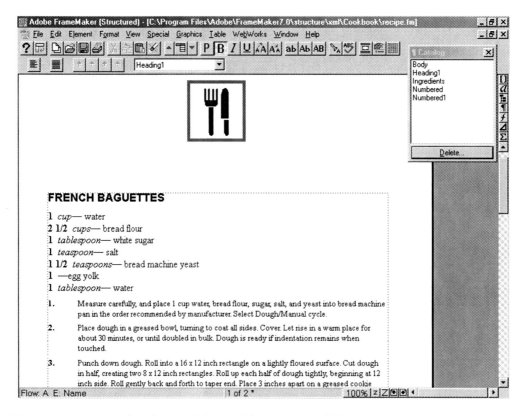

Figure 10–16. A marker element is inserted in a structured document.

Cross-Reference Element

Elements defined as this type become FrameMaker cross references when used in structured documents. Upon insertion, the Cross Reference dialog box is launched in FrameMaker so that you can link to the desired source. Once you select the source, inserting adds a marker to the structure and a *linked* cross reference to the Document window view.

In Figure 10–17, the portion of the EDD containing a UniqueID attribute is shown.

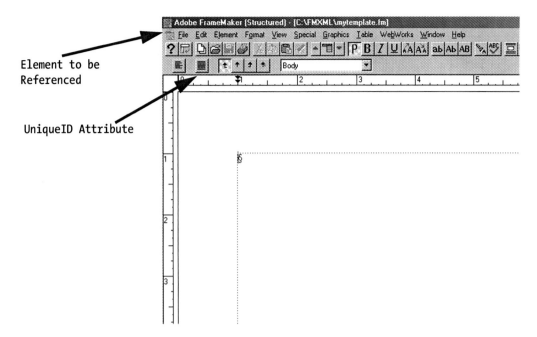

Figure 10–17.   The UniqueID *attribute is created for the* QuestionBlock *element in the EDD.*

NOTE   These elements must have attributes. While attributes are optional on most elements, Cross-Reference elements require an attribute that can hold a referenced unique identifier, allowing it to maintain the link in FrameMaker (and outside FrameMaker). Sources to be referred to must also have attributes to hold this unique identifier; elements without it cannot be referenced. If you are familiar with XML, you may recognize that these correspond to the ID and IDRef attribute relationship in XML.

Any elements to which you wish to build cross references will have that same type of attribute (UniqueID), although the attribute name is allowed to differ from element to element.

In Figure 10–18, the portion of the EDD corresponding to the CrossReference element and its attributes are shown.

The final piece of this—after creation of elements with unique IDs and the creation of a cross reference-producing element—is including the cross reference in another element's content model (General Rule). This makes them available in the Element Catalog—

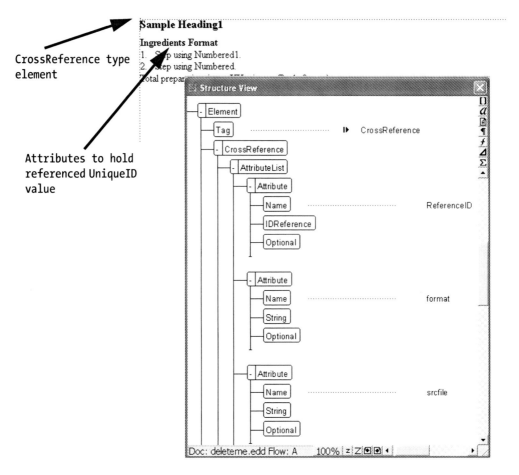

CrossReference type
element

Attributes to hold
referenced UniqueID
value

Figure 10–18.   A Cross Reference element and its attributes (FrameMaker 7.1) are displayed.

inside those elements—so that you may insert cross references into your structured documents. In this example, the cross reference is allowed to be inserted in Para elements. The Para element and its General Rule are shown in Figure 10–19.

Once the EDD is set up, the elements may be tested by importing element definitions into a sample document and trying to insert elements.

Cross references and their attributes will look similar to that shown in Figure 10–20. This figure shows an element with a unique ID that matches to an attribute on a cross reference in a separate document.

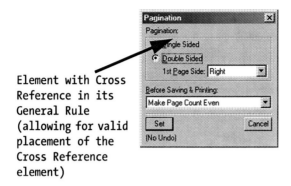

Element with Cross
Reference in its
General Rule
(allowing for valid
placement of the
Cross Reference
element)

Figure 10–19.   An element is shown with the CrossReference *element included in its General Rule.*

Equation Element

Elements in this type become Equation elements when inserted. You may select a default size (small, medium, or large) and then, in a structured document, insertion of the element produces a sized equation.

Figure 10–21 shows an Equation element created within the EDD. In this case, it has been set up to always—in all contexts—come up as a medium-size equation.

Graphic Element

These elements produce anchored frames when placed in a FrameMaker structured document. Figure 10–14 shows a Graphic element called Frame being created in an example EDD. This would then be available for insertion in structured documents using this EDD.

On the left in Figure 10–22, the insertion point is in the Figure element being created. In the Structure View on the right, a Graphic element has been created along with an InitialObjectFormat that can be used to drive the behavior of FrameMaker (Anchored Frame versus Import File dialog box). An All Contexts rule is being created, although context rules are also available. Now look at the Element Catalog and note that there is an AnchoredFrame elem1ent that may be inserted. There is also an ImportedGraphicFile element. Choosing one of these over the other will change the behavior that you get in FrameMaker.

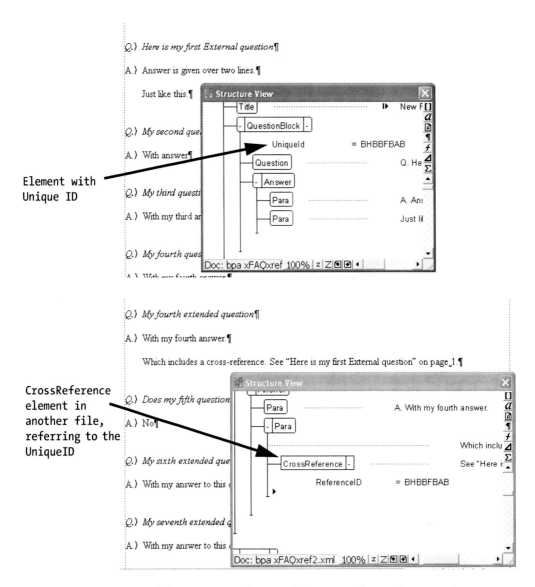

Element with Unique ID

CrossReference element in another file, referring to the UniqueID

Figure 10–20.   Structured documents are shown with a cross reference between them.

NOTE   Using an Attribute/Context Rule would allow you to drive to one or another in different situations within your document.

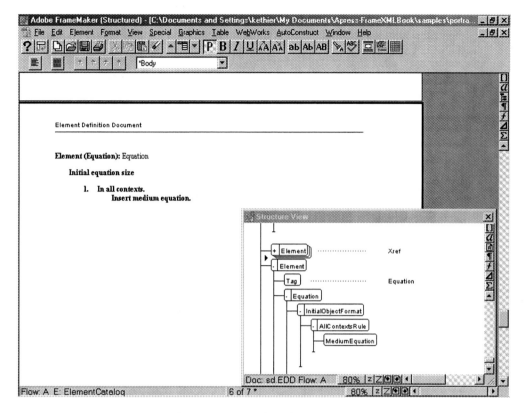

Figure 10–21.   An equation element is created in the EDD.

Once the Graphic element is created, it can be inserted within a structured document. Depending on the settings for the element, and the presence of any attributes to drive behavior, you may be taken to the Anchored Frame dialog box or to the *File>Import>File* menu, as mentioned previously.

Rubi and RubiGroup

These two types of elements allow for use of special characters that are required for conventional Japanese publications. The Rubi characters are small characters that appear above a word to shown its pronunciation. The RubiGroup is used in structure to hold both the Rubi text and the text it appears above (the Oyamoji text).

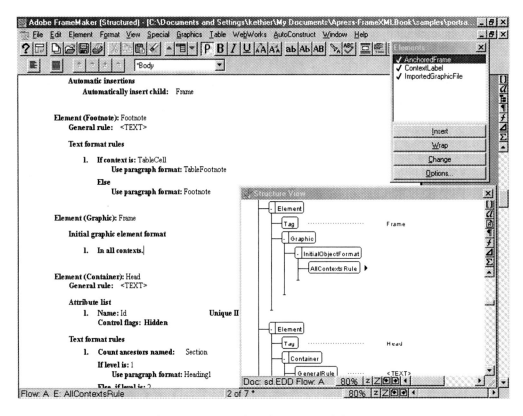

Figure 10–22.   A Graphic element is created in the EDD (at left).

Defining Elements

For now, make sure that you understand that there are different types of elements that can be defined within an EDD. Setting an element as a specific type will drive its behavior within your structured documents.

In Chapter 12, you will use multiple types of elements to create an example EDD. This can then be used to create a structured document. An example EDD for a simple document is shown in Figure 10–23.

Using this EDD as an example, take a look at the syntax needed to build elements and set up the rules for how elements may fit together to create valid documents.

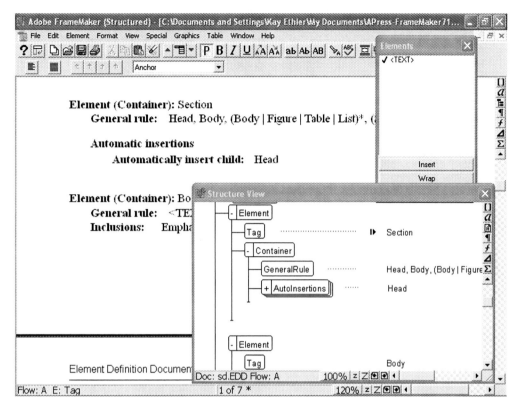

Figure 10–23. The simpledoc *EDD is displayed.*

General Rule Syntax

The General Rule has a very specific syntax and order of application. As mentioned in Chapter 7, there are specific symbols within the EDD's General Rule that need to be understood. These symbols are the same for Container, Table, and Footnote element *types*. The first are shown in Table 10–1.

Along with these symbols for indicating frequency, the punctuation between child elements is important. Punctuation is used to indicate the order of occurrence of child elements listed in the General Rule.These indicators and explanations are shown in Table 10–2.

Some elements you will not design to contain other elements, but to contain text or other special content. The General Rule for allowing text to be typed is simply <TEXT>. If you are familiar with DTD syntax, this would be the equivalent of the PCDATA specification in a DTD. To clarify, <TEXT> and several similar content rules are shown in Table 10–3.

Table 10–1.   General Rule Syntax Indicators for Frequency

GENERAL RULE SYMBOL	EXAMPLE	MEANING	
		REQUIRED OR OPTIONAL	HOW MANY
(No Symbol)	Para	The element is required for the structure to be valid.	Only one can be inserted at the specified location.
Question Mark	Para?	The element is optional and can be used or omitted.	Only one can be inserted at the specific location, or you can have none since it is optional.
Plus	Para+	The element is required for the structure to be valid.	As many as you want can be inserted at the specific location, but you have to have at least one since it is required.
Asterisk	Para*	The element is optional and can be used or omitted.	As many as you want can be inserted at the specific location, or you can have none since it is optional.

Table 10–2.   General Rule Occurrence Indicators

SYMBOL	EXAMPLES	MEANING
comma: ,	Head, Para Head, Para+, Graphic?	The elements must occur in the order given. The symbols mentioned in the previous table do not lose their meaning.
pipe: |	Para | List Para | List | Table | Graphic	One of the elements may occur. Thinking of this as an OR, as in *this element OR that element* may be helpful.
ampersand: &	Para & List Para & List & Table & Graphic	All of the elements may occur in any order. Thinking of this as an AND, as in *this element AND that element* may also be helpful. With the ampersand the elements can occur in any order but all must occur (unless an asterisk or question mark appears with it).
parentheses: ( )	Head, (Para | List) Head, Para, (Para | List | Table)+	Parenthesis may be used to group elements. This can allow you to hone the rule so that child elements are controlled the you want.

Table 10–3.   General Rule Syntax for Content Types

GENERAL RULE	EXPLANATION
<TEXT>	Specifying this in the General Rule means that the element can contain text and inclusions if desired. Sometimes this is included in the General Rule along with element names, allowing the element to contain a mix of text and child elements.
<TEXTONLY>	Using this in the General Rule means that the element can contain only text, and cannot contain child elements (not even inclusions).
<ANY>	Using this in the General Rule means that the element can contain any combination of text and elements defined in EDD. This could be opening a can of worms, as *anything goes* within the element!
<EMPTY>	Specifying this in the General Rule means that the element cannot contain any text or elements; it will have nothing in it.

Consider the syntax options carefully when creating your General Rules. Once they are created, test them by creating sample documents. Watch the Element Catalog closely as you create the sample documents, to ensure that elements which should be valid are showing with bold checkmarks.

Also watch to make sure all elements are available when you want them to be. If the elements are not appearing in the Element Catalog as you want, then adjust the General Rules for your elements and reimport from the EDD into the test document (this process is explored further in "Importing Element Definitions" on page 221).

Attribute Types

As you define your elements within the EDD, you will need to define attributes for some of your elements. As you determine the elements that you need during document analysis, you will need to determine the corresponding attributes for those elements.

When you create an element, one of the choices that you have for child elements is an AttributeList element.

Just as elements may be of different types, attributes may be of different types. The types of attributes FrameMaker allows you to create are listed in Table 10–4.

Examples of attributes and steps regarding their creation are discussed in Chapter 12, which describes EDD creation.

Table 10–4.   Attribute Types

TYPE	PURPOSE
String or Strings	Text may be typed as the attribute value. The plural means that multiple values may be supplied. For example, an Author attribute may have a string attribute with a value of *John Doe* or strings listing multiple author names.
Integer or Integers	The attribute value may be any whole number, positive or negative (integer values are 0, 1, 2, 3, and so forth). A range of values may also be specified to restrict allowed numbers. The plural allows more than one integer to be provided.
Real or Reals	The attribute value may be any real number, positive or negative (a real number is any number, including decimals: 0, 1.25, 4.999999, and so forth). A range of values may also be specified to restrict allowed numbers. The plural allows more than one integer to be provided.
Choice	The attribute value must be selected from a list of provided choices. These choices are defined in the EDD (or DTD). For example, in the cookbook example documents, the Recipe element has an attribute called Category. The Category attribute has choices of Entree, Appetizer, Dessert, and Other. These may be seen in Figure 10–5—at least the view that the user sees. The corresponding EDD definition may be seen in the *cookbook.edd* document.
UniqueID	Used mostly for cross references, this allows the attribute value to be a string of characters that uniquely identifies an element. No two elements within a file may have the same value for this type of attribute. (If you are familiar with HTML, this is the equivalent of <a name="something"> where something is provided by the user or inserted by FrameMaker when a cross reference is made to the element.)
IDReference or IDReferences	Used for referencing to elements that have a UniqueID attribute, this stores the value of a UniqueID to complete the link. The plural allows multiple UniqueID values to be stored. (Again, referring to HTML, the equivalent of this would be <a href="filename.html#something">.)

Entities

An entity in a markup document is a string of characters that you may reference. Similar to the way that a FrameMaker user variable can be defined and then dropped into FrameMaker documents, you may define a phrase as an entity and then use the entity in an XML document wherever you want the phrase inserted. This type of entity is referred to as an internal entity.

The entity and its replacement text are specified in an entity declaration in the XML file.

External entities are stored in a separate file or XML fragment and work much the same way. These might be compared to the FrameMaker text inset feature. The external entity is declared in a document and then the referenced entity is placed in the XML wherever the fragment should be inserted.

NOTE   Graphics handling may similarly be done using entities, with the graphics filenames referenced using entities.

Importing Element Definitions

Any time you want to create a file that will use an EDD's structure, the EDD's element definitions need to be imported into that file. You may then make a structured document within that file.

The process goes something like this:

1. Open your template.

2. Open your EDD.

3. Create a new document (*File>New>Document*).

4. Save the new document.

5. Import the formats from the template by selecting *File>Import>Formats* and choosing the template from the Import from Document drop-down menu. Make sure that you checkmark all the formats that you want to import, then click the *Import* button.

6. Import the element definitions from the EDD by selecting *File>Import>Element Definitions* and choosing the EDD

from the Import from Document drop-down menu. Under *While Updating, remove* in the dialog box, you may also checkmark *Format Rule Overrides* and *Information Inherited from Book*—the formats that you want to import—then click the *Import* button.

You now have a document that has the structure and formatting needed to produce a structured document.

7. Start creating your structured document by inserting elements.

An alternative procedure includes the following steps:

1. Open your structured template (this is a FrameMaker template into which the EDD element definitions have been imported).

2. Save your structured template with a new name.

3. You now have a document that has the structure and formatting needed to produce a structured document. Start creating your structured document by inserting elements.

NOTE   If you have structured documents, and at any point you adjust the EDD, you will need to import the element definitions from the revised EDD into the existing structured documents (and the template, if your template is a structured one).

NOTE   *File>Import>Element Definitions* is a complete replacement of the structure. The structure that existed before the import is completely deleted and the structure currently in the EDD (or structured template if importing elements from this) is put in its place.

This is unlike FrameMaker's *Import>Formats* command, which only modifies formats that match the names of the imported formats. Therefore, importing elements is a much *cleaner* process.

The differences between the previous two sets of procedures are minimal. Either way, you are pulling in the latest version of your formats and the latest version of your element definitions. There is an advantage to putting the element definitions into the template, which is that you can distribute just one file to your users that they can import into their documents. The EDD can be safely stored somewhere with the original template, and you will only need to open the EDD when structure changes are needed. You may not want to make your EDD accessible because that may encourage others to modify it. See Chapter 12 for information on creating an EDD from scratch.

Moving Forward

Once the EDD has been imported into a template or document, that template or document can be used to import into other documents. You should still save your EDD for a time when you might want to change it in the future.

Validating a Document

Valid XML is XML that follows all the content rules (General Rules) within your DTD. The validation tool within FrameMaker allows you to ensure your FrameMaker document structure follows the general rules in your EDD. If your EDD General Rules are equivalent to your DTD content model, the FrameMaker validation may indirectly help you create valid XML.

If you plan to use your XML outside FrameMaker and need the content to follow the rules set up in the DTD, you will want to have valid content. Validation can be done on FrameMaker documents using the *Element>Validate* command. Validation can also be done on your XML after exporting from FrameMaker.

Validating a FrameMaker document is easy, if you know your structure. Understanding the rules of your content is as important as understanding what FrameMaker's validation error indicators look like.

FrameMaker uses red indicators to show you where you have structure errors (invalid structure in your documents or books). These indicators are described next.

NOTE It may be helpful to you to open the sample documents described and view the red indicators firsthand.

An example Recipe document is used to demonstrate the red indicators. This file is available in the cookbook subfolder that you copied into your *FrameMaker7.x\structure\xml* folder in Chapter 6.

Open the *badtaste.fm* file. Open your Structure View window.

When you place your insertion point in this recipe, the Structure View window shows the structure for this document. It appears with many validation errors indicated in red (the document window does not show any errors).

Red Box

Red boxes indicate that something is missing that is required to be there. A red box attached to a line descending from any element indicates a missing element or elements at that location.

For example, in the Structure View under Item, note the red box between Quantity and ItemName. The red box indicates that an element—in this case Unit—is missing.

If the red box is located next to an attribute name, it means that the attribute has been defined (in the EDD) to require a value, but no value has been given.

For example, in the Structure View of the *badtaste.fm*, expand the attributes for the Recipe element by clicking on the plus on the right side of its element bubble.

Red X

A red X next to an attribute name indicates that an incorrect value has been given to that attribute. It may also indicate that an attribute does not belong in the document. In this second case, the name of the attribute will show up in red next to the red X.

While FrameMaker prevents you from entering an incorrect value for an attribute, you could get incorrect attribute values if you import XML or even *paste* content from a FrameMaker document using a different EDD.

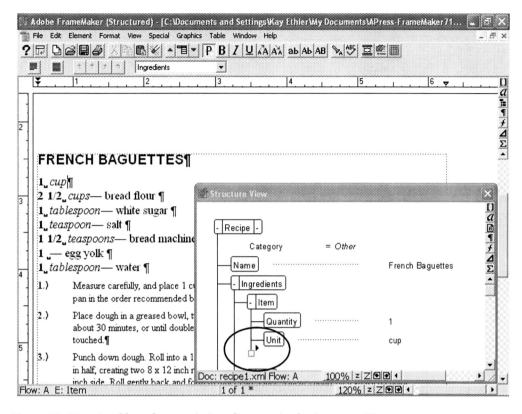

Figure 10–24.   A red box shows missing elements in the Structure View.

When an attribute is defined in an EDD, it is given certain settings. For example, you could set a draft attribute to hold values that are numeric and must be between 0 and 3. If you import XML and a value of 4 is given, then the red X will appear.

In this figure, the red X also appears next to the Author attribute. In this case, Author is also in red, which indicates that the Author attribute is not an allowed attribute within the structure.

Red Element Bubble

If the entire element bubble is red, that means the element is not defined in the document's structure. This can happen if you *paste* content from a document that uses a different EDD (see Figure 10–27).

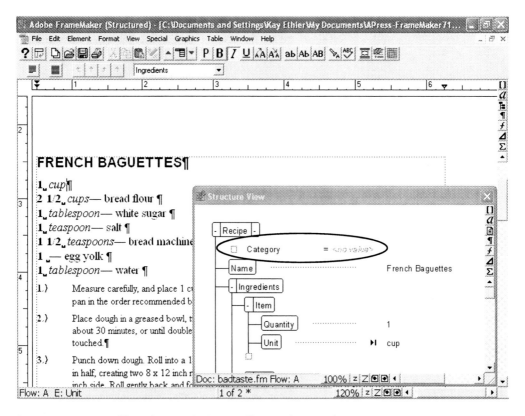

Figure 10–25.   A red box shows missing attribute values in the Structure View.

Red Dashed Line

The red, dashed vertical line indicates that an element is in a location where it does not belong—it is invalid as placed. The red will begin at the element that is out of place, and can continue for long distances throughout the structure. An example is shown in Figure 10–28.

Once the out-of-place element is corrected, the red dashed line will disappear.

Red Plus

A red plus will show up if an element is collapsed and one of its descendants has an error. In Figure 10–29, there is a child element missing within an Item element, so the plus on the Item element bubble is red.

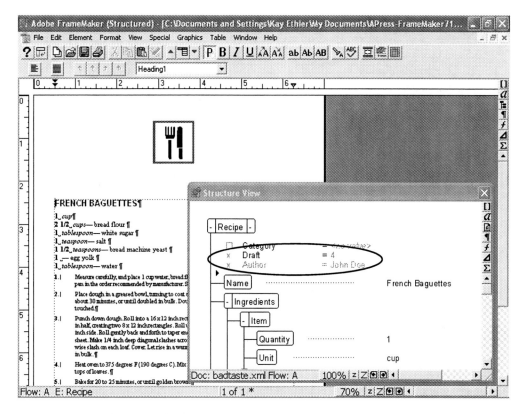

Figure 10–26.   Red Xs show bad attributes and attribute values in Structure View.

No-See-Ums

There is also a type of error that does not show up in red, and it is one of the reasons that you need your validation tool. The error that does not flag in red is a missing *first required child* element.

> **NOTE**   Another reason is that validating saves you time in searching through your documents. Because it leaps you from one error to the next, it saves you time. Because it doesn't miss any errors, it is more accurate than you and your eyes may be.

If you drop in an element that requires one or more child elements, and you do not put in any child elements, there will be an

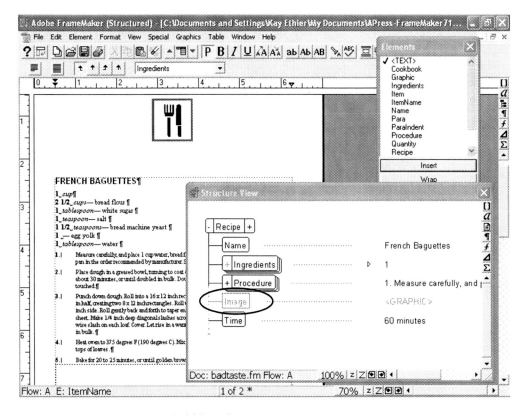

Figure 10–27. A red element bubble is shown in Structure View.

error. But because there is no line of descent to which to attach the red box indicator, no red shows up in the Structure View. The element is incomplete and therefore not valid. However,

- as soon as you drop in any child, the line of descent will show up (and show a red box if a child element is still missing)

- if you collapse the parent of the element with the missing required child, the parent element will show the red plus indicator

- when you validate, these errors are caught

Using the *badtaste.fm* recipe sample as an example, you can cause this error to see what it looks like first hand. Inside the Ingredients parent element, click between two Item elements. Open your Element Catalog and you will see one or more available child elements.

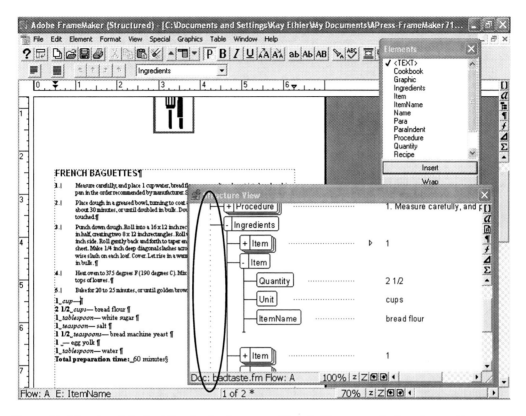

Figure 10–28. A red dashed line in the Structure View indicates a misplaced Ingredients *element.*

NOTE   The number of elements that you see in the Element Catalog will vary depending on how you have the Element Catalog options (or *Element>Set Available Elements*) set. If you have All Elements showing, you will see many more elements than if you have selected *Valid Elements for Working from Start to Finish*. This was covered in "Authoring a Document With Structure" on page 190.

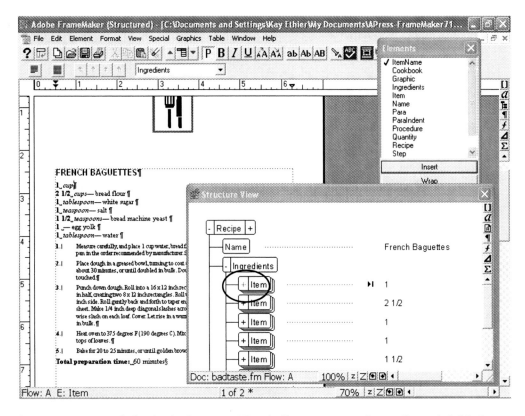

Figure 10–29.   A red plus in the Structure View indicates an error in a collapsed child element.

Summary

FrameMaker uses an EDD to drive document formatting and structure. Additional tools like the Element Catalog assist you in creating your structured documents.

Once a document is created, you may validate it against the rules of structure by using the Validate command within FrameMaker. This ensures your FrameMaker structure is correct, which increases the likelihood that exported XML instances will be valid.

PART III

Breaking Apart the XML Round-Trip Process

CHAPTER 11

Exploring the FrameMaker Application File

IN THIS CHAPTER, the Structured Application Definitions file is checked out, its components explained, and options for adjusting and adding Structured Applications noted.

Using Applications

When using XML content with FrameMaker— importing or exporting—you may need to create an Application for your documents. While optional, a structured Application really is necessary for automating the use of XML with FrameMaker.

An XML Application is not as mysterious or complex as it may sound. A FrameMaker structured Application is—simply put—a set of pointers to files and information that relate to a FrameMaker publishing project. The structured Application file is called *structapps.fm* and it is a structured document. It begins with the StructuredSetup element.

Once set up, an Application allows you to automatically access your template and other useful files (like a DTD and Read/Write rules) as an XML instance is imported/exported. There are also a few special things that you can add to your Application to change the default XML translation (for example, specifying a particular style sheet).

Depending on the types of documents you are publishing, and your requirements, you may be able to use one of the Applications that installs with FrameMaker. You should try to determine this before spending any time creating a custom XML Application. In the next section, the installed structured Applications are reviewed.

Reviewing the Installed Applications

Several structured Applications install with FrameMaker 7.0 and 7.1. These include several flavors of DocBook for SGML, as well as XDocBook and XHTML for XML. To open the structured Application file and view the installed Applications, select *File>Structure Tools>Edit Application Definitions.* In this *structapps.fm* file—part of which is shown in Figure 11–1—you can review the Applications and even modify them if desired.

You might want to open it in your FrameMaker installation to get a better view than is provided here.

DocBook and DocBook 2.1

Notice that the structured Application shown in Figure 11–1 is *DocBook*—one of the pre-made Applications that installs with FrameMaker (except on the UNIX platform). The DocBook Application is an updated version (4.1) of DocBook Application that has been included in FrameMaker since the days of FrameMaker+SGML. This updated version includes new entity references for 4.1. Figure 11–2 shows the DocBook Application in FrameMaker 7.1.

Also in the FrameMaker 7.0 and 7.1 installations, you have the DocBook 2.1 Application. This is the older version, included for those who are already using it from prior versions. Figure 11–3 shows the DocBook 2.1 Application from FrameMaker 7.1.

It is important to note that both the DocBook and DocBook 2.1 Applications are SGML Applications. They are designed for working with SGML Import/Export, not XML.

An XML-specific version called XDocBook also installs, and if you want to work with DocBook for XML, this is the one that you would choose—or use as a starting point to make your own, scaled-down version.

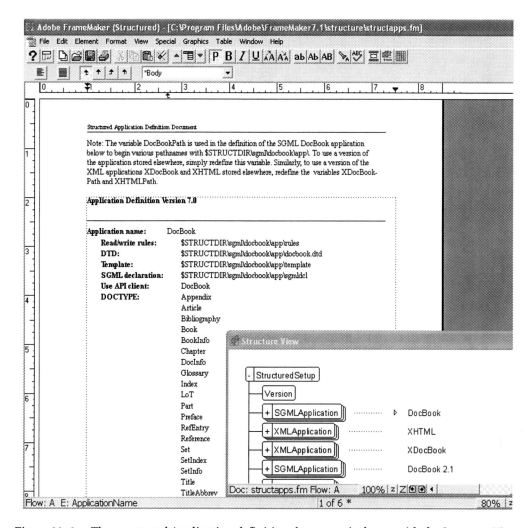

Figure 11–1. *The structured Application definition document is shown with the Structure View.*

The two pre-made SGML Applications are not explored further in this book. Additional information is available in Adobe's *Structure Application Developer's Guide* that installs with FrameMaker 7.0 and 7.1.

XDocBook

This XML version of DocBook installs with FrameMaker 7.0 and 7.1. XDocBook is not an Adobe creation, but the results of years of work by the Organization for the Advancement of Structured Information Standards (OASIS) and markup language experts like Norm Walsh.

```
Application name:              DocBook
    Read/write rules:             $STRUCTDIR\sgml\docbook\app\rules
    DTD:                          $STRUCTDIR\sgml\docbook\app\docbook.dtd
    Template:                     $STRUCTDIR\sgml\docbook\app\template
    SGML declaration:             $STRUCTDIR\sgml\docbook\app\sgmldcl
    Use API client:               DocBook
    DOCTYPE:                      Appendix
                                  Article
                                  Bibliography
                                  Book
                                  BookInfo
                                  Chapter
                                  DocInfo
                                  Glossary
                                  Index
                                  LoT
                                  Part
                                  Preface
                                  RefEntry
                                  Reference
                                  Set
                                  SetIndex
                                  SetInfo
                                  Title
                                  TitleAbbrev
                                  ToC
Entity locations
    Public ID:  -//OASIS//DTD DocBook V4.1//EN
        Filename:  $STRUCTDIR\sgml\docbook\app\docbook.dtd
    Public ID:  -//OASIS//ENTITIES DocBook Notations V4.1//EN
        Filename:  $STRUCTDIR\sgml\docbook\app\dbnotn.mod
    Public ID:  -//OASIS//ENTITIES DocBook Character Entities V4.1//EN
        Filename:  $STRUCTDIR\sgml\docbook\app\dbcent.mod
    Public ID:  -//OASIS//ELEMENTS DocBook Information Pool V4.1//EN
        Filename:  $STRUCTDIR\sgml\docbook\app\dbpool.mod
    Public ID:  -//OASIS//ELEMENTS DocBook Document Hierarchy V4.1//EN
        Filename:  $STRUCTDIR\sgml\docbook\app\dbhier.mod
    Public ID:  -//OASIS//ENTITIES DocBook Additional General Entities V4.1//EN
        Filename:  $STRUCTDIR\sgml\docbook\app\dbgenent.mod
    Public ID:  -//USA-DOD//DTD Table Model 951010//EN
    Filename: $STRUCTDIR\sgml\docbook\app\cals-tbl.dtd
```

Figure 11–2.   This details the DocBook Application (DocBook Version 4.1).

The XDocBook version installed with FrameMaker 7.1 is XDocBook 4.1.2. This is reflected in the Application, which is shown in Figure 11–4.

XHTML

If you produce HTML for a website, your next shift may be to use XHTML. XHTML is, basically, HTML done to XML rules.

XHTML uses the HTML tag set. Unlike HTML files, though, an XHTML document starts with an XML declaration. The HTML tags used within the file conform to XML's rules as shown in the section in Chapter 1 called "Understanding XML Rules" on page 8.

```
Application name:              DocBook 2.1
    Read/write rules:              $STRUCTDIR\sgml\docbook\app\docbook2.1\rules
    DTD:                           $STRUCTDIR\sgml\docbook\app\docbook2.1\dtd
    Template:                      $STRUCTDIR\sgml\docbook\app\docbook2.1\template
    SGML declaration:              $STRUCTDIR\sgml\docbook\app\docbook2.1\sgmldcl
    Use API client:                DocBook
    DOCTYPE:                       Appendix
                                   Article
                                   Bibliography
                                   Book
                                   BookInfo
                                   Chapter
                                   DocInfo
                                   Glossary
                                   Index
                                   LoT
                                   Part
                                   Preface
                                   RefEntry
                                   Reference
                                   Set
                                   SetIndex
                                   SetInfo
                                   Title
                                   TitleAbbrev
                                   ToC
    Entity locations
        Public ID:  -//HaL and O'Reilly//DTD DocBook//EN
        Filename: $STRUCTDIR\sgml\docbook\app\docbook2.1\dtd
```

Figure 11–3.   This is the earlier DocBook 2.1 Application still used by some.

Figure 11–5 shows the structured Application for XHTML in FrameMaker 7.1.

Understanding Structured Application Elements

Taking a closer look at structured Applications, you will see that they are made of many elements. The *structapps.fm* file itself is a structured FrameMaker document and each Application is made up of elements. These elements are described here, with the XDocBook Application used for example purposes.

The XDocBook Application Elements

Each element of the XDocBook Application is explained in this section, with a screen shot showing the Structure View for that part of the Application. This Application as it appears in the Document window may be seen back in Figure 11–4.

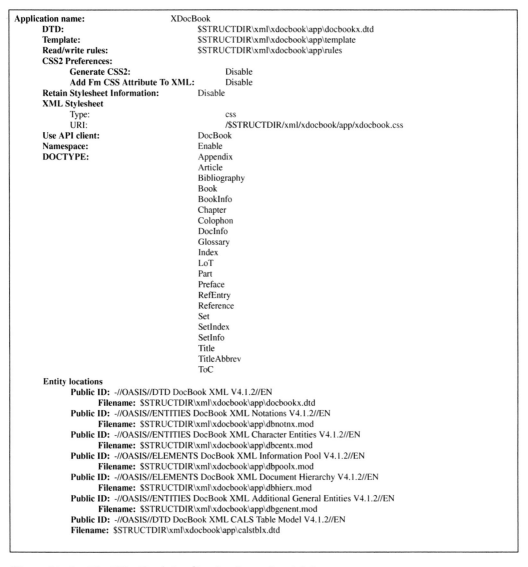

Application name:	XDocBook
DTD:	$STRUCTDIR\xml\xdocbook\app\docbookx.dtd
Template:	$STRUCTDIR\xml\xdocbook\app\template
Read/write rules:	$STRUCTDIR\xml\xdocbook\app\rules
CSS2 Preferences:	
Generate CSS2:	Disable
Add Fm CSS Attribute To XML:	Disable
Retain Stylesheet Information:	Disable
XML Stylesheet	
Type:	css
URI:	/$STRUCTDIR/xml/xdocbook/app/xdocbook.css
Use API client:	DocBook
Namespace:	Enable
DOCTYPE:	Appendix
	Article
	Bibliography
	Book
	BookInfo
	Chapter
	Colophon
	DocInfo
	Glossary
	Index
	LoT
	Part
	Preface
	RefEntry
	Reference
	Set
	SetIndex
	SetInfo
	Title
	TitleAbbrev
	ToC
Entity locations	

Public ID: -//OASIS//DTD DocBook XML V4.1.2//EN
   Filename: $STRUCTDIR\xml\xdocbook\app\docbookx.dtd
Public ID: -//OASIS//ENTITIES DocBook XML Notations V4.1.2//EN
   Filename: $STRUCTDIR\xml\xdocbook\app\dbnotnx.mod
Public ID: -//OASIS//ENTITIES DocBook XML Character Entities V4.1.2//EN
   Filename: $STRUCTDIR\xml\xdocbook\app\dbcentx.mod
Public ID: -//OASIS//ELEMENTS DocBook XML Information Pool V4.1.2//EN
   Filename: $STRUCTDIR\xml\xdocbook\app\dbpoolx.mod
Public ID: -//OASIS//ELEMENTS DocBook XML Document Hierarchy V4.1.2//EN
   Filename: $STRUCTDIR\xml\xdocbook\app\dbhierx.mod
Public ID: -//OASIS//ENTITIES DocBook XML Additional General Entities V4.1.2//EN
   Filename: $STRUCTDIR\xml\xdocbook\app\dbgenent.mod
Public ID: -//OASIS//DTD DocBook XML CALS Table Model V4.1.2//EN
Filename: $STRUCTDIR\xml\xdocbook\app\calstblx.dtd

Figure 11–4.   The XDocBook Application is version 4.1.2.

When created, a structured Application is given a name. This is what you use when calling the Application into action. In the preceding screen shot, the XDocBook Application name is seen. This name was given by the creator typing it into the corresponding element.

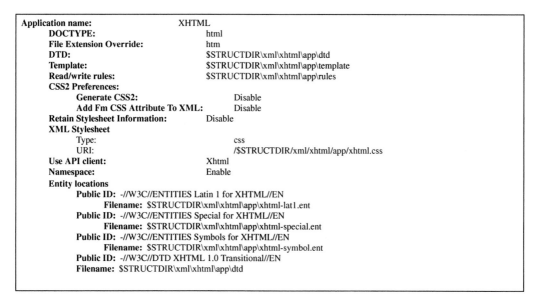

Figure 11–5.   FrameMaker shows the XHTML Application.

Once an Application is named, its elements may be added pretty much in any order (the Element Catalog guides you through this and lists available components). One that you may wish to add is the DTD. This element contains the path to the DTD file, seen here as

`$STRUCTDIR\xml\xdocbook\app\docbookx.dtd`.

The first part—`$STRUCTDIR`—is shorthand for typing the path to the *FrameMaker7.x\structure* subfolder. The remainder of the path is shown, ending in the name of the DTD file—*docbookx.dtd*.

Including the DTD in the Application allows FrameMaker to validate XML against the DTD as instance documents are imported. It also causes the DTD declaration to be included in XML instance documents exported from FrameMaker.

The template may be included in the Application alongside the DTD. In this example, the path to the file is seen with the filename being Template.

Including the template in an Application makes the template available for FrameMaker to use for formatting imported XML. Without a template, you cannot format a document automatically on import. With the template, you are putting the XML into a formatted documents automatically as the XML file is opened. The included template must be a structured template—a template with an EDD's element definitions imported into it—in order for the formatting to be automatically applied to the XML elements.

In some cases, just listing the DTD and template may be enough for you to work with XML. If, however, you find some of the default round-trip settings are not working well enough, you can adjust the default behavior using Read/Write rules.

In this case, the Read/Write rules file is named *rules*. It is a text file, although these files may also be FrameMaker files or structured FrameMaker files.

Read/Write rules files are discussed in more detail in Chapter 13.

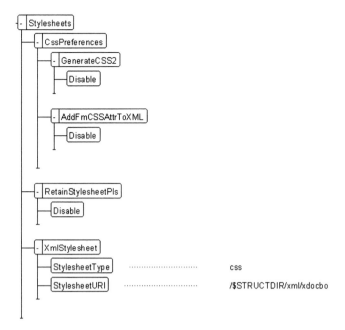

When XML is exported from FrameMaker, a CSS may be created on the fly. FrameMaker can create CSS2, which is a second level language built on the original CSS level 1 specifications.

While CSS is not dealt with in detail here, more information on it is available at the World Wide Web Consortium website (*w3c.org*) and in the FrameMaker *Structure Application Developer's Guide*.

What you need to understand for the Application is that you may specify what style sheet is included in the XML instance upon export. You may include a reference to an existing style sheet (XSL or CSS) or have FrameMaker create a CSS from your EDD. More details on this—and the specific Application components shown here—may be found in Chapter 9.

If you use Read/Write rules and your XML round trip still is not working well, you may need to use a FrameMaker API client that has been written for your Application. If an API client has been written for an Application, then this may be specified in the UseAPIClient element. In the XDocBook application, a DocBook API client is specified as shown in the preceding screen shot. For more information on this, refer to the *DocBook Starter Kit* PDF within your FrameMaker installation's OnlineManuals folder.

If there are no API clients being used within a structured Application, then another element—UseDefaultAPIClient—could be included instead (although these elements are optional).

FrameMaker supports namespaces within XML, which allows you to specify a namespace within your XML and import elements into FrameMaker without losing this information.

This element, when included in an Application, is set to *Enable* or *Disable*—this is set to *Enable* in XDocBook so that a namespace will be properly handled if used in an XML instance.

DOCTYPE	....	Appendix
DOCTYPE	....	Article
DOCTYPE	....	Bibliography
DOCTYPE	....	Book
DOCTYPE	....	BookInfo
DOCTYPE	....	Chapter
DOCTYPE	....	Colophon
DOCTYPE	....	DocInfo
DOCTYPE	....	Glossary
DOCTYPE	....	Index
DOCTYPE	....	LoT
DOCTYPE	....	Part
DOCTYPE	....	Preface
DOCTYPE	....	RefEntry
DOCTYPE	....	Reference
DOCTYPE	.... ▶I	Set
DOCTYPE		SetIndex

Due to the length, all of the XDocBook Application's DOCTYPE elements are not shown in the preceding graphic. If you are familiar with markup languages, then you know that a DOCTYPE may be specified for an XML file.

If one (or more) DOCTYPE is specified in an Application—such as the many specified for XDocBook— this information is used by FrameMaker when opening XML documents. Any time an XML instance is opened that lists a particular DOCTYPE, FrameMaker will select the Application that has that DOCTYPE automatically, instead of prompting the user to select a structured Application. If several Applications have the same DOCTYPE, then FrameMaker adjusts the list of structured Applications to only show the Applications that include that DOCTYPE.

For example, if you open an XML document with the following DOCTYPE,

```
<!DOCTYPE Part SYSTEM "docbookx.dtd">
```

FrameMaker will automatically select the DocBook Applications from its available Applications. The other Applications will not be shown.

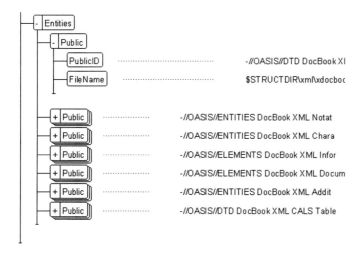

XDocBook includes some predetermined entity information. Entities are of different types that are not explored here. In the XDocBook Application shown in the preceding screen shot, you can see pointers to several files within the installation that hold entity data. Special characters and other entities specific to XDocBook have been predefined and may be viewed in the directory referred to in the Application (*$STRUCTDIR\xml\xdocbook\app*).

If an Application includes entities, FrameMaker uses the paths specified in the Application to locate the entities.

Additional Elements (FrameMaker 7.0 and 7.1)

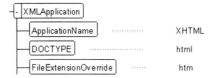

While not included in the XDocBook Application, another component of a structured Application is `FileExtensionOverride`. This particular component is used in the XHTML Application.

In this case, the File Extension Override is provided to force FrameMaker to save files with an *.htm* extension.

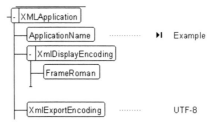

Other options within the Application are the `XmlDisplayEncoding` and `XmlExportEncoding` elements—both elements are shown in the above screen shot. The display encoding allows you to specify the character encoding to be used in displaying XML. The options are shown in the Element Catalog in Figure 11–6.

The XML export encoding allows you to type in the encoding you wish to use when exporting. UTF-8, for example, is specified in Figure 11–6.

Additional Elements (FrameMaker 7.1)

FrameMaker 7.1 includes two new elements within the structured Application setup. These are the `ExternalXRef` element and the `ConditionalText` element.

Both elements may be seen in the Element Catalog shown in Figure 11–7, although neither is used in XDocBook as explored in the previous section.

The `ExternalXRef` element helps with handling of cross references between XML documents. External cross-reference handling is new

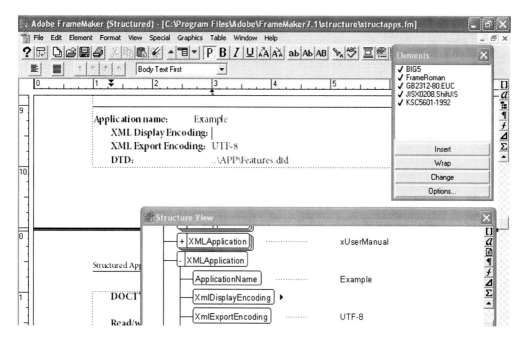

Figure 11–6.   XML display encoding options are shown in the Element Catalog.

to FrameMaker 7.1, as external cross references were broken when FrameMaker 7.0 documents were exported to XML.

FrameMaker 7.1 handles references between XML documents by maintaining both documents as XML and retaining the XML settings. To allow users some control over references during XML round trip, however, the ExternalXRef element includes the following options:

- ChangeReferenceToXML   If you enable this within your *structapps.fm*, all references to *.fm* extensions will be converted to *.xml* when a FrameMaker document with external cross references is saved as XML. If you plan to save all the referenced files to XML, you will want to enable this; make sure, however, that you actually do save the referenced files to XML as FrameMaker will not automatically do so

- TryAlternativeExtensions   If you open an XML file within Framemaker and it contains cross references to *.fm* and *.xml* files, then it will check for the alternate file extensions if the referenced file is not found (for example, if you have opened the XML file and saved it as a FM file)

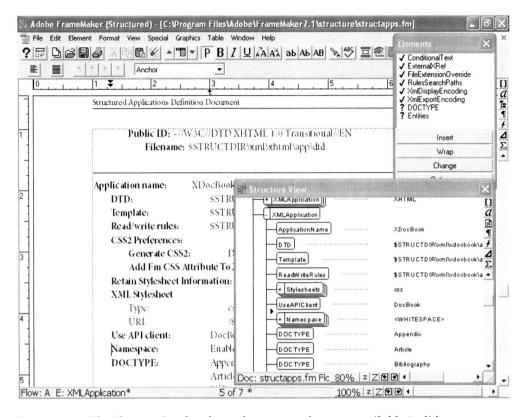

Figure 11–7.   The Element Catalog shows the new 7.1 elements available (valid).

Enabling this is preferable to having FrameMaker consider a reference unresolved. If you plan to open XML in FrameMaker 7.1, and Save As to FrameMaker format, you will want to enable this so that references are maintained. Otherwise, references will continue to look only for the original *.xml* extension on cross references, which may cause them to break and may cost you time in fixing them.

Both the TryAlternativeExtensions and the ChangeReferenceToXML elements may be seen in Figure 11–8. Each of the options is enabled (notice the Enable child element). To disable these options, these elements may be removed from the Application or their child element may be changed to Disable.

The second new component, ConditionalText, allows you to control how conditional text is exported to XML.

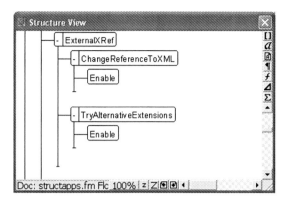

Figure 11–8. `ExternalXRef` *element and its descendents are detailed.*

With FrameMaker 7.0, conditions were not saved when files were exported to XML. Instead, FrameMaker saved the document to XML and output only the visible text. No conditional data was retained.

With FrameMaker 7.1, conditions now may be output as process instructions within the XML. After inserting the `ConditionalText` element and its child `OutputTextPI` element into your Application, you will have four elements available:

- `OutputAllTextWithoutPIs` If this option is included in your Application, FrameMaker outputs all conditional text in the document, whether it is shown or hidden. Process instructions are not included in the output

- `OutputAllTextWithPIs` If you include this option in your Application instead, FrameMaker outputs all conditional text in the document, whether it is shown or hidden. Conditional text is enclosed in process instructions (this is used by default if you specify nothing)

- `OutputVisibleTextWithoutPIs` If you use this option instead, FrameMaker outputs all the visible conditional text and does not include process instructions in the output (this is equivalent to the behavior of FrameMaker 7.0)

- `OutputVisibleTextWithPIs` If you use this final option, FrameMaker outputs all the visible conditional text and includes process instructions in the output

This structure can be seen in Figure 11–9, with the four options showing as valid (bold checkmark) in the Element Catalog.

If you plan to work with FrameMaker conditional text, you should consider including the ConditionalText element in your Application.

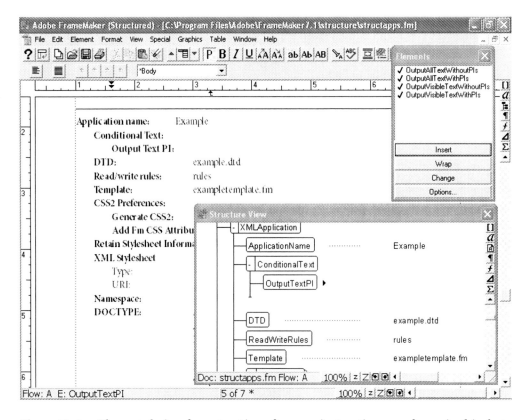

Figure 11–9. Element choices for outputting of process instructions are shown in this shot.

Other Applications

The structured Application file within FrameMaker includes several Applications upon installation, including XDocBook and XHTML. If you determine that these will work for your content, you may use the Applications as created.

If, however, these will not work as they are, another option is to copy one of the premade structured Applications and then modify it. Be sure to copy its XMLApplication element in your *structapps.fm* file and copy its files under the FrameMaker $STRUCTDIR so that you have the originals to refer to as you create your custom Application.

Another alternative is that you may build your own DTD, template, and other related files, and then create your own Application. Because the Application Definition Document is a structured document, its elements will lead you through the Application creation process (see Chapter 14). Elements such as the template, DTD, style sheet, and DOCTYPE can be selected, and then the paths to your files can be typed.

Summary

A round-trip structured Application may be set up to allow you to publish fully-formatted documents with FrameMaker and still produce nonproprietary XML. Once an Application is set up, you have all of FrameMaker's strengths at your disposal and are able to work with your XML regardless of its source.

Whether you create your XML in Notepad, export it from another program, or draw it from a database, the XML for your document types will work within FrameMaker using a standard or customized XML Application.

CHAPTER 12

Creating Your Structure (EDD Development)

THIS CHAPTER OUTLINES potential workflows for moving into the publishing of structured documents. Included are descriptions of the FrameMaker EDD's structure and the EDD authoring process.

Starting Points

There are different starting points for moving into structured document publishing. You might

- start with a DTD

- start with a sample FrameMaker structured document

- start with a FrameMaker template

- start from scratch

If you begin with a DTD or a FrameMaker structured document, the move to structured documents is easier than if you do not have these. One of the big tasks you face in moving to structured FrameMaker is structure creation. If you begin with a DTD or a FrameMaker structured document, the structure is already created—that is, the elements and the attributes have been defined—and you can begin working on your formatting and layout.

If you start with a FrameMaker template, you have your template and a sense of the FrameMaker features you will use; however, the job of analyzing your documents and creating a structure (DTD/EDD) based on those documents requires a lot of effort.

Starting structure from scratch requires the most effort, although it also has the benefit of being a clean slate, and is the path that you may be taking if you have just started working with FrameMaker and you do not have a DTD or template to use. Unfortunately, you cannot always choose what you start with, as it is usually chosen by what you have available (or by nothing being available).

Each of these tasks are described in the sections that follow. Be sure to note what portions apply to your particular situation.

Starting with a DTD

If you already have a DTD, the best starting point for you is to open your DTD within FrameMaker. This allows FrameMaker to use the DTD elements and attributes to create an EDD because your DTD elements become EDD elements.

Choose *File>Structure Tools>Open DTD* in FrameMaker to create your EDD. Browse to your DTD, select it, and then choose *Open*. Your attributes also come in and become attributes for those elements. You end up with an EDD that corresponds to your DTD.

Once you have created your EDD from a DTD, it is suggested that you validate the EDD to ensure there are no errors introduced during the creation process.

You might wonder why you should validate your EDD after it is created. Well, when the DTD information and content models become FrameMaker elements and General Rules, there is a chance that the content that FrameMaker needs to have within the EDD has not been provided by the DTD. Validation ensures there are no missing or misplaced components. Validation is an opportunity for you to do some cleanup and ensure the element definitions are correct. Then, you may import the elements into your templates and documents. If an EDD is not valid, you cannot import its element definitions—you will get an error message instead.

After you validate, you may add formatting data to your new EDD. Your template development will go hand-in-hand with adding the formatting to the EDD elements, as you begin creating your formats and adding them to elements.

As you add formats and create the template, be sure to test the template by using elements in a test document and checking for appropriate formatting.

NOTE If you have a schema instead of a DTD, you might be able to use it with Framemaker, even though FrameMaker will not use schema directly.

FrameMaker 7.0 and 7.1 do not support schema. To use a W3C XML schema with FrameMaker 7.0 or 7.1, you must first convert the schema to a DTD. Tools like *TurboXML®* will do this for you, and quickly. Once you have created a DTD from your schema, and have validated it and checked it to ensure all your important elements have come through, you can open the DTD in FrameMaker to make an EDD from it.

Starting with a FrameMaker Structured Document

If you have a structured FrameMaker document, you can export the EDD from the structured document plus use the document as a template. You have what you need to publish immediately, or to use as a start for editing and optimizing both the EDD and the template for your documents.

Exporting the EDD from a Structured Document

To export an EDD from a structured FrameMaker document, open your structured document in FrameMaker. Select *File>Structure Tools>Export Element Catalog as EDD*. The EDD will appear and you can save it.

The only negative thing about EDDs that have been reclaimed in this way is that the elements are listed alphabetically. After such an EDD is created, it may makes sense for you to group related elements together.

To group elements, just drag and drop them to put them in the order you want. You can even add Section elements from the EDD's structure and sort your elements into sections.

Creating a DTD from an EDD

Once you have an EDD, you may save your EDD as a DTD using *File>Structure Tools>Save as DTD*.

After you have saved your file as a DTD, you need to check the DTD to ensure all of your elements and attributes have come through and are using accepted DTD syntax. Sometimes when the EDD General Rule is converted to the DTD content model, problems are introduced. Some rules that are perfectly acceptable in FrameMaker will be rejected in XML.

For example, XML does not like text mixed in with elements in the content model. In tools like TurboXML, you are prompted on these errors when you open the DTD and can adjust the DTD to make content models with text and elements together—referred to as mixed content models in TurboXML.

Part of the job in creating a round trip XML Application is making sure that what you are doing in FrameMaker and what you are doing in XML are going to work together. Take the time to do the testing as you create your DTD and EDD.

Creating a Template from a Structured Document

To use the document as a template, just empty it of content and save it as whatever you want to call it—for example, *mytemplate.fm*. FrameMaker templates are not a special file format, so you can just use the regular file extension and save it to create the template.

A FrameMaker template has the formatting needed for pages, text, and other FrameMaker objects. A structured template has all of this, plus the EDD element definitions imported into it. If you start with a FrameMaker structured document, the element definitions are already in it and are saved along with all the formatting.

Starting with a FrameMaker Template

This path entails analyzing your existing documents and template to determine the structure that you need. You will have an idea of what you want the documents to look like but need to determine what the pieces are that make up your documents. Then, you create an EDD that contains those elements and ties the formatting in your template to the elements. You turn your structure into a DTD and EDD, linking the EDD to the template.

Starting from Scratch

If you do not have any other starting point such as those described previously in this chapter, then you will need to create your EDD, DTD, and template from scratch—after document analysis to determine your structure. Basically, you start from nothing and need to create everything.

Document Analysis

If you do not have a DTD or EDD, you need to determine what structure you need. What elements do you need? What are the types of data you will have in your documents? Examining your documents to determine the structure is document analysis.

 NOTE If you already have a DTD or a structured FrameMaker template, you are pretty much beyond the document analysis phase—unless you wish to modify your structure.

Document analysis involves examining your documents to determine their implied structure. All documents have structure. Even a letter has a structure, though the structure may be a simple one. The letter, for example, at a very basic level has a heading, address, salutation, body, and closing.

You need to determine the high view structure and the detail structure as best you can. You then use the structure as the basis for creating your elements (EDD).

To analyze your documents, select a few of them that are representative of your document collection. Those you select should be the type of document that you need to structure and should contain examples of all the main document constructs (lists, tables, figures, headings, and whatever else is important in your documents).

Once you have selected the samples, print a few representative pages so that they may be easily referenced or marked up. Then, begin examining the pieces that make up your documents. You may start at the high level (book, files in your book, main pieces of each file) or the lower level (paragraphs, items in lists, components of figure captions).

NOTE   With structure, there is no right or wrong answer as to what your structure should look like. Put the best information at your disposal and your best efforts into your structure, and you can end up with a usable structure. Keep in mind that your structure needs to work for you and for the types of output you plan to produce from the structure (XML, print, PDF).

You should consider the following things during document analysis:

- Type of content

- Relationship to other content

- Element types

- Attributes types

You may benefit from drawing diagrams that show the relationship between elements. It may help to include the attributes that you believe you will need, even though you will probably only have attributes for some of your elements.

Diagrams often look like the starting point of a FrameMaker structure view—a tree view of the document. Diagrams may also look like *mind maps* with the main elements at the center connecting to descendent elements around it. Choose sketches that work for you. It can help speed up EDD production later if you note frequency and order of elements as you map the structure. An example is shown in Figure 12–1.

After document analysis, you will know what your elements and attributes need to be for your data structure. Once you have this information, you can begin creating your structure (DTD/EDD). Information on building elements is included in the next section.

Do not be afraid to make mistakes. Also, do not be discouraged if—after beginning your EDD—you find that some elements need to be rethought or the structure adjusted to make your documents work as needed. Rethinking and adjusting are just part of the structure creation process.

For the purposes of the examples, you will build elements similar to those named in Figure 12–1 in the remainder of this chapter. These are just example names, not special or reserve names, so feel free to modify with your own names.

As mentioned before, there are several element types available in FrameMaker. The types, listed within the Element Catalog, are shown in Figure 12–2.

The best way to help you understand these types is to have you create them. In the steps that follow, you will create a small EDD[1] with specific elements. Although names do not have to match types, it is all right if they do (such as the Footnote type named Footnote).

Element names should indicate their purpose within the structure, or the data they will contain, rather than the content appearance. For example, naming an element Heading1 and using it throughout a document dooms the content of Heading1 elements to generic, undifferentiated existence. Setting up elements for Introduction, Scope, Summary, and so forth, for major headings within a document differentiates their contents. Table 12–1 below provides example names, several of which you will use when building elements in the upcoming section.

---

1. Rubi and RubiGroup are skipped in these exercises.

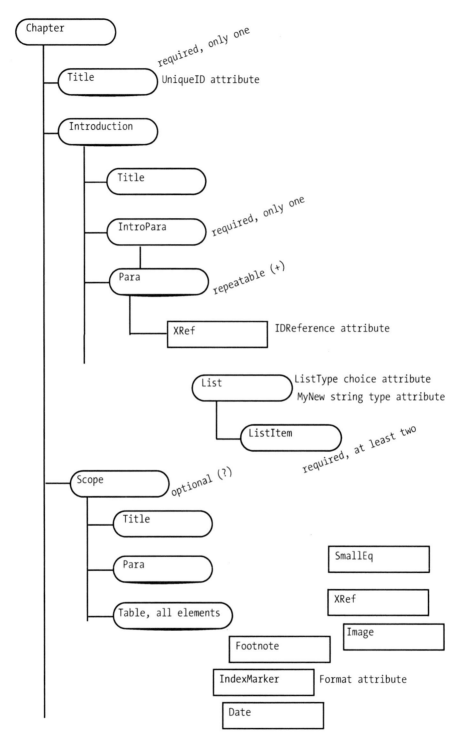

Figure 12–1.   A sketch shows the beginnings of a document structure.

Figure 12–2.   These are the available element types.

Table 12–1.   Example Element Names

TYPE	ELEMENT NAME
Container	Chapter
	Title
	Introduction
	IntroPara
	Para
	Section
	AnotherElem (bad name, just for example)
	List
	ListItem
Cross Reference	XRef
Equation	SmallEq
Footnote	Footnote
Graphic	Image
Table Related (types shown at right)	Table (type=Table)
	TTitle (type=TableTitle)
	THeading (type=TableHeading)
	TBody (type=TableBody)
	TFooting (type=TableFooting)
	TRow (type=TableRow)
	TCell (type=TableCell)
Equation	SmallEq
System Variable	Date

Creating an EDD

To create a new EDD, select *File>Structure Tools>New EDD*. An EDD with no elements appears, as shown in Figure 12–3, and you can begin creating your elements. The EDD is a structured document, and its structure assists you in creating elements; pieces needed in the structure appear in the Element Catalog for easy selection.

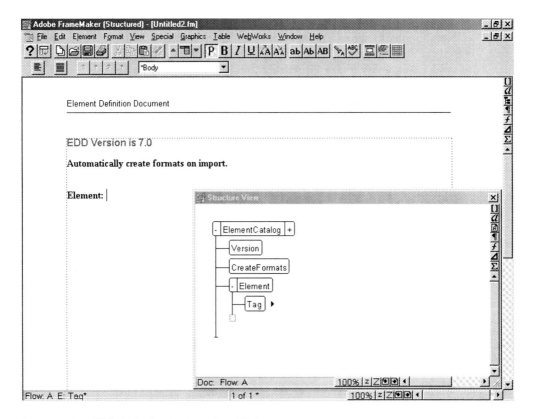

Figure 12–3. This is the beginning of an EDD.

Once you have the EDD started, you may save it to whatever name you like. Saving it with a EDD extension may make it easier to find later.

NOTE On Microsoft Windows, if you want to be able to double-click an EDD in Windows Explorer and have it open in FrameMaker, you may need to assign the EDD extension to FrameMaker. This is done through the Windows setup for *File Types.* Refer to Windows *Help* for instructions.

Now open your Structure View and Element Catalog so that you can see the EDD's structure and can access elements from the EDD's structure to build it.

When the EDD is started, it has the first Element element in place, along with a Tag child element. In this Tag element is where you type the element name—for example, you might name your first element Chapter (see Figure 12–4).

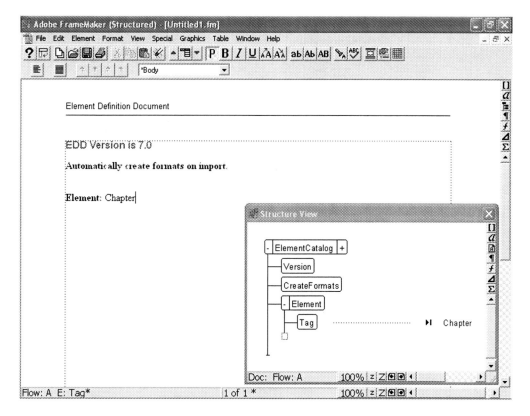

Figure 12–4. A Chapter *element being created in EDD.*

When the Chapter element name is typed within the Tag element, the name appears in the Document window (as content) and in the Structure View (as a text snippet).

NOTE   Whatever the element is named in the EDD, it will have the same name in XML. Chapter within a FrameMaker structured document will become a <Chapter> beginning tag and matching </Chapter> end tag upon export to XML. Case is retained, so choose how you wish to represent the elements and then stick with that case. Do not mix case to the point of confusing yourself and those using your XML.

Clearer: Chapter, Section, Title, ...
Confusing: CHAPTER, section, Title, ...

A red box appears just below the Tag element, signifying that an element is required but missing. You need to continue defining this element. The next step is to set the element type (types were initially explored in Chapter 10).

Defining Element Types

All elements must have a type specified, which means that the type needs to be included in the element definition. As you create an element within the EDD, the types will become available. The types are shown in Figure 12–5, listed in the Element Catalog, and awaiting insertion in the EDD.

The following sections provide information on the element types available for use in your FrameMaker structure and the steps needed to create each of them. The element type is set in the EDD for each element created.

Container Elements

In the Chapter element being created, place your insertion point below the Tag element so that you can insert an element that will be a

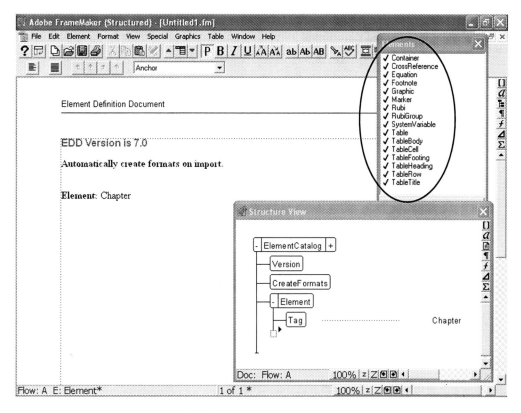

Figure 12–5.   Element types are listed in the Element Catalog.

sibling to Tag (and a child of the Element element). Proper insertion point placement is shown in Figure 12–5.

For the Chapter element, since it is going to contain other elements within the structure (subheading elements, paragraph elements, and so forth), it needs to be a Container type. Container type elements are allowed to contain text and other elements.

NOTE   You may find that 90 percent or more of the elements in your EDD are of the Container type.

To make the Chapter element a container (with your insertion point still next to the red box below the Tag element), select Container in the Element Catalog and click the *Insert* button at the bottom of the catalog. The result will be a Container element inserted in your structure, as shown in Figure 12–6. It brings with it a child element (GeneralRule).

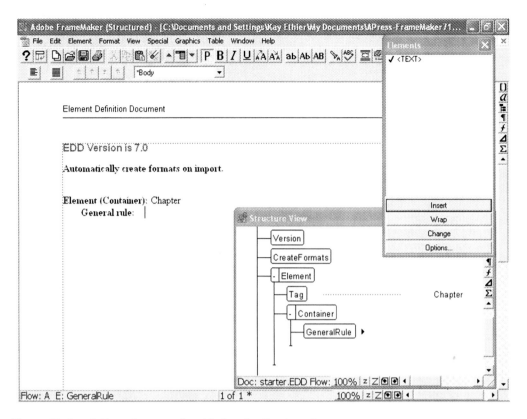

Figure 12–6. A Container type is added to the Chapter *element.*

In the GeneralRule element, you will list the elements or other content that you want Chapter elements to contain within your documents. For example, if you want Chapter elements to contain Section elements within your structured documents, then you would make the Chapter element's General Rule Section+.

Syntax for the General Rule was initially shown in Chapter 7. The syntax included symbols (including the plus sign as used in the Section+ example) to specify the order and frequency of child elements or other content within elements. In this case, a Section+ General Rule means that a Section child element may be inserted within Chapter, and it will be repeatable—allowing you to insert additional Section child elements within the Chapter element.

If you prefer to control the frequency to, say, force at least two sections to occur within your document chapters, then you would modify the rule to force a minimum of two sections. Thus, the rule would be Section, Section+. The first Section within the General Rule tells FrameMaker that Section is a required child. The *comma* means that the elements must appear in the order shown (although techni-cally they both have the same name here and you do not see that effect). The second Section means that a second section is required, and it has a *plus* so that it may be repeated. With this rule, you would get two or more sections. With the prior rule, you could get a single section or many sections.

You might also define the General Rule for the Chapter element as Introduction?, Section, or Section+. What do you think this does? See the footnote[2] for the answer.

Now that you have your Chapter element in place, you may finalize it by inserting some or all of the elements described in "Final-izing Container Elements" on page 275. If you wish, you may also create the rest of your Container type elements so that they are all available for testing as you finalize each of them, using the elements mentioned in the section on Container types.

To create more Container type elements in your *starter.edd*, follow the upcoming steps. If you are comfortable with the process, feel free to experiment or adjust as you go. Just remember if you change any names or settings, as this may affect exercises coming up later in this chapter.

---

2. This rule adds an optional Introduction child element within the Chapter element, before any Section elements are inserted. The result is that you will be able to author a chapter with an introduction if you like, but may also skip the introduction and still maintain a valid structure (since the Introduction is optional, per the *question mark*).

1. If not open, open the *starter.edd* file.

2. Place your insertion point inside the ElementCatalog element, below the last Element element.

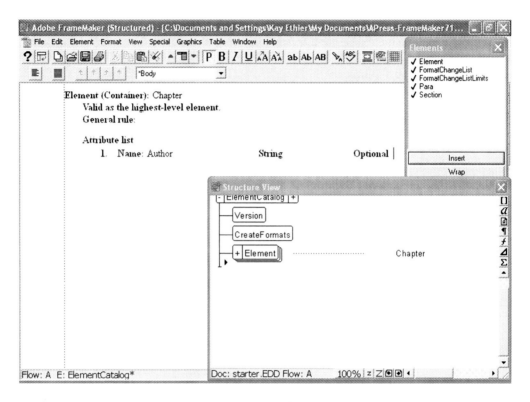

3. Insert an Element element.

4. In the Tag element that autoinserts with the Element element, type **Title** for the element name.

5. Insert a Container element to set the element type.

6. In the `GeneralRule` element that automatically inserts, type a general rule of **<TEXT>**.

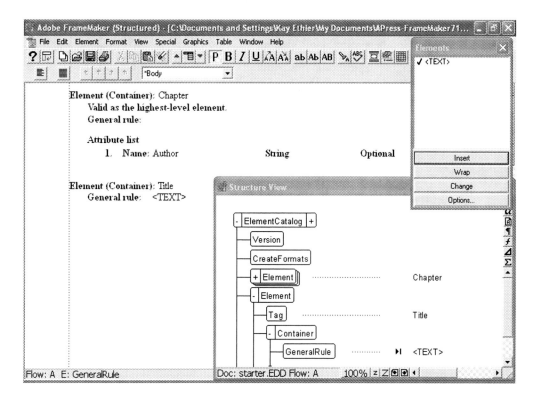

7. Move your insertion point to the right of the line descending from `ElementCatalog`, just below the `Element` element just created.

You may wish to collapse the `Element` element above your insertion point. This may make it easier for you to properly place your insertion point below those already created.

8. Insert another `Element` element.

9. Insert the `Container` element below the `Tag` element to set the element type.

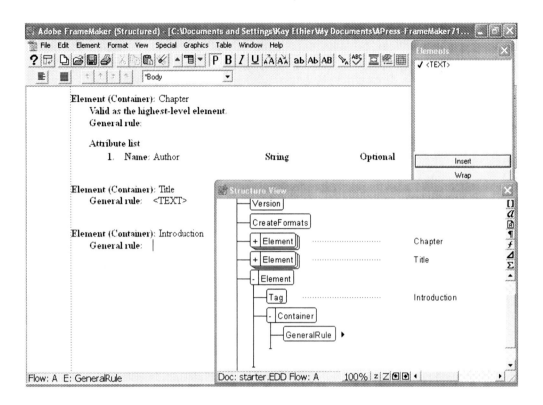

10. In the `GeneralRule` element, type **Title**, **IntroPara**, **Para+**.

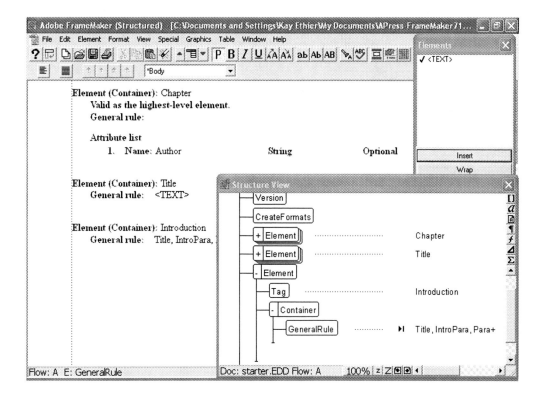

11. Insert an Element element and give it the name IntroPara by typing this within the Tag element.

12. Insert the `Container` element to set the element type.

13. In the GeneralRule element that autoinserts, type <TEXT>.

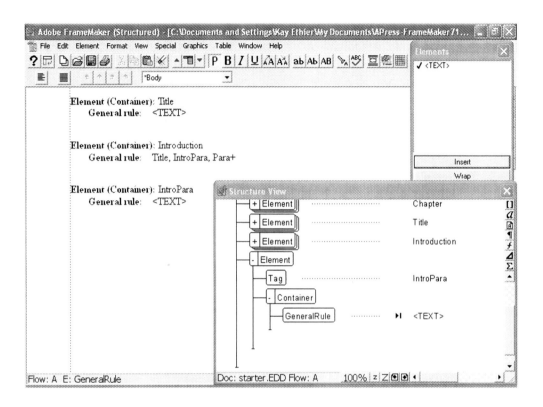

14. Insert another `Element` element.

15. Name this element `Para` by typing it in the `Tag` element.

16. Move your insertion point and insert the `Container` element beneath the `Tag` element.

17. Give this element a general rule of <TEXT>.

NOTE   For now, this rule only allows text within Para elements. You will change this later in these exercises, adding child elements to the Para element's general rule.

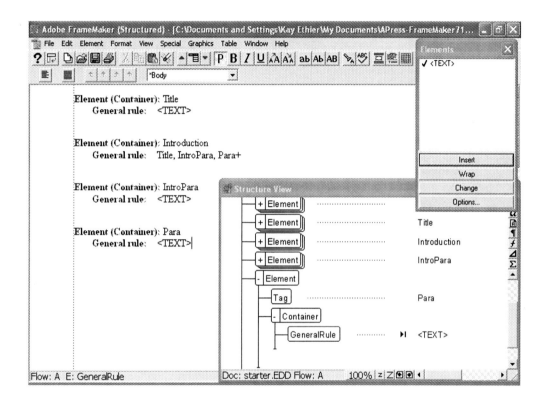

273

18. Using similar steps, create an element called Section and set it as a Container type.

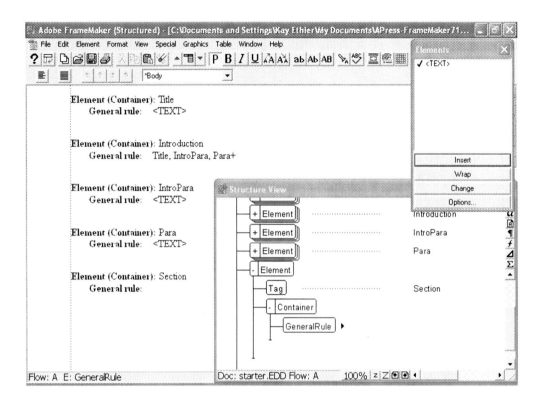

19. For the Section element you just created, type **Title, Para+, Section*** in its GeneralRule element.

    The last part of the General Rule (Section*) allows Section elements to nest inside Section elements. If you wish to force a minimum of two nested sections within higher-level sections (similar to the way the chapter forces a minimum of two at that level), then feel free to adjust the general rule to Title, Para+, (Section, Section+)?.

20. Create an element called List and make it a Container type element.

21. Give the List element a general rule of ListItem, ListItem+.

22. Now create an ListItem element for use inside the List element you just created.

23. Give the ListItem element a general rule of <TEXT>.

24. Save your EDD file.

25. Create a new document (*File>New>Document* and choose *Portrait*).

26. Save the new document as *test.fm*.

27. Import the element definitions into *test.fm* from your *starter.edd* file.

NOTE Both files need to be open before you can import from one into the other.

28. Test your elements by inserting them into the *test.fm* document, checking what is available in the Element Catalog against what you expect (based on the general rules you wrote) as you insert each element.

Based on the General Rules that you created, you will see elements become available in the Element Catalog.

Finalizing Container Elements

Also within the Container element are elements that allow you to control formatting, attributes, insertion behavior, and more. These Container child elements are shown in Figure 12–7.

The AttributeList Element

The AttributeList element is available within Container type elements. It is also available in Table type elements.

The AttributeList element contains child Attribute elements that are used to add attributes to each element. You may add one or more Attribute elements within an AttributeList element.

Figure 12–7. Additional elements are shown within the Container *element definition.*

Because attributes require as much thought and setup as elements, their creation is discussed in a separate section called "Defining Attributes for Elements" on page 319.

The Autoinsertion Element

The Autoinsertion element is available within Container type elements. It is also available in Table type elements. It allows you to automate element insertion for your users. Autoinsertions work in the following way:

1. Elements are created in the EDD.

2. Parent element/child element pairings are found—generally through testing—that recur throughout the structure.

3. In the EDD, autoinsertions are defined for these parent elements, allowing the child elements to insert when the parent element is inserted.

4. When element definitions are used for documents, authors turn their autoinsertions on from the *Element>New Element Options* menu.

5. Authors insert parent elements and the child elements come in with them.

The Exclusion and Inclusion Elements

The Inclusion element is available within Container type elements. It is also available in Table-related and Footnote type elements.

Inclusions are a kind of shortcut for EDD developers. An inclusion allows for an element to be inserted into many other elements within a structure, without the EDD developer adding the inclusion element into the other elements' General Rules. The inclusion is specified at a high level—for example, in a Chapter or Section element—and then all of the descendents of that high-level element may have the inclusion in them.

Inclusions appear in the Element Catalog with a bold checkmark (valid) and a small bold plus. It is the plus that identifies them as an inclusion at that point in the structure.

The Exclusion element is available within Container type elements. It is also available in Table-related and Footnote type elements.

An exclusion is used to negate, or cancel out, an inclusion that has been set for use at a high level. For example, if you set an inclusion within a Section element (and its descendents) but do not want that included element to be allowed within List elements inside sections, you would need to exclude that inclusion element within the List element's definition.

It is recommended that inclusion and exclusion not be used if you are importing or exporting XML. There is not an equivalent within a DTD. Any Inclusion or Exclusion elements would be considered out of place (invalid) in the resulting XML exported from FrameMaker because the XML DTD would not show them within its content model (they may be used for SGML export because they are supported by SGML DTDs, which is why they are still included in the FrameMaker EDD settings).

The FirstParagraphRules and LastParagraphRules Elements

The FirstParagraphRules element is available within Container type elements. It is also available in Table-related and Footnote-type elements.

This element allows you to specify formatting that should be applied to the first paragraph within a parent element. For example, you could specify additional spacing above a first bullet within a bulleted list.

The LastParagraphRules element is available within Container type elements. It is also available in Table-related and Footnote type elements.

This LastParagraphRules element allows you to specify formatting that should be applied to the last paragraph within a parent element. For example, you could specify additional spacing below a last bullet within a bulleted list.

The PrefixRules and SuffixRules Elements

The PrefixRules element is available only within Container type elements.

Adding a prefix to an element allows you to add characters or text in front of an element's content. It behaves in a similar fashion to the Numbering properties within the Paragraph Designer.

The SuffixRules element is also available only within Container type elements.

Adding a suffix to an element allows you to add characters or text at the end of an element's content. It behaves in a similar fashion to the Numbering properties within the Paragraph Designer.

In the Paragraph Designer, however, you are limited to selecting either *Start of Paragraph* or *End of Paragraph* within a paragraph's definition. You may use both a prefix and a suffix in structure. This is a formatting advantage that structure has over regular FrameMaker documents.

This would allow you, for example, to place square brackets before and after an element's content.

The TextFormatRules Element

The TextFormatRules element is available within Container type elements. It is also available in Table-related and Footnote type elements. Follow these steps to add a `TextFormatRules` element to your `Title` element:

1. In your *starter.edd* file, locate the `Title` element's definition.

2. If collapsed, expand the `Title` element by clicking the plus in front of the `Title` element bubble in the Structure View.

3. Place your insertion point inside the `Container` element and below the `AttributeList` element (or below the `GeneralRule` element if there is no `AttributeList` element).

4. From the Element Catalog, insert the `TextformatRules` element.

5. Save your EDD.

Text format rules require pretty significant explanation. Refer to "Adding Formatting to Elements" on page 327 for information on formatting and the child element available within the `TextformatRules` element.

The `ValidHighestLevel` Element

The `ValidHighestLevel` element is available within Container type elements. It is not available in any other type of element.

When you started your cookbook sample document in Chapter 10, you inserted a `Recipe` element into the empty text frame. This began your structure. If you take a look back at Figure 10–8, you will see the `Recipe` element's definition from the EDD. It includes "Valid as the highest-level element" in its definition. This means that this element may be used to start a structure in an empty FrameMaker document.

If you would like to specify this for your Chapter element in the *starter.edd,* follow these steps:

1. Place your insertion point inside the Chapter element's Container element, above the GeneralRule element.

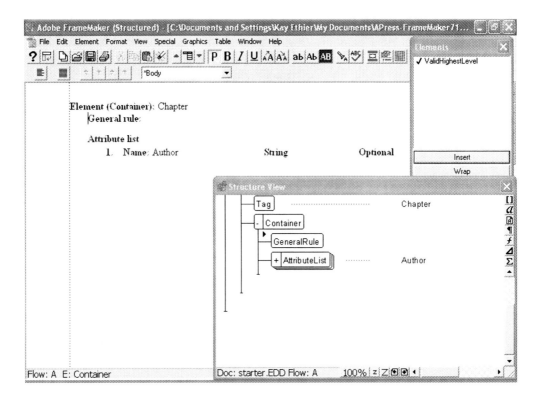

2. Insert the ValidHighestLevel element from the Element Catalog.

   The ValidHighestLevel element and Yes child element will appear in the Structure View. You will see the "Valid as the highest-level element" text in the Document window inside the Chapter element.

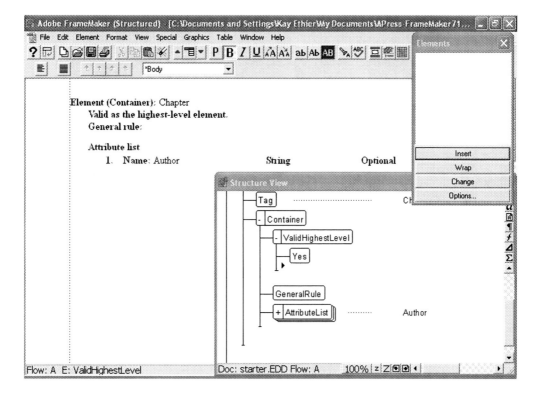

3. Save your EDD.

On export to XML, this element will be the *root element* in the resulting XML instance.

CrossReference Type Elements and Related Attributes

CrossReference type elements work best (for XML round trip) when attributes are included in the EDD and DTD. The attributes hold the information FrameMaker needs to link the cross reference to its destination, and to set the FrameMaker cross reference format to control what the cross reference looks like.

With FrameMaker 7.1, specific attributes are needed to make new external cross-reference features link properly.

An external cross reference (from a cross-reference element in one document to an element in another document) output to XML might look something like this,

```
<CrossReference format = "Heading &#x0026; Page" srcfile =
"file:///C:/folder/mydocument.xml#BHBIGBAB"/>
```

using a relative path from one file to another. You may instead see a relative path in the XML if the files are *close* to each other in the folder tree.

```
<Xref format = "Heading &#x0026; Page" srcfile =
"../simpledoc/xref_uniqueIDexample.xml#CEGHGHCE"/>
```

In the above example, the name of the XML element is `CrossReference`. The attribute format has a value of `"Heading &#x0026; Page"` which, in FrameMaker, becomes the Heading & Page cross-reference format. The `srcfile` attribute includes the path to the referenced document, including the unique ID to which it refers (the sequence after the pound symbol). This path would not be included if these files were in the same folder. Instead, the reference would be to the filename and unique ID:

```
<Xref format = "Heading &#x0026; Page" srcfile =
"xref_idref_example.xml#BHBDHEFF"/>
```

An internal cross reference, from a cross-reference element to another element in the same document, might look like this:

```
<Xref RefID = "BHBDHEFF" format = "Heading &#x0026; Page"/>
```

The difference is that no path is included in the internal reference.

To define an `XRef` element and its corresponding attribute, follow these steps.

1. If not open, open your *starter.edd*.

2. Insert an `Element` element and name it **XRef**.

NOTE   XRef is not a reserved name so you may feel free to
name this element something else.

3.   Move your insertion point below the Tag element.

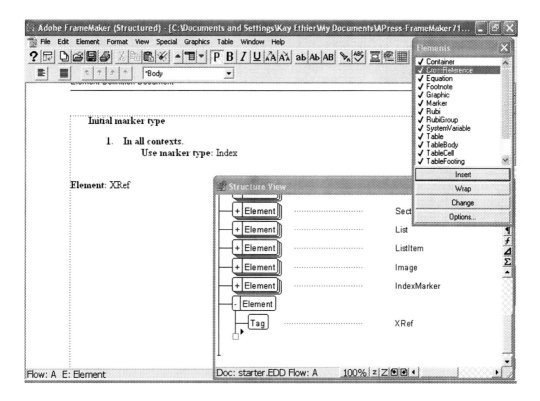

4. Insert the `CrossReference` element from the Element Catalog.

The `CrossReference` element bubble appears in the Structure View, and the Element Catalog will show two available child elements: `AttributeList` and `InitialObjectFormat`.

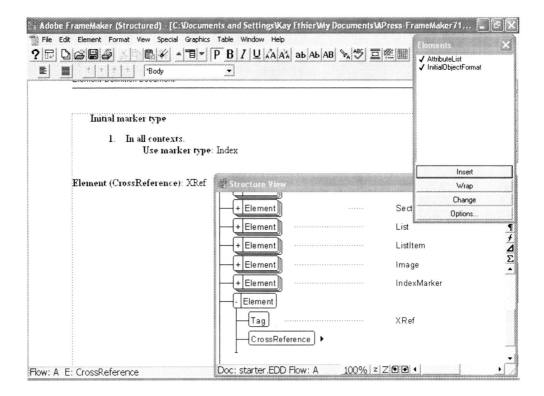

NOTE In the EDD, all element bubbles appear as rounded-edge rectangles. It is only within structured documents created from the EDD that FrameMaker differentiates object-type elements (cross references, markers, etc.) with square-edged rectangular bubbles.

5. Insert the `InitialObjectFormat` element.

    The `InitialObjectFormat` element bubble appears in the
    Structure View. The Element Catalog now has three element
    choices available: `AllContextsRule`, `ContextRule`, and
    `LevelRule`.

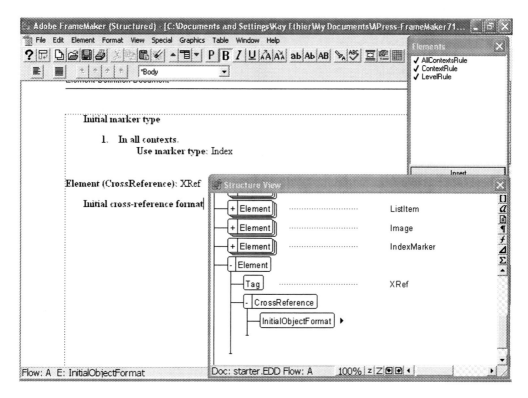

6. Insert the `AllContextsRule` element.

7. The Element Catalog now shows two available child elements: ContextLabel and CrossReferenceFormat.

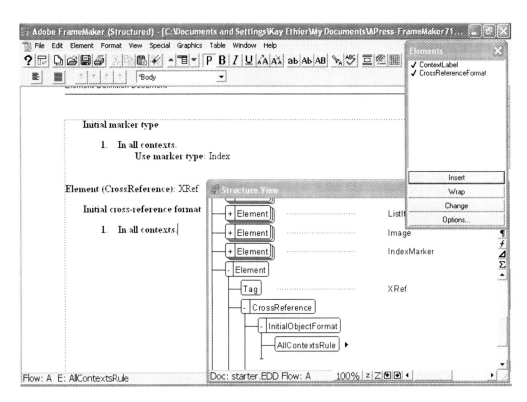

NOTE The ContextLabel element allows you to specify an element's alternative label to appear within FrameMaker's dialog boxes. It is useful for elements that will be used at different levels or in different contexts within a structure document, or to provide more descriptive phrases next to an element name.

8. Insert the `CrossReferenceFormat` element from the Element Catalog.

   The `CrossReferenceFormat` element appears and the Element Catalog displays `<TEXT>`, meaning that you may type inside this element.

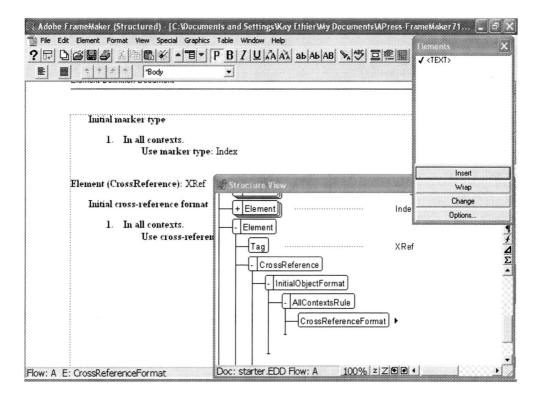

9. Type the name of your cross reference format.

   If you are still creating your template, decide what you want the format name to be and type that name here. Be sure to note that you need to create a format in your template with the exact same name (case and spacing matters).

10. In this example, the cross-reference format name *See Heading* was given.

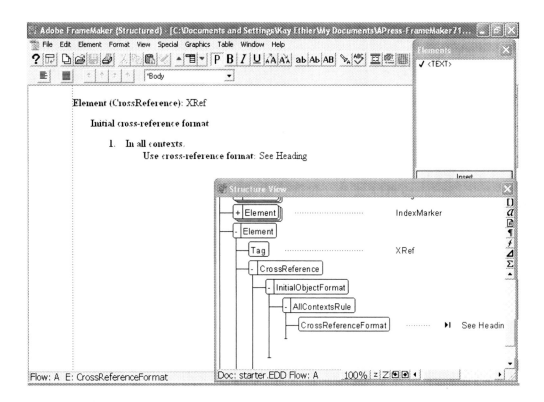

11. Save your *starter.edd* file.

12. If you wish to add attributes to your XRef (at least one is required), place your insertion point above the InitialObjectFormat element, as shown in the screen shot below.

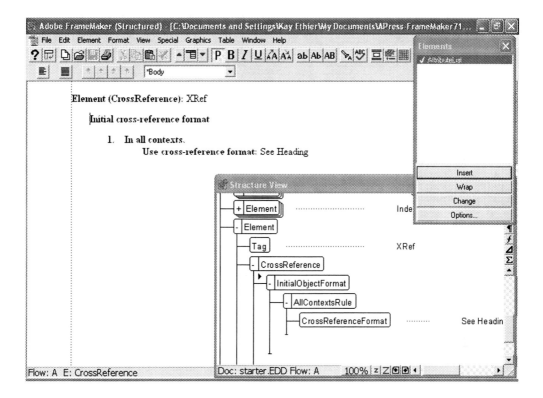

The AttributeList element may only be inserted as shown, above the InitialObjectFormat element

13. Insert the AttributeList element.

14. The `AttributeList` element and `Attribute` child element should appear in the Structure View, along with a nested child element `Name` inside the `Attribute` element.

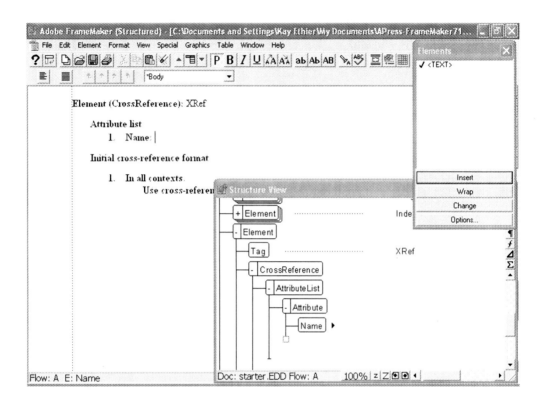

15. Name this attribute **IDRef** by typing that text within the Name element.

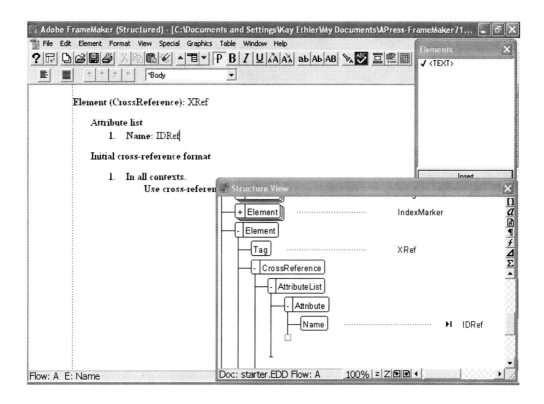

16. Move your insertion point below the Name element and to the right of the line descending from the Attribute element.

NOTE The red box near your insertion point denotes that a required element is missing. Once you perform the next few steps, the red box will disappear.

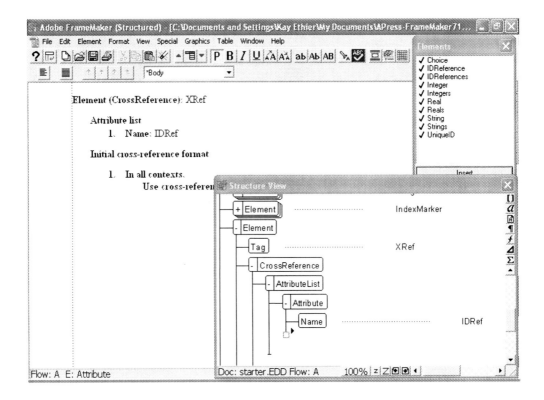

17. From the Element Catalog, insert the IDReference element to
set this attribute's type.

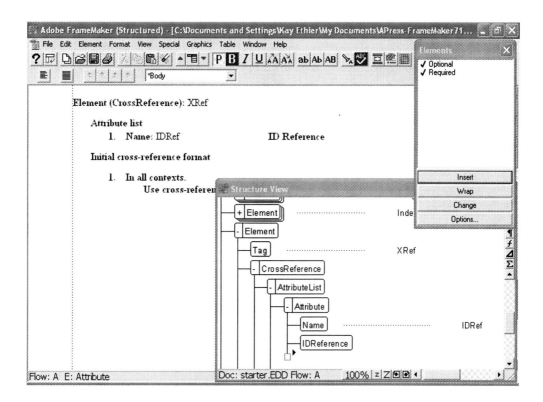

18. Move your insertion point below the IDReference element in the Structure View, and insert the Required element from the Element Catalog.

    The Required element specifies that, when this element is used in a structured document, its IDRef attribute must be given a value for the document to be valid.

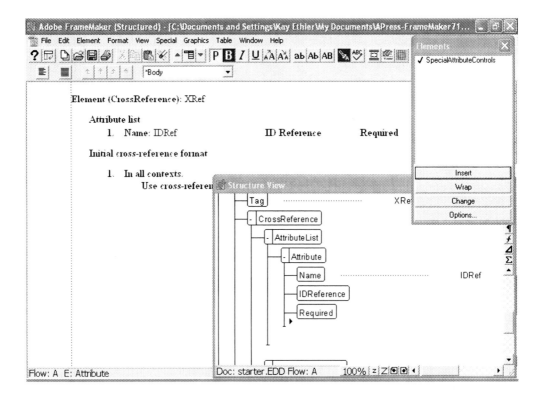

19. Place your insertion point below the Required element.

    The Element Catalog will show an optional child element: SpecialAttributeControls.

    You do not need to insert this element in your EDD if you do not want to use it. In this example, you will.

20. Insert the `SpecialAttributeControls` element.

    Two child elements are now shown in the Element Catalog:
    `Hidden` and `ReadOnly`.

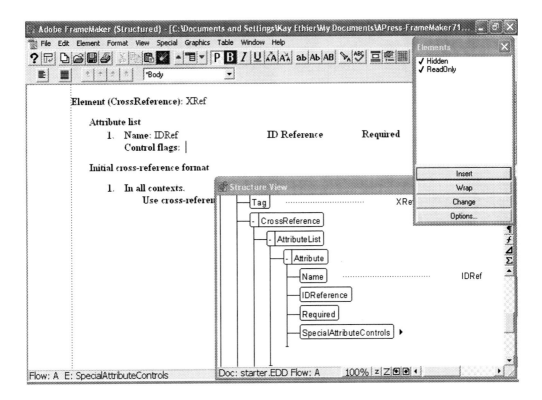

Hidden   if used, the attribute will not appear in your
structured documents. This setting is not recommended for
normal use.

ReadOnly   if used, the attribute will not allow users to
access the value nor to change it. While this is not a
requirement for your cross references to work, it is suggested.

21. Insert the ReadOnly element.

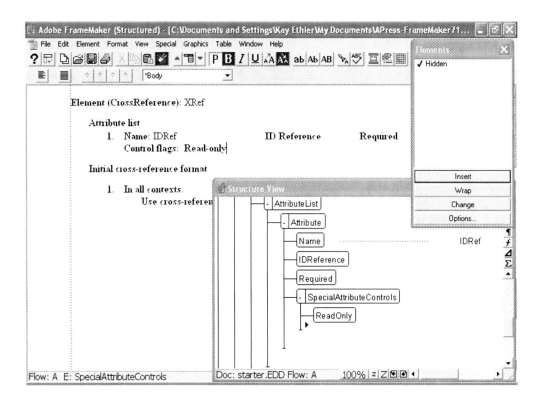

22. Save your EDD.

Now add an attribute to the `Title` element, so you can cross reference to titles within your documents.

1. Place your insertion point under the `Title` element's `GeneralRule` element.

2. Insert the `AttributeList` element from the Element Catalog.

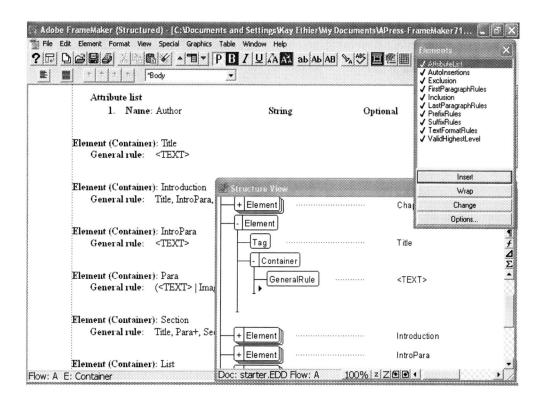

3. The `AttributeList` element, `Attribute` child element, and nested child element, `Name`, appear in the Structure View.

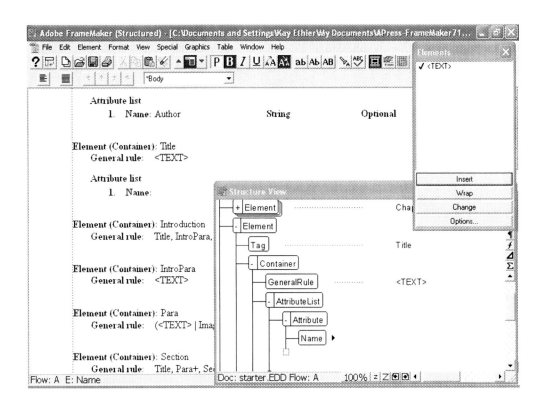

4. In the Name element, type **srcfile** as the name for this
    attribute.

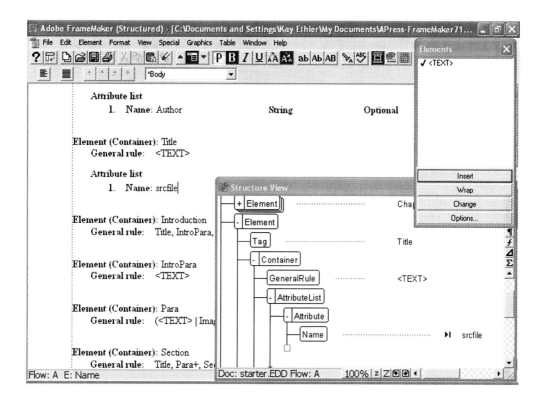

5. Place your insertion point below the Name element.

The attribute types will be listed in the Element Catalog.

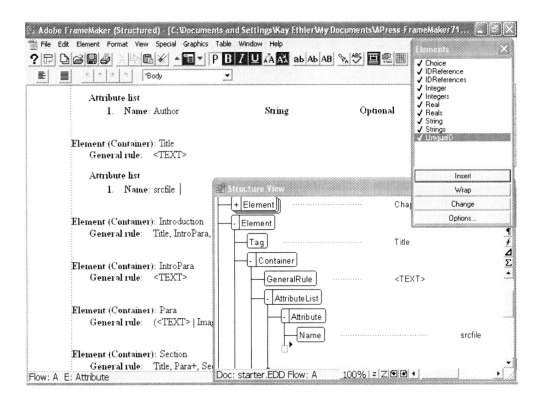

6. Insert the `UniqueID` element to set this attribute's type.

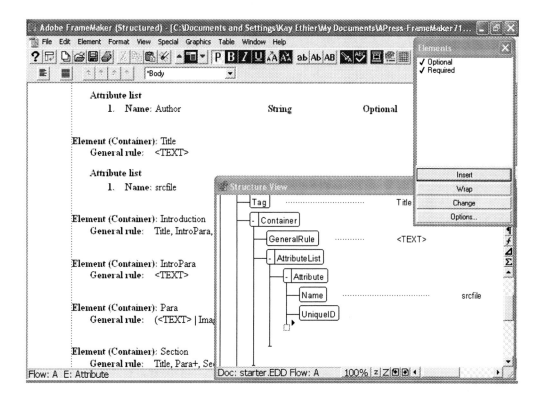

7. Place your insertion point below the UniqueID element.

The Element Catalog shows two elements as available for insertion (valid): Optional and Required.

Optional   you will not have to specify a value for this attribute when authoring your structured document, though you may specify a value if you wish.

Required   You *must* specify a value for this attribute when authoring your structured documents. This is not a recommended setting, because the result is that you would have to enter a value every time you insert the element with this attribute. This would be tedious and would result in your creating attribute values that are not referenced (a waste of time).

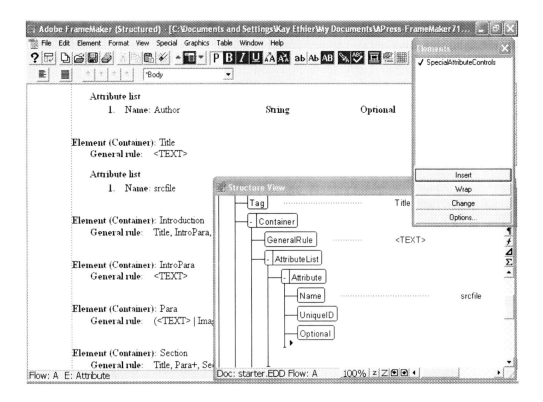

8. Save your EDD file.

A little later in these exercises, you will add *XRef* to another element's general rule so that the XRef element will appear in the Element Catalog as available for insertion (valid) inside that element. In this example, the element you will adjust is Para.

Table Type Elements and Related Types

Tables have a specific structure to them that must be built into the structure for XML round trip tables to work properly. If set up improperly, the XML you import will form paragraphs instead of forming into a table. To understand the proper way, it is important for you to understand FrameMaker tables.

For structured tables, you need to create the main table element and elements for all the following parts of a FrameMaker table:

- Table

- TableTitle

- TableHeading

- TableBody

- TableFooting

- TableRow

- TableCell

Because FrameMaker table rows are divided into three different types—body, heading, and footing—you must include these designations in your table structure. Each of these types of rows is defined as an element that wraps around TableRow type elements. The TableRow type elements, in turn, wrap around TableCell type elements. Inside the cells, you may either type directly (by giving the TableCell type elements a General Rule of <TEXT>) or insert child elements (by instead giving a General Rule that lists allowed child elements). The TableTitle type element is the only other type of table element that may include text or non-table child elements.

NOTE Because FrameMaker does not allow nested tables, you may not nest table elements inside table elements. Any XML imported with such a structure will drop the nested table content in the resulting FrameMaker structured document.

While FrameMaker does not have a way of handling nested tables, the Frame Developer's Kit (FDK) does allow work arounds to be created for this type of issue (among other things).

Create your table elements, and take care to select the correct element type or your tables will not form properly.

1. In your *starter.edd*, place your insertion point below the last Element element created and to the right of the line descending from the ElementCatalog element.

2. Insert an Element element.

3. Name this element *Table*.

4. Place your insertion point below the Tag element and to the right of the line descending from the Element element.

   The Element Catalog shows the available element types.

5. Set the element type by inserting the Table element from the Element Catalog.

6. Specify a General Rule of TTitle, THeading?, TBody, TFooting?.

7. Repeat the preceding steps, replacing the element name (Tag) and type with the following:

NAME	TYPE	GENERAL RULE
TTitle	TableTitle	<TEXT>
THeading	TableHeading	TRow+
TBody	TableBody	TRow+
TFooting	TableFooting	TRow+
TRow	TableRow	TCell+
TCell	TableCell	<TEXT>

8. Add *Table* to the Para element's General Rule, similar to the way you added *Image* to allow placement of these elements inside Para elements. For example, (<TEXT> | Image | IndexMarker | Table)*.

9. Save your EDD.

10. Open the *test.fm* document, if it is not already open.

11. Import your element definitions into the example document and test them by inserting a Table element within a paragraph.

Table attributes that allow you to retain table dimensions throughout the XML round trip process are listed in Table 12–2. You may wish to include these in the EDD (and related DTD). These are common in XML based on CALS tables.

Table 12–2. Example Table Attributes

NAME	TYPE	OPTIONAL/REQUIRED
Name: Cols	String	Optional
Name: Widths	String	Optional
Name: Colsep	String	Optional
Name: Rowsep	String	Optional
Name: Frame	String	Optional
Name: Tabstyle	String	Optional

Graphic Elements

To insert graphics into your documents, you need to include at least one Graphic type element in your EDD. This will allow you to insert elements that are FrameMaker anchored frames.

Only anchored frames may be used for images in your XML. While FrameMaker does allow you to place images directly on the page, graphics placed on a page in a structured document are not considered to be part of the structured flow—they will not export to XML. Anchoring them within the structured flow ensures they are a part of that flow and will export.

To create a Graphic type element, follow these steps.

1. In your *starter.edd*, place your insertion point below the last Element element.

2. Insert a new Element element.

3. Name this element *Image* by typing this in the Tag element.

4. Place your insertion point below the Tag element.

5. Insert the Graphic element to set the element's type.

   Two elements are now available in the Element Catalog: AttributeList and InitialObjectFormat.

6. Insert the InitialObjectFormat element.

   Choices in the Element Catalog are now AllContextsRule, ContextRule, and LevelRule.

7. Insert the AllContextsRule element.

   The Element Catalog now allows you to insert an AnchoredFrame, ImportedGraphicFile, or ContextLabel element.

   Anchored Frame   when the element is inserted in a structured document, FrameMaker will open the Anchored Frame dialog box.

Imported Graphic File   when the element is inserted in a structured document, FrameMaker will open the Import File dialog box.

8. Insert the `ImportedGraphicFile` element.

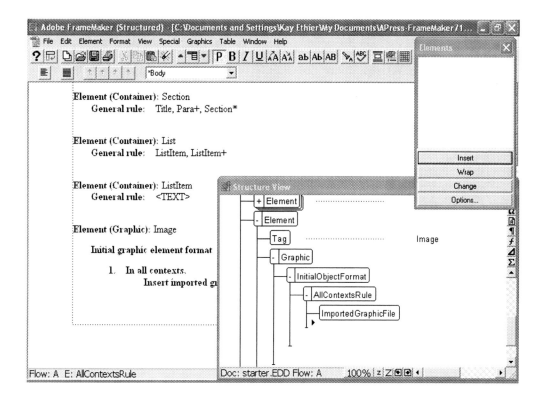

9. Save your EDD.

If desired, you might also add an element to your EDD that is the Graphic type, but select `AnchoredFrame` for that element. Then you would have an alternative to the `Image` element.

Another option that you have is to set up one Graphic type element with an attribute choice that allows you to choose *anchored frame* or *imported file* each time you insert the element. You would add an attribute to the `Image` element. Then, you would define a context rule. Within the context rule, you would set the context based on the attribute value, so that as you use the element in a structured document and set the attribute value, the attribute will drive which dialog box appears (Anchored Frame versus Import File dialog box). Context rules are described a little later in this chapter.

An example of a Graphic type element with an attribute context rule may be found in this book's *simpledoc* sample files.

Marker Elements

If you wish to include markers in your structured documents, then a Marker type element needs to be added to your EDD.

When the Marker type elements are inserted, FrameMaker's Marker dialog box automatically opens. If a marker type has been built into the element settings, the Marker type will automatically be selected in the window. This is an advantage of working in structure, since the user must remember to select the correct marker type in unstructured FrameMaker documents. Here, you may set up the structure to select it for you—that way, you do not need to think about it.

1. Place your insertion point below your last Element element in your EDD.

2. Insert an Element element.

3. Name this element *IndexMarker* by typing that text inside its Tag element.

4. Place your insertion point below the Tag element.

5. The Element Catalog will list the available elements, which
   are the element types.

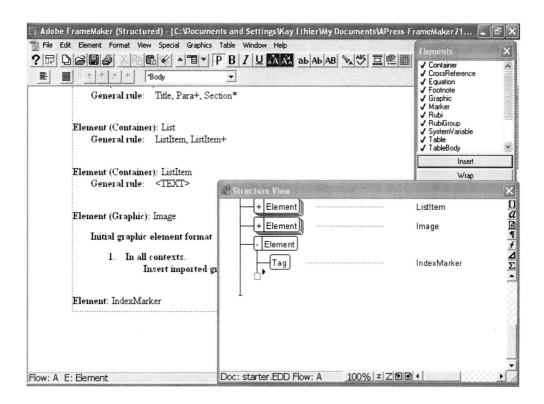

6. Choose the Marker element from the Element Catalog and click *Insert*.

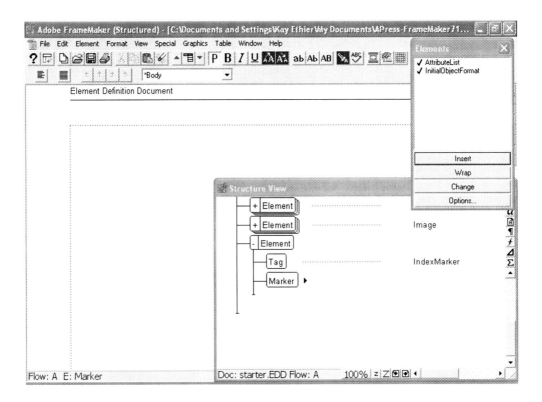

The Element Catalog will now show AttributeList and InitialObjectFormat as available (valid).

7. For our example, insert the InitialObjectFormat element.

8. Now the Element Catalog displays choices of
   AllContextsRule, ContextRule, and LevelRule.

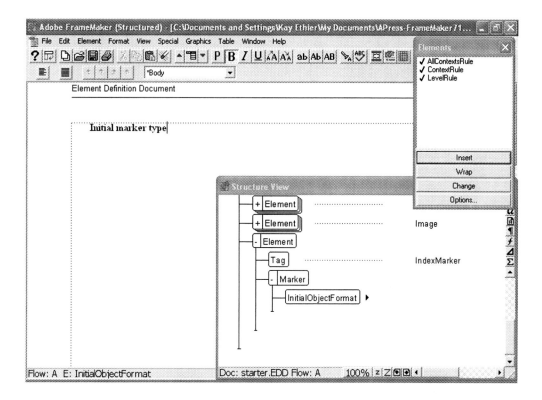

9. Insert the AllContextsRule element.

10. You now have choices of `ContextLabel` or `MarkerType` in the Element Catalog.

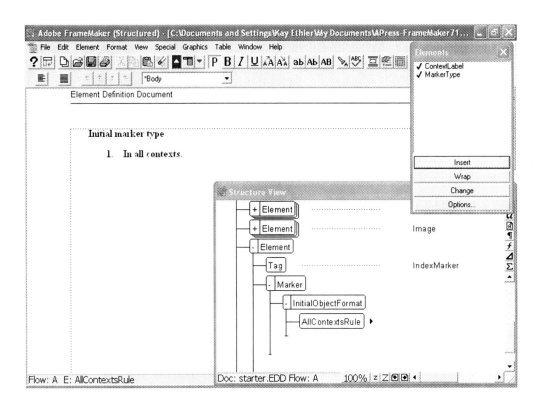

11. Insert the MarkerType element.

    The Element Catalog now shows all of the available types of
    FrameMaker markers.

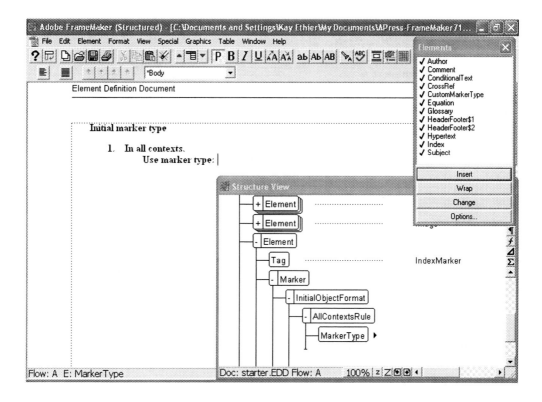

313

12. Insert the Index element so that FrameMaker will automatically select this in the Marker window when you use this element in strulctured documents.

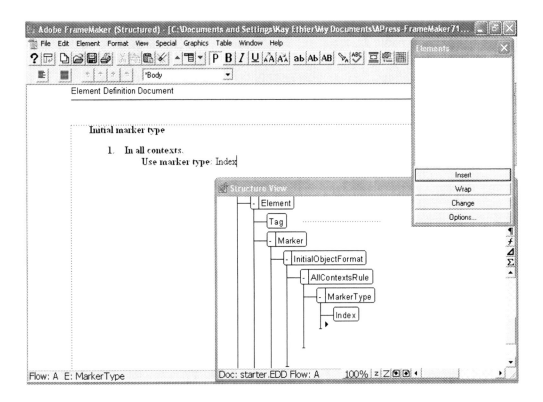

13. If you wish to add attributes to this element, move your insertion point to above the InitialObjectFormat element bubble in the Structure View and Insert the AttributeList element. In this example, we will not add any attributes.

14. Save your EDD.

Once you have added IndexMarker and other elements (such as the Image element), you may need to adjust the General Rules for the container elements. Elements may only be used if they are referenced within the General Rules of other elements. So, IndexMarker and Image cannot be validly placed in a structured document until another element has them in its General Rule. In this example, we will add both the Marker and the Graphic type elements to the Para element. This will allow placement of the Image element and the IndexMarker element within any Para, when inserted in a structured document.

1. In your EDD, locate the Para element's definition.

2. Change the Para element's General Rule to (<TEXT> | Image | IndexMarker)* so that child elements and text may be included in this element.

> **NOTE** Because of the way XML content models must be written, <TEXT> must appear first in the General Rule, and the entire sequence must be enclosed in parentheses and followed by an asterisk. Otherwise, saving your EDD to a DTD may yield a DTD with content model errors.

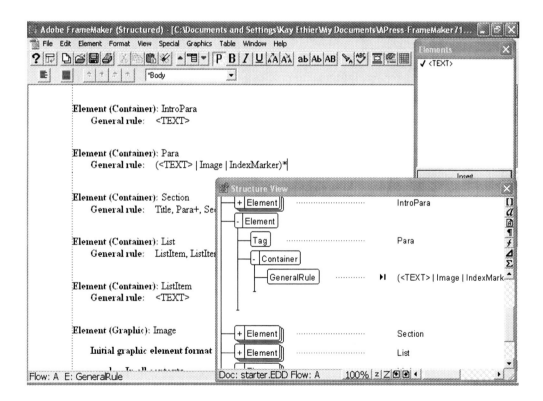

Now you will be able to insert Para elements in your test document and have these other two (Image, IndexMarker) available as valid choices within Para in your structured documents.

3. Open your *test.fm* file.

4. Import your element definitions from *starter.edd* into *test.fm*.

NOTE   If an error log appears when importing element definitions, read the errors carefully and hyperlink from the errors back into your EDD to adjust them. Then, save your EDD and reimport the element definitions.

5. Test your elements by inserting them in your test document.

Footnote Elements

You may also create a Footnote type element within your EDD. FrameMaker will ensure that this element behaves as a footnote when it is inserted. The footnote properties within your template will be used for the element.

1. Create a new element in your EDD and name it *Footnote*.

NOTE   This is not a reserved name, so feel free to name it something else.

2. Set the element type as Footnote.

3. Give it a general rule of <TEXT>.

4. If you wish, add any desired attributes or text format rules.

5. Adjust the Para element's General Rule so that the Footnote element is an option: (<TEXT> | Image | IndexMarker| Footnote)*.

6. Save your EDD.

7. Reimport your element definitions and test the Footnote element in your test document.

Equation Elements

You may also create Equation type elements within your EDD. If you plan to use equations, then you may add an element of this type. You may also specify for it to come in as a small, medium, or large equation.

Similar to the way that you could drive the FrameMaker dialog boxes for Graphic type elements, you can drive the equation size by using an attribute. This is optional, but not necessary if you plan to always use the same size equation.

1. Create a new element in your EDD and name it *SmallEq*.

NOTE   This is not a reserved name, so feel free to name it something else.

---

2. Set the element type by inserting the Equation element.

3. Insert the InitialObjectFormat element.

4. Insert the AllContextsRule element.

5. Insert the SmallEquation element to set the size of equations within your structured documents.

6. If you wish, add any desired attributes or text format rules.

7. Adjust the Para element's general rule so that Footnote element is an option: (<TEXT> | Image | IndexMarker| Footnote | SmallEq)*.

NOTE   While this example shows adding these special items within a Para element, you may include them in any Container, Table-related, or Footnote type elements. Feel free to add these within other elements—for example, by modifying the Section element general rule to allow SmallEq as a sibling to the other child elements of Section.

---

8. Save your EDD.

9. Reimport your element definitions and test the `Equation` element in your test document.

SystemVariable Elements

System variables are used in FrameMaker to drop text into a document and have FrameMaker manage the display. Examples of System variables are *Current Date* and *Current Page #*.

If you would like to include a system variable in your structure, then define it as a SystemVariable type element.

1. Create a new element in your EDD and name it *Date*.

2. Set the element type by inserting the `SystemVariable` element.

3. Insert the `SystemVariableFormatRule` element.

4. Insert the `AllContextsRule` element.

5. Insert the `UseSystemVariable` element.

6. Select the `CurrentDateLong` element from the list of available system variables in the Element Catalog.

7. Add any desired attributes or text format rules, if you wish.

8. Adjust the `Para` element's General Rule to include the `Date` element.

9. Save your EDD.

10. Reimport your element definitions and test the `Date` element in your test document.

Defining Attributes for Elements

Just as elements are of different types, attributes are also of different types. And, just as elements could be specified as *required* (plus symbol or no symbol) or *optional* (question mark or asterisk) in the General Rule, attributes can be specified as required or optional within the element's definition.

Attributes are defined in the EDD inside of elements. The EDD allows elements within its structure to build attributes, name them, specify their type (see Table 12–3), and mark them as required or optional.

There are also some special attribute controls that elements do not have, such as the ability to fill in a default value and the ability to hide them within the resulting FrameMaker structured documents. To define an attribute, you must first have an element in which you plan to include an attribute. In the EDD, your insertion point must be inside that element along the line of decent from the Type element within the element.

NOTE Attributes are an optional part of elements and may be built into any type of element. If you do have attributes, you may have as many as you like. Neither FrameMaker nor XML limit the number of attributes on any single element.

Table 12–3.   Attribute Types

TYPE	PURPOSE
String or Strings	Text may be typed as the attribute value. The plural means that multiple values may be supplied.
Integer or Integers	The attribute value may be any whole number—positive or negative (integers are 0, 1, 2, 3, and so forth). A range of values may also be specified to restrict allowed numbers. The plural allows more than one integer to be provided.
Real or Reals	The attribute value may be any real number—positive or negative (a real number is any number, including decimals: 0, 1.25, 4.999999, and so forth). A range of values may also be specified to restrict allowed numbers. The plural allows more than one integer to be provided.
Choice	The attribute value must be selected from a list of provided choices. These choices are defined in the EDD (or DTD).
UniqueID	Used mostly for cross references, this allows the attribute value to be a string of characters that uniquely identifies an element. No two elements within a file may have the same value for this type of attribute. (If you are familiar with HTML, this is the equivalent of <a name="something">, where something is provided by the user or by FrameMaker.)
IDReference or IDReferences	Used for referencing to elements that have a UniqueID attribute, this stores the value of a UniqueID to complete the link. The plural allows multiple UniqueID values to be stored. (Again referring to HTML, the equivalent of this would be <a href="filename.html#something">.)

To add an attribute to your Chapter element, for example, follow these steps:

1. In your EDD, place your insertion point below the Chapter element's GeneralRule element.

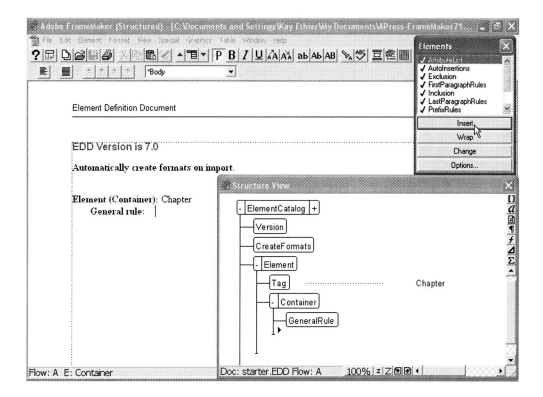

2. Insert the `AttributeList` element from the Element Catalog.

The `Attribute` child and `Name` nested child elements appear with the `AttributeList`.

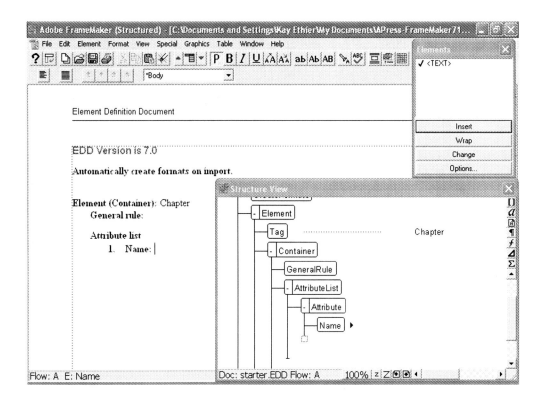

3. Type the name **Author** for this attribute.

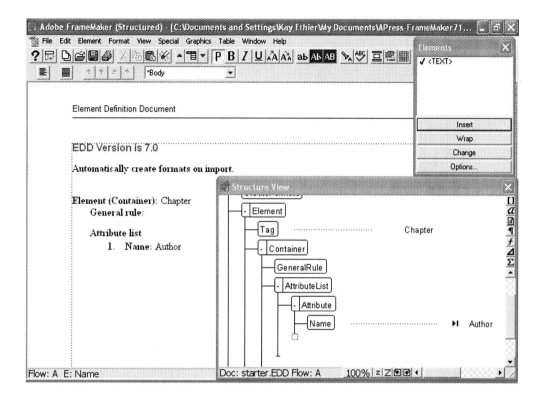

4. Place your insertion point below the Name element.

The attribute types will be listed in the Element Catalog.

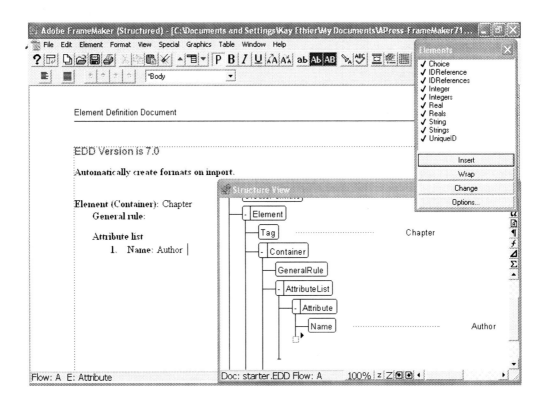

5. Insert the String element to set the attribute's type.

    The Element Catalog will show Optional and Required as
    available elements.

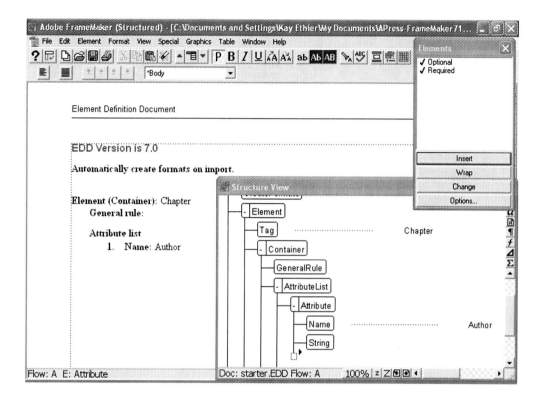

6. Insert Optional so that you do not have to enter a value for
    this attribute for the document to be valid.

7. The Element Catalog now shows optional choices of Default and SpecialAttributeControls (do not insert these for this example).

Default allows you, as the EDD developer, to specify a value for this attribute if it is not given a value in the structured document.

Special Attribute Controls give you the option of making the Hidden or ReadOnly attributes, as described earlier in this section.

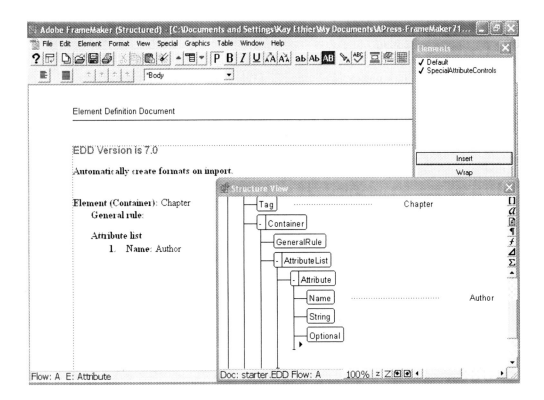

8. If you wish to add more attributes to this element, move your insertion point below the first attribute.

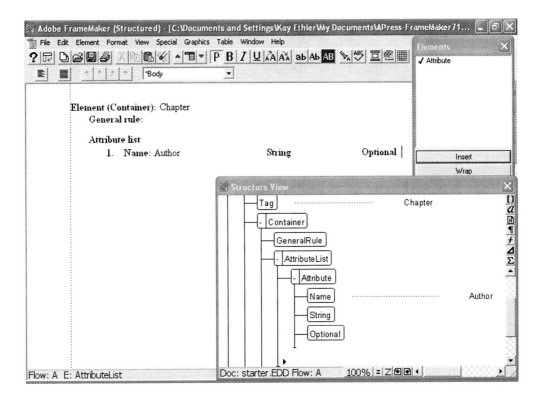

9. After you finish adding your attributes, save your EDD.

At this point, you have many elements and may wish to reimport and test your elements in your test document to ensure they work. Importing will also allow you to check your EDD to ensure there are no errors—an error log will be generated upon import if any errors are detected.

Adding Formatting to Elements

Another important part of element creation is adding formatting. Your *test.fm* document is very plain looking, with all elements not formatted and using the Body paragraph format by default. Whether you are adding a Table format to a Table type element, or setting up complex rules for text formatting, this information needs to be included in the EDD for your resulting structured documents to be formatted consistently.

Before walking through creation of elements and their formatting, it is important that you understand how formatting may be applied.

Formatting in All Contexts

Once you have your Container elements, Footnote type elements, Table type, and other table-related elements, you may add formatting to them. When you specify text format rules to be used in all contexts, then the element will format as specified every time it is inserted.

Figure 12–8 shows a `TextFormatRules` element with a `AllContextsRule` child element. The Element Catalog shows options within the all context rule.

Once the `AllContextRule` is in place, then you may choose a `ContextLabel`, `NoAdditionalFormatting`, `ParagraphFormatting`, or `TextRangeFormatting` element.

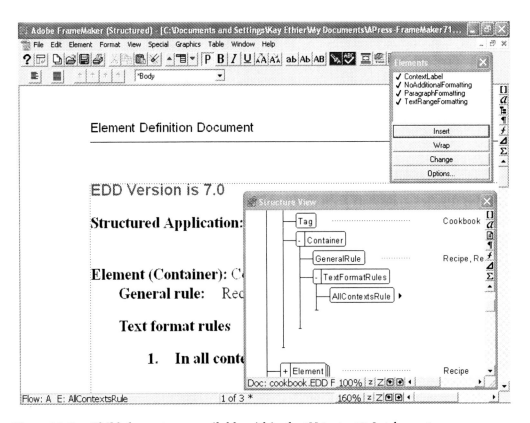

Figure 12–8. Child elements are available within the `AllContextRule` element.

Understanding the FrameMaker Paragraph and Character Designers may help you locate text format rule options more easily. The Paragraph Designer is shown in Figure 12–9, and was explored in more detail in Chapter 2.

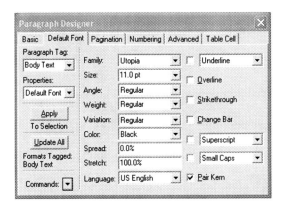

Figure 12–9.   The Paragraph Designer is shown with default font properties sheet showing.

Once you drop in the TextFormatRules element, the child elements that become available (marked as valid with the dark checkmark) are shown in Figure 12–10.

Within the TextFormatRules element, you may specify a Paragraph Format from your template by inserting the ElementPgfFormatTag element and then typing the name of the format that should be used. The format must then exist in your template and have exactly the same name.

Figure 12–11 shows instead the ParagraphFormatting element inserted and the options that become available. Notice the similarity to the settings within the FrameMaker Paragraph Designer. You may either specify a named format from the template by selecting ParagraphFormatTag, or you may select from the different properties-named elements to format your elements property by property.

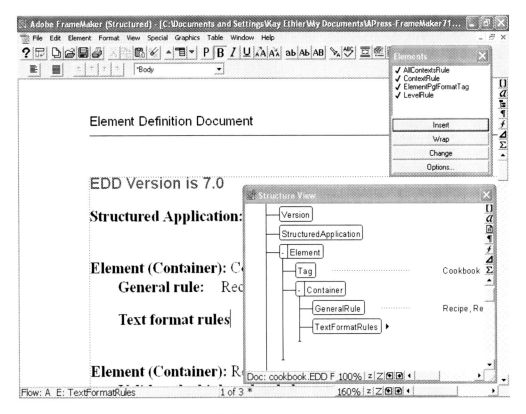

Figure 12–10.   Child elements are available within the TextFormatRules *element.*

There are three ways to format text within an element:

- Format by specifying a named paragraph or character format from your template

- Specify the formats piece-by-piece using the properties-named elements

- Use a FormatChangeList to specify piece-by-piece text property adjustments (such as an indent increase) in a change list and then invoke the list when needed

You may also format using a combination of these options.

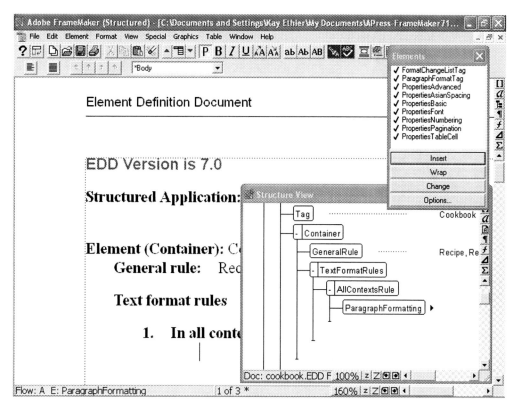

Figure 12–11. Writing an "all contexts rule" can be done within an element's text format rules.

NOTE   While there are no hard and fast rules regarding how text should be formatted, if you plan to share your content with users of other word processors, plan to create PDFs with bookmarks based on paragraph styles, or plan to adjust content by adjusting the template (without needing to adjust the EDD). Then, the best choice for you will be to name formats (Option 1 in the preceding bullet list).

Using the TextRangeFormatting element allows you to set up elements as text ranges so that they will format a range of text rather than creating an entire paragraph when they are inserted.

NOTE The default behavior for an element is to create an entire paragraph. If you wish for an element to contain words or phrases within larger paragraphs instead (such as a Term element for terminology within text), then you need to set that element up as a text range.

Formatting Based on the Context

If you plan to format your elements differently based on the context, then you would use a context rule. Context rules are written as *If-ElseIf-Else* statements, with you specifying the element's contexts and the formatting to be used in each context.

For example, if you are using the example EDD to create a document, you may want the Title element used in both the Chapter element and the Section element. In this case, you might want to format the text differently for the chapter's title than for the section's title.

Figure 12–12 shows an example ContextRule element with the beginning of the specification: an If element with a Specification child element.

The Specification element allows you to type text. Depending on what you want the context to be, you write the rule accordingly. The example specifications—referring to the Title element—demonstrate the syntax options available (see Table 12–4).

Any combination of these may be used to refine the context. You may also use the indicators in Table 12–5 along with element names to refine the context, by using any of these indicators within the specification.

In the amount of space we have here, it is difficult to provide full examples of when to use these. One example may be helpful.

In a bulleted list, you may want to use a special paragraph format for the first bulleted item. So, you would specify that the *first* item within the list should use a specific format. If desired, you might specify that the *last* item within the list should use a specific format. In this instance, you would not need to specify for the *middle*, as you could just write an Else specification that handles everything else. Or, you could include a special formatting specification if there is only one item within a list.

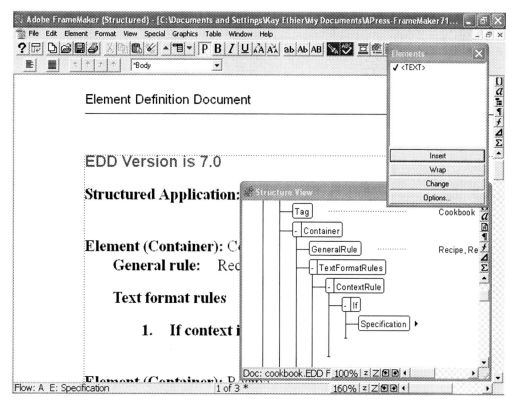

Figure 12–12. Child elements are available within the ContextRule *element.*

Table 12–4. Example General Rule Specifications

SPECIFICATION	MEANING
Chapter	The Title is inside the Chapter parent element
Section	The Title is inside the Section parent element
Section < Section	The element is inside a Section parent element, which is inside a Section (you could take this further if desired, such as *Section < Section < Section* or perhaps *Section < Section < Chapter*)
Chapter [Author=*John Doe*]	The element is inside a Chapter parent element, which has its Author attribute set to a value of *John Doe* (if the attribute were of the element itself, then you would drop the element name before the beginning square bracket)

Table 12–5. Element "Location" Indicators Used in General Rules

INDICATOR	MEANING	EXAMPLE
{after *sibling*}	The element is after the element named	{after Title}
{before *sibling*}	The element is before the element named	{before IntroPara}
{between *sibling1*, *sibling2*}	Between the elements named	{between Title and Para}
{first}	The first element inside its parent	{first}
{notfirst}	Other than the first element in its parent	{notfirst}
{last}	The last element inside its parent	{last}
{notlast}	Other than the last element in its parent	{notlast}
{middle}	Not the first nor the last element in its parent	{middle}
{only}	The only element in its parent	{only}

If you plan to format your elements differently, based on the context, you would use a ContextLabel element and then specify the label to be added to the element name. This allows you to differentiate elements—such as the example Title element—when accessing them via dialog boxes like the Cross Reference dialog box.

For very complex structures, you may find it necessary to use a Subrule element inside your ContextRule element to further refine the formatting—or to make the ContextRule easier to edit by combining similar rules. Within the Subrule element, the settings are very similar to those within a ContextRule element.

Formatting Based on the Level

An alternative to context rule formatting is level rule formatting. If elements are reused within other elements to multiple levels, then you can drive the formatting by counting the number of times an element has been used in the hierarchy.

In Figure 12–13, you can see a Head element used in several places. The resulting text uses different text sizing because the number of Section elements above each Head element is different.

If you use a LevelRule element within your text format rules, then you may specify the levels using a CountAncestors element (see Figure 12–14). This only works if you are using the same elements at

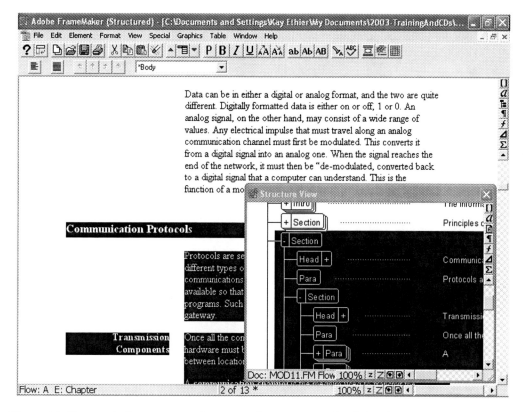

Figure 12–13. Head *elements nested* Section *elements to multiple levels.*

multiple levels. It would not work if you, for example, used SectionLevel and SectionLevel2 elements instead of just Section elements.

Formatting Tables

Table elements pick up their formatting from the table format that you place upon them. Table formats may be built into the Table type element using the InitialTableFormat child element.

Once you have your Table type element created, you will be able to insert the InitialTableFormat child element within that element. Inside this element, the table format may be specified for all contexts, or adjusted using a context rule or level rule. Type the format name exactly as it exists in the table format catalog when you are prompted to type the name.

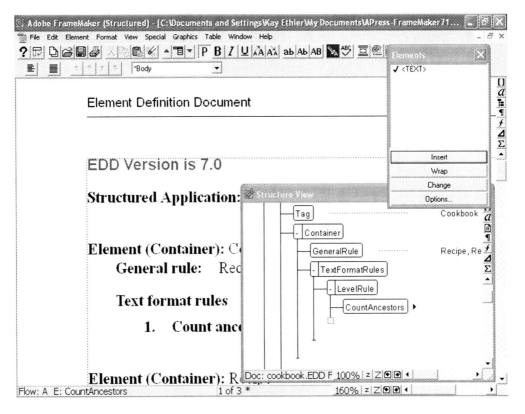

Figure 12–14. The CountAncestors *element in the Structure View.*

When you insert the Table type element in your structured documents, the Insert Table dialog box will appear and the table format you specified in the EDD will be preselected.

NOTE FrameMaker will allow you to select another format. While you can use the EDD to select it, there is no way within FrameMaker to prevent authors from changing the selection.

Once a format is selected, you may then set the number of rows and columns and insert the table. The table will come into the document as structured, and all of the child elements will be automatically inserted. In the Document Window, you will see the table. In the Structure View, you will see a long stream of elements inside the Table type element.

Updating EDDs and DTDs

If your DTD or EDD changes after you have set up your structured publishing files, you might need to update the EDD. FrameMaker's Import DTD function is designed for just this need.

When you choose *File>Structure Tools>Import DTD*, FrameMaker imports your DTD into your EDD. FrameMaker then does the following:

- Adds the element's definitions for any elements in the DTD but not in the EDD

- Removes definitions (which can be problematic if you want the elements in your EDD) for any elements in the EDD but not in the DTD

- Adjusts the content rules and attribute definitions to match the DTD (which can be problematic if you have customized the DTD or EDD and you do not want them to match) for elements in both the DTD and the EDD

After the import, you may need to adjust your EDD to tie formatting to any new elements. DTDs do not contain any formatting information. You may wish to make other changes or adjustments, as well. Once you have the EDD the way that you want it, you may import the revised EDD's element definitions into your structured template (to update its element definitions) and into any of your structured documents that need the new element definitions.

NOTE   If you modify an existing EDD, be sure to import the element definitions into your template and any related structured documents.

If the import changes your EDD, you should know that this may affect existing documents when you import the revised element definitions. Validate the documents after import to locate any validation issues and determine changes that you may need to make to your documents.

Referencing an Application in the EDD

If you wish to have your files associated with a structured application, you may wish to specify this within the EDD. Then, any FrameMaker document structured by that EDD will have its application set directly by use of the EDD.

To set the application, insert the StructuredApplication element within the EDD, as shown in Figure 12–15.

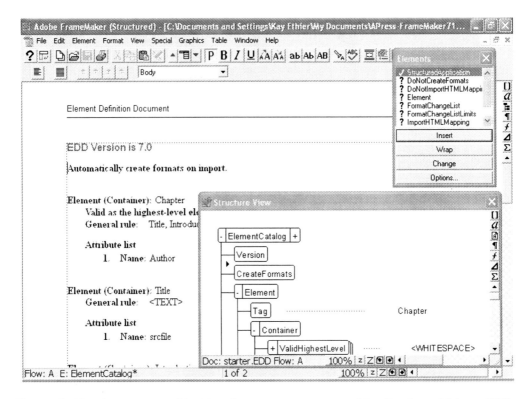

Figure 12–15.   A StructureApplication *element sets a structured Application within an EDD.*

Summary

Creating structure involves understanding the structure you need and creating all the necessary pieces. Several options for creating structure were explored in this chapter, along with information on validating structured documents.

Once you know what your structure should look like, you create it. Where you begin depends on what you choose as your starting point. And, depending on what you have to begin with, the hours required to build your EDD will vary.

CHAPTER 13

Understanding Read/Write Rules

This chapter explores the Read/Write rules file. This file, sometimes used with an XML Application, allows you to adjust the way FrameMaker imports or exports structured content.

Understanding Read/Write Rules

Sometimes moving content between FrameMaker and XML does not work exactly as you need it to work. Whether it is due to special needs in your XML, formatting you need to invoke in FrameMaker, or a FrameMaker-specific markup you wish to adjust, Read/Write rules are available to optimize the flow of content between XML and FrameMaker.

A Read/Write rules file is used by FrameMaker as XML is brought into FrameMaker (the read) or as XML is saved out of FrameMaker (the write). The Rules file fits into your structured Application setup alongside your DTD, structured template, and whatever other elements your Application is using.

Example rules are provided in this section to show you some of the possibilities that rules provide for you.

Example Rules files may be found in the book's sample folders. Additional rules are located in the FrameMaker installation folder in subfolders under *structure\xml*.

Basics of Read/Write Rules

The Read/Write rules file provides you with the ability to adjust elements, attributes, or FrameMaker-specific settings. Many of the actions you can control with rules are described in this chapter. Rules act as a kind of *filter* between your FrameMaker and XML.

A Read/Write rules file may be:

• A structured document (using a special setup available online)

• A text file

• A FrameMaker document (*.fm*)

Different examples of rules, demonstrating the proper syntax, are included in the next section. These include simple rules and complex rules with nested subrules.

Rules Syntax

In a basic Read/Write rule, you specify some FrameMaker property for an element. Most rules are bidirectional, meaning that they perform one adjustment during the *read*, then reverse that adjustment when performing the *write*.

A rule may also be written so that one or many adjustments are made by the rule. Therefore, the syntax allows you to write one simple rule or put several subrules (for multiple adjustments) together using curly braces as delimiters. This syntax, as defined in the *Structure Application Developer's Guide*, is:

```
element "gi"          XML element name
{
is fm type "fmtag";   frame element name
fm property prop value is val;
}                     a FM property    value for the property
```

[handwritten annotations: "XML element name", "frame element name", "value for the property", "a FM property", "replace w/ Fm element Type - see next pg."]

where

gi	is a placeholder for an XML element name
fmtag	is a placeholder for a FrameMaker element name
type	is a placeholder for one of the following:

cross-reference element

marker element

graphic element

equation element

table element

table row element

table cell element

colspec

spanspec

prop   is a FrameMaker property

val   is a value for the property

Substituting for the placeholders, for example, you might produce a rule such as

```
element "blah"
{
  is fm footnote element "Blah";
}
```

When an XML instance is *read* into FrameMaker, a blah element in the XML would become a FrameMaker footnote type element named Blah. When the document is saved from FrameMaker to XML (the *write*) this rule will take the FrameMaker footnote type Blah element and rename it so that the XML contains the markup blah.

NOTE   The curly braces do not have to be placed on separate lines, but it may help you with future editing to use this open style.

You may also combine rules if desired. The next example rule adjusts an element name plus ensures that the element becomes a FrameMaker marker. The text of the marker becomes the content in the FrameMaker marker box. Upon export, the rule ensures a marker in an element named Filename becomes an XML element.

```
element "filename"
{
  is fm marker element "Filename";
  marker text is content;
}
```

NOTE   Because rules syntax is picky and typos problematic, you may benefit from using a structured Read/Write rules template. This template is not available in the FrameMaker installation, but may be downloaded from *www.txstruct.com*. ~~Rules~~zip Rules7.zip

More information on the properties, which you may specify for cross references, graphics, equations, markers, and table elements, may be found in the *Structure Application Developer's Guide*.

Rules for Renaming Elements

One use of a rule is renaming an element so that it has a different name in the XML than it does in FrameMaker. This includes renaming for changes in the case of the name.

NOTE   Many of the rules examined here are examples pulled from the FrameMaker installed Applications (XDocBook, XHTML); some shown here, however, are custom rules written to demonstrate a variety of options.

For example, reading the following rule from top to bottom, an XML appendix element will become an element called Appendix in FrameMaker.

```
element "appendix"
{
  is fm element "Appendix";
}
```

Because many rules are bidirectional, looking at it from the other direction (the *write*) you may discern that this rule renames a FrameMaker element Appendix to appendix when exporting XML.

Rules for Dropping or Removing Elements or Content

Rules may be written to remove elements from a structure upon import into FrameMaker. In the following example, an XML area element is dropped from the resulting FrameMaker structured document.

```
element "area" drop;
```

Rules that drop content are not bidirectional. There is not a way to recover content that is dropped.

The next rule drops an element's content upon import into FrameMaker.

```
element "toc"
{
  is fm element "TOC";
  reader drop content;
}
```

The idea behind this rule and the dropping of the TOC element's content upon import (the read in *reader*) is that the TOC element will be emptied and an automatically-generated FrameMaker table of contents may be substituted.

Another option is unwrapping an element, which allows you to keep its content but get rid of the beginning and end tags around that content.

```
element "term" unwrap;
```

These drop and unwrap options allow you to manipulate the structure without having to hand-edit to remove unwanted elements or data.

Since these rules are not bidirectional, bear in mind that once you drop content you cannot get it back.

Rules for Setting the Element Type (Used Internally by FrameMaker)

Another use for rules is to make certain XML elements become special element types in FrameMaker. This allows you to then use special FrameMaker features, such as markers, that do not have an equivalent in XML. For example, the callout XML element not only changes its name to Callout on import to FrameMaker, it becomes a FrameMaker footnote. If the footnote feature was not identified this way, the element might appear as a paragraph in FrameMaker

```
element "callout"
{
  is fm footnote element "Callout";
}
```

NOTE   If the Callout element is defined in the EDD as a FrameMaker footnote element, then using such a rule may be redundant. FrameMaker should automatically use the EDD settings. This example rule is only necessary because of the name (case) difference that must be dealt with.

In addition to changing the case in names, complete name changes may be done.

```
element "topic_data"
{
  is fm marker element "TopicAlias";
}
```

The key to determining what changes to make is knowing your structure. Know what the element names are in your XML (and DTD, if you are using one) and what the corresponding element names are within your FrameMaker structure (the EDD/structured template). Once you know these names, you will know where there are mismatches and when rules need to be written.

Rules for Managing Graphics and Settings

Moving images between FrameMaker and XML can sometimes be problematic. Graphics may not size properly, nor position properly, unless the import/export process is refined using rules.

In the following example, a graphic XML element is renamed Graphic, plus it is identified as a FrameMaker graphic element (which tells FrameMaker to create an anchored frame), and the filename referenced by FrameMaker is written to an attribute. It also, when exported to XML, creates the attribute and corresponding value that will allow the XML to point to the image—without the user needing to put the value in the attribute.

```
element "graphic"
{
  is fm graphic element "Graphic";
  attribute "fileref" is fm property file;
  attribute "entityref"
  {
    is fm property entity;
    is fm attribute;
  }
}
```

NOTE Note that the graphic element name is not a reserved name. You may just as easily call it *image* or *file* or anything else that you want to within your structure.

This next rule does many things. It specifies that an element is a graphic type element. It takes attributes and uses their values to perform sizing. It also uses some information (such as the *alignment* property values) to set the alignment of the resulting anchored frame on the page.

```
element "Image" {
        is fm graphic element;
        attribute "File" is fm property file;
        fm property import by reference or copy value is "ref";
        attribute "Width" is fm property width;
        attribute "Height" is fm property height;
        attribute "Impsize" is fm property import size;
        attribute "XOffset" is fm property horizontal offset;
        attribute "YOffset" is fm property vertical offset;
        attribute "Align"
        {
        is fm property alignment;
        value "left" is fm property value align left;
        value "middle" is fm property value align center;
        value "right" is fm property value align right;
        value "aoutside" is fm property value align outside;
        value "ainside" is fm property value align inside;
        }
        attribute "BlOffset" is fm property baseline offset;
        attribute "Position"
        {
        is fm property position;
        value "below" is fm value "below";
        value "inline" is fm property value inline;
        value "top" is fm property value top;
        value "bottom" is fm property value bottom;
        value "sleft" is fm property value subcol left;
        value "sright" is fm property value subcol right;
        value "snear" is fm property value subcol nearest;
        value "sfar" is fm property value subcol farthest;
        value "sinside" is fm property value subcol inside;
        value "soutside" is fm property value subcol outside;
        value "tleft" is fm property value textframe left;
        value "tright" is fm property value textframe right;
        value "tnear" is fm property value textframe nearest;
        value "tfar" is fm property value textframe farthest;
        value "tinside" is fm property value textframe inside;
        value "toutside" is fm property value textframe outside;
        value "runin" is fm property value run into paragraph;
    }
```

This last set of values for the *position* property are used to set the **anchoring position** within the anchored frame (positions available include *Below Current Line, At Insertion Point,* and so on).

Rules for Managing Tables and Settings

Tables may also be a special case. The width of columns, straddling of columns, and related settings may be managed by using rules to automatically produce attribute values.

If you do not include a rule similar to the one below, certain settings within your FrameMaker table will not perform a round trip properly—settings in the original FrameMaker tables will be lost when tables are exported to XML and then brought back in to FrameMaker.

```
element "specialtable"
{
  is fm element "SpecialTable";
  attribute "colsep" is fm property column ruling;
  attribute "frame" is fm property table border ruling;
  attribute "orient" drop;
  attribute "pgwide" is fm property page wide;
  attribute "rowsep" is fm property row ruling;
  attribute "tabstyle" is fm property table format;
}
```

The rule above does the following:

- When XML is imported into FrameMaker, the element is renamed SpecialTable. Then, attributes in the XML are used to set FrameMaker properties: column ruling style, table border style, page width, row ruling style, and the FrameMaker table format. An attribute for table orientation is dropped

- When a FrameMaker file is exported to XML, table formatting information is automatically placed in attributes so that sizing information is retained

This next rule is very similar, with some minor differences in names, case, and settings retained. This second example is provided to give you a broader set of examples to reference, and to clarify that there are not reserved names on the elements and attributes.

```
element "Table" {
is fm table element;
attribute "Cols" is fm property columns;
attribute "Widths" is fm property column widths;
attribute "Colsep" is fm property column ruling;
attribute "Rowsep" is fm property row ruling;
attribute "Frame" is fm property table border ruling;
attribute "Tabstyle" is fm property table format;
}
```

If you do not care to retain some (or all) of these settings, you may feel free to simplify the rule. The next example merely renames a table and drops an attribute.

```
element "table"
{
  is fm element "Table";
  attribute "orient" drop;
}
```

To specify a Table type element and the related FrameMaker table format name,

```
element "tgroup"
{
  is fm table element "TGroup";
  attribute "tgroupstyle" is fm property table format;
}
```

You may even specify values such as the number of columns for a table. The next example rule would create a two-column table upon import to FrameMaker.

```
element "table" {
is fm table element;
fm property columns value is "2";
}
```

In addition to affecting the Table type element, you may wish to affect other types of elements within tables. The other element types include TableCell, TableRow, TableTitle, TableBody, TableFooting, and TableHeading.

NOTE   As mentioned before, element *types* in the EDD are specific to FrameMaker and do not have a DTD equivalent.

For a table cell, for example, you may wish to retain the straddling when moving from FrameMaker to XML (or vice versa).

```
element "TableCell" {
is fm table cell element;
attribute "Straddle" is fm property horizontal straddle;
attribute "Vstraddle" is fm property vertical straddle;
}
```

You may also wish to retain the properties of a table row. (TableRow type elements contain TableCell type elements and any settings for the row may impact the cell or layout.)

```
element "TableRow" {
is fm table row element;
attribute "Rowsep" is fm property row ruling;
}
```

To specify that an element will become a FrameMaker TableBody type element, you might have a rule similar to this one:

```
element "tbody"
{
  is fm table body element "TBody";
}
```

Using similar rules, you might specify that an element is a Table-Footing or TableHeading type element, as the following two rules specify.

```
element "tfoot"
{
  is fm table footing element "TFoot";
}
element "thead"
{
  is fm table heading element "THead";
}
```

Or, simply add a rule to recognize an element as a TableTitle type element.

```
element "caption" is fm table title element;
```

This could be rewritten using curly braces. The action would be the same as with the one-line version.

```
element "caption"
{
is fm table title element;
}
```

Additional examples may be found in the installed Application files within the Structure folder and the XMLCookbook folder within the FrameMaker installation. You may also refer to the *Structure Application Developer's Guide* chapter on CALS.

CALS = Computer Aided Logistics System, though when developed was initially Continuous Acquisition and Life-cycle Support

Rules for Book Components

Rules may also be used to manage the XML import and export from FrameMaker books. The following example is from the XDocBook Rules file.

```
/* Book structure */
reader generate book for  doctype "set", "book", "part"
  {
    put element "appendix" in file "app.fm";
    put element "article" in file "art.fm";
    put element "bibliography" in file "biblio.fm";
    put element "bookinfo" in file "info.fm";
    put element "chapter" in file "chap.fm";
    put element "colophon" in file "colo.fm";
    put element "dedication" in file "dedicate.fm";
    put element "glossary" in file "gloss.fm";
    put element "index" in file;
    put element "lot" in file;
    put element "part" in file;
    put element "preface" in file "preface.fm";
    put element "refentry" in file "refent.fm";
    put element "reference" in file "ref.fm";
    put element "setindex" in file "setind.fm";
    put element "setinfo" in file "info.fm";
    put element "title" in file;
```

```
      put element "titleabbrev" in file "titlea.fm";
      put element "toc" in file "toc.fm";
  }
writer do not output book processing instructions;
```

The elements within the book XML file will be split to form the separate *.fm* files listed above. The last part of the rules above (the *writer*) tells FrameMaker when it writes XML to not include book-related process instructions within the XML markup.

Rules for Cross-References

Cross references require some special explanation. The following is a Read/Write rule that you may have used within FrameMaker 7.0.

```
element "xref"
{
  is fm cross-reference element "XRef";
  attribute "role" is fm property cross-reference format;
  attribute "linkend" is fm property cross-reference id;
}
```

In FrameMaker 7.1, however, there is a special attribute assigned to cross references to enable external cross-references. The *reserved name* for the attribute in FrameMaker 7.1 is srcfile.

Rules should not be needed to make cross references work properly in FrameMaker 7.1. If the default translation is not working or if you wish to use different naming conventions in your XML, however, you might write a rule to rename your attribute to srcfile on import into FrameMaker.

Rules for Special Characters or Symbols

The *isoall.rw* rules file included in the FrameMaker installation—and referenced in the initially-created Read/Write rules—contains many special characters. These are predefined to save you time.

The *isoall.rw* file includes rules for special symbols you use in your documents. If you use these symbols within FrameMaker, they will translate to the proper character code when saving as XML. In reverse, if you use the character code in your XML, the rule will help

FrameMaker display the proper character in FrameMaker when XML is imported. Example ISO Read/Write rules are:

```
entity "mdash" is fm char 0xd1;
entity "ndash" is fm char 0xd0;
entity "dash" is fm char 0x15;
entity "blank" is fm char 0x11;
entity "hellip" is fm char 0xc9;
```

This may include specifying the font to be used to create the symbol in FrameMaker. For example,

```
entity "marker" is fm char 0x79 in "FmDingbats";
entity "cir" is fm char 0x6d in "FmDingbats";
entity "bull" is fm char 0xa5;
entity "clubs" is fm char 0xa7 in "FmSymbol";
entity "diams" is fm char 0xa8 in "FmSymbol";
entity "hearts" is fm char 0xa9 in "FmSymbol";
entity "spades" is fm char 0xaa in "FmSymbol";
```

For any special characters that are not specified in the *isoall.rw* rules file, you may need to add rules to your own Read/Write rules file. Use the same syntax as above, and be sure to test the character Import and Export functions.

Creating New Read/Write Rules

To create Read/Write rules, you type the rules that you need inside a file and save it. Then, from within your Application (*structapps.fm*) setup you point to the rules file that you have saved. For the following examples, you will use FrameMaker's menus to start your rules file and to check the rules once they are written.

To create an initial Read/Write rules file in FrameMaker:

1. Choose *File>Structure Tools>New Read/Write Rules.*

   The Read/Write rules file appears. If you are using FrameMaker 7.1, then it will appear as shown in Figure 13–1.

The initial Read/Write rules file contains the FrameMaker version and a reference to a Read/Write rules file called *isoall.rw* that installs with FrameMaker.

2. Save the file.

    You may name the file whatever you like, but using a *.rw* extension may help you to manage and track the files.

3. Type the rules that you need and Save the file again.

> **NOTE**   If you are just starting out with Read/Write rules, you might add the nearly-empty rules file to your structured Application (see Chapter 14 on building an Application). As you determine the rules that you need, you may modify your rules file and FrameMaker will be able to immediately access the changed file via the Application.

4. Check the rules to ensure the syntax is correct by choosing *File>Structure Tools>Check Read/Write Rules*.

    FrameMaker will display a log if there are any errors in your rules. Adjust and recheck until you have no errors.

5. Test the rules by importing and exporting XML from FrameMaker.

```
fm version is "7.1";

/*
 * Include all ISO entity mapping rules.
 */

#include "isoall.rw"
```

Figure 13–1.   This exhibits the initial Read/Write rules file.

Summary

Sometimes moving content between FrameMaker and XML does not work exactly as you need it to. The solution provided by FrameMaker is a Read/Write rules file.

The Read/Write rules file provides you with the ability to adjust your markup between XML and FrameMaker. You may add the rules as needed to make your Application work as you desire.

While rules are not required within an Application, they may help you hone your round-trip results.

CHAPTER 14

Steps to Creating Your XML Application

FrameMaker structured Applications may be created fairly easily once you have a template and DTD available—even if they are still being refined. To adjust the Import and Export functions, you may need to create an Application designed specifically for your documents. XML Application creation is detailed in this chapter.

Creating Your Application

You can create multiple structured Applications if desired, with each used for a particular document type or using a specific template. Then, when importing and exporting XML, you use your Application by selecting its name when the dialog box appears.

Elements may change from one type of document to another, thus *Document Type Definition*.

The process is much simpler than you may think to create a structured Application. Its creation begins with *File>Structure Tools>Edit Application Definitions*. This opens a file called *structapps.fm*. This file contains information on the structured Applications set up for your copy of FrameMaker.

NOTE The default Applications were discussed in Chapter 11.

Adding Pointers to Related Files

When you import your XML, FrameMaker displays it pretty much as-is (plain). Because XML contains no formatting, the results in FrameMaker are not formatted. FrameMaker being a layout and formatting tool, you will probably want to apply formatting by telling FrameMaker to use your templates as XML documents are opened. You do this by creating an Application pointing to your template and then selecting this Application as you import the XML.

The steps below walk you through creating an Application called *simpledoc* that points to a template file.

NOTE While some steps include the details needed to access the necessary files, there are no steps in this chapter on creating the template or DTD.

When creating your own Application, you need to use your own files. While DTD creation is discussed in Chapter 12, template creation is dealt with only on a small scale (as part of Chapter 3).

The files you will use to create the *simpledoc* Application are located in this book's example files, which are available from this book's website. If you followed the instructions in Chapter 6, these files will be in the *simpledoc* folder that you created using those instructions.

NOTE   As noted in Chapter 6, the sample files are available at *www.apress.com/book/download.html*.

To create your Application, you need to first open the Application Definition document. If you do not have it open already, click *File>Structure Tools>Edit Application Definitions* to open it.

Since the structured Application file is a structured document, you must open the Structure View along with the Element Catalog. The latter will guide you as you create your Application.

1. In the *structapps.fm* file just opened, place your insertion point to the right of the line descending from the StructuredSetup element.

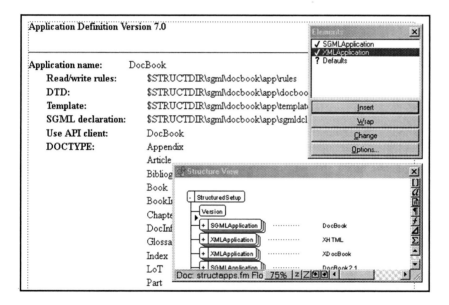

2. Select the XMLApplication element and click ***Insert***. The XMLApplication and child ApplicationName elements appear.

3. Type the name simpledoc for your new Application, as shown.

4. Move your insertion point to just below your `ApplicationName` element and keep the file open.

File Locations

Before continuing, make a place for the Application's files. For purposes of this example, you will create a folder. Some explanation of paths is needed, however, so that you understand your options for folder placement.

Placing your files in the same location as your XML may be easiest during testing, because it means you can move the files as you go through various revision phases and the paths are treated as *relative* to the XML.

For long-term use, you may wish to make a folder specifically for your files. This may be on a network or a local folder. You can then use its absolute path in your Application setup (see Figure 14–1).

Another option is to place the files within the FrameMaker installation, in an area designed for this purpose. There is a *FrameMaker7.x\structure\xml* folder provided for XML Application files that already includes the DocBook and other installed files. If you choose to make a folder in this location, you may easily copy the file paths from FrameMaker's existing Applications and adjust them to point to your Application files (absolute path).

Once you decide where to put your Application files, put your template in your new folder, noting the complete path for inclusion in your Application—or noting no path, which allows FrameMaker to keep pointers relative to the XML.

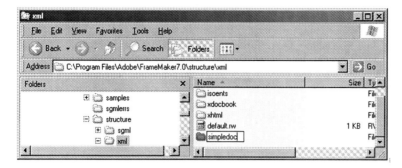

Figure 14–1. The Microsoft Explorer dialog box is where you create the Application's folder.

1. To continue with this example, create a folder under the *structure\xml* folder for your Application files, called *simpledoc.*

2. Save your template, DTD, and any other appropriate files into the new folder, and be sure to note their filenames. An example of this is shown in Figure 14–2.

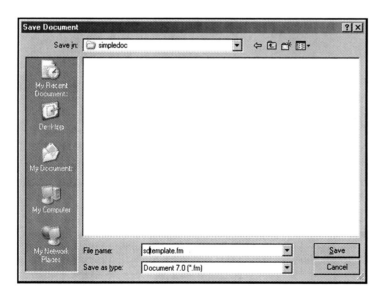

Figure 14–2. Save the template in the Application folder in the Save Document dialog box.

NOTE Even though your EDD is not needed by the Application, you might also put your EDD in this folder to keep everything together. That way, the structured template will be right with the EDD if you need to make adjustments and reimport the EDD elements into the structured template.

The paths may be anywhere, including on a network, although it may be easier to start by dropping the files into the structure folder provided within FrameMaker's installation directory: *FrameMaker7.1\structure\xml*.

Accessing a Template

Now, let's return to the *structapps.fm* file to add a template to the Application, using the following steps:

1. With your insertion point still below the ApplicationName element, select the Template element from the Element Catalog and click **Insert**.

2. Type the file path, or use a variable containing the path (as used in the preinstalled structured Applications like XDocBook), and include the template's filename. In this example, the template is *sdtemplate.fm* as shown (circled) in the following screen shot.

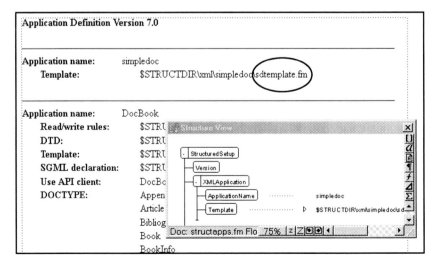

3. Save the *structapps.fm* file.

4. On the File menu, choose *Structure Tools>Read Application Definitions.*

NOTE   Any time that you adjust the Application definitions file, you must reread it so that FrameMaker has a chance to register the adjustments.

5. After FrameMaker has read (or more precisely, reread) the Application definitions, Close the *structapps.fm* file.

First, open your XML document without an Application to review FrameMaker's out-of-the-box behavior. The results are not formatted (see Figure 14–3).

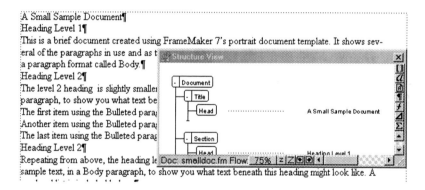

Figure 14–3.   XML is shown opened in FrameMaker without Application (no formatting).

Now, follow the steps below to open your XML document and (from the Use Structured Application dialog that appears) select the Application you just created. It is called *simpledoc*, and selecting it allows FrameMaker to access the *sdtemplate.fm* template—it can do this because you put the template's file path in the *structapps.fm* structured Application file.

1. Select *File>Open* and browse to the book's sample documents in the *structure\xml* folder.

2. From the *simpledoc* folder, select *simpledoc.xml*, then click *Open*.

3. When prompted, select the *simpledoc* Application from the list.

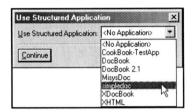

4. Click *Continue*.

NOTE Because the Application only has the template in it right now, you will probably get an error that the DTD is not available for validation. This is shown in Figure 14–4. You can ignore this error for now.

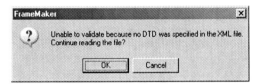

Figure 14–4.   The dialog box shows an error regarding the DTD.

5. Do not worry about this error and click *OK* to continue.

You will now see a formatted file that uses your XML tags and displays your XML document *content*. This formatted result is shown in Figure 14–5. You may see different results if you used files other than the XML instance and template provide on the book's website.

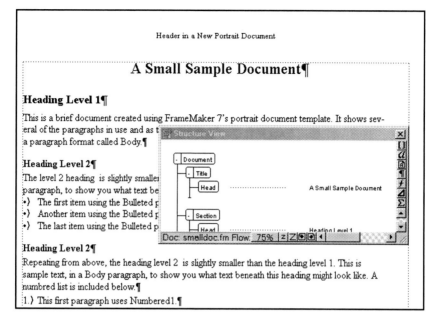

Figure 14–5. `simpledoc.xml` *is shown opened in FrameMaker using the simpledoc Application.*

NOTE   As noted in Chapter 6, the sample files are available at *www.apress.com/book/download.html.*

Because the Application points to the template, and the template includes page layout data, text styles, and information on which styles to use with each XML tag, the structured document is formatted just as it was originally (as shown previously in Figure 4–1). Pretty cool, right?

Please note that if your template path is incorrect in the Application, you may get an error such as the one in Figure 14–6. If such an error appears, check your file path and filenames.

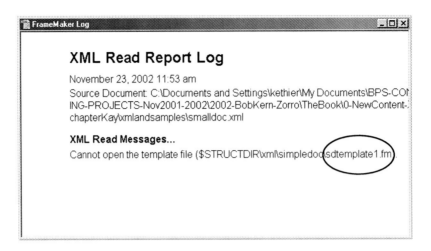

Figure 14–6. *An error log can be caused by typos in the template file pathname.*

NOTE The example error shown in Figure 15-6 was forced to occur by editing the *structapps.fm* file and adding a *1* to the template's name—making it not match the template's filename. This shows a mismatch between the template filename and the *structapps.fm* pointer.

Accessing a DTD for Validation

The error message shown in Figure 14–4 mentioned that a DTD was not available for the Application. To allow validation of your XML, make sure that you copied your DTD into the directory with your template when instructed to do so earlier in the chapter. Then, you need to add the DTD path to your Application.

1. Click in the structure of the *structapps.fm* file, just below the Template element.

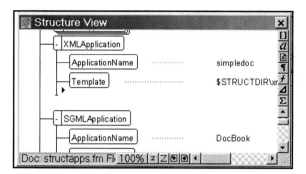

2. Insert the DTD element from the catalog.

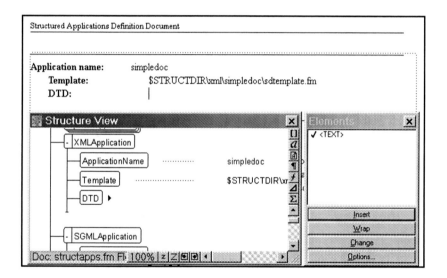

3. Type the pathname to the DTD in the directory you made—much like you did in the previous section for your template. The adjusted Application might look like the one in the following screen shot.

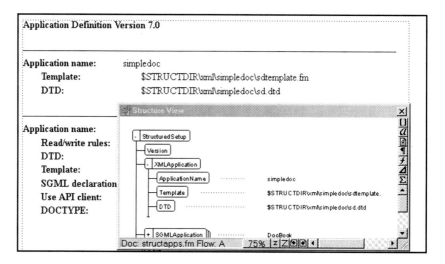

4. Save the *structapps.fm* file.

5. On the File menu, choose *Structure Tools>Read Application Definitions.*

Now, open the *simpledoc.xml* document again using the *simpledoc* Application, and the DTD error message should not appear. If there are any validation errors, they will appear in a log file similar to the error log shown in Figure 14–6. If a log appears, check that your DTD pathname and filename are correct.

Adding Read/Write Rules

In this section, several examples are given of items that might require adjustment when XML is opened in (imported into) FrameMaker. Some common uses for Read/Write rules are:

- To identify an element as a specific type of FrameMaker element (such as a TableTitle)

- To adjust an element name (such as changing chaptitle to ChapterTitle), allowing you to take advantage of FrameMaker's ability to include spaces in element names

- To map your XML entities to FrameMaker element types

- To drop an element or attribute not needed or desired in FrameMaker

Read/Write rules are used as FrameMaker *reads* the XML into a FrameMaker document, and *writes* a FrameMaker document as XML. Many rules are bidirectional, and are used for both reading and writing.

Before adding the link to a Read/Write rules file, look at a simple rule. This Read/Write rules file only has one rule, which is to change an element name. The entire content of the file is seen in Table 14–1.

Table 14–1.   Read/Wrige Rule File

`/*fm version is "7.0";`	Line 1
`/*`	Line 2
` * Include all ISO entity mapping rules.`	Line 3
` */`	Line 4
	Line 5
`#include "isoall.rw"`	Line 6
	Line 7
`/* Element rules. Rules herein capitalize letters other`	Line 8
`than the initial one or perform name changes.*/`	Line 9
	Line 10
`element "document"`	Line 11
`{`	Line 12
`  is fm element "Document";`	Line 13
`}`	Line 14
`/*`	Line 15

Lines 1 through 7 come in automatically when you create Read/Write rules. Lines 8 through 10 are a comment, which is an optional but helpful addition if you plan to have extensive rules. Comments allow you to describe what a rule is doing so that you or others who need to edit the rules can fully understand their purpose.

The rule to change the element is shown on Lines 11 through 14. This rule says that an XML element called *document* should change its name to *Document* when imported into FrameMaker (the *read*). If instead you *write* by saving as XML, the rule goes in reverse and the FrameMaker element *Document* will be renamed to *document*.

NOTE Element names and case need to match those in the element definitions. This means that names for the XML elements should match the DTD, and names for the FrameMaker elements should match the EDD.

If you have a Read/Write rules file, make sure it is in the same directory as your template and DTD, and then add the pointer to your Application.

1. Click in the structure of the *structapps.fm* file just below the DTD element.

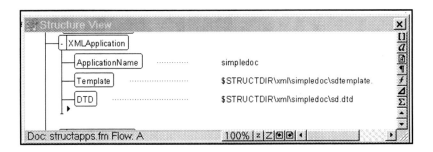

2. Insert the `ReadWriteRules` element from the catalog.

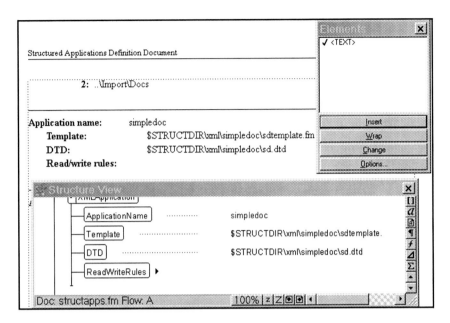

3. Type the pathname to the Read/Write rules in the directory you made—much like you did in the previous section for your DTD.

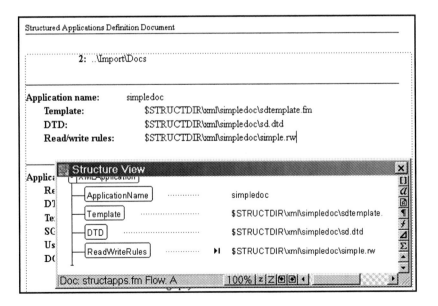

4. Save the *structapps.fm* file.

5. On the File menu, choose *Structure Tools>Read Application Definitions*.

6. Close the *structapps.fm* file.

Now that the Read/Write rules are added, if you perform a round trip, you will see the name change. By opening the structured document from Figure 4–1, and saving it to XML using the Application, you will end up with XML containing the name change (lowercase *d* in document). This XML is shown in Figure 14–7.

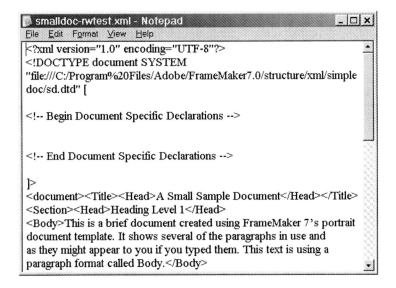

Figure 14–7.   This XML shows a change from the Read/Write rules.

Please note that you may get an error log if the resulting element names do not match your DTD or EDD.

Examples of Read/Write rules are in the XML Cookbook—a resource that installs with FrameMaker 7.0 and 7.1. The XML Cookbook is well over a hundred pages long and includes steps for setting up an Application, writing Read/Write rules, and more. It may be a good next step in your round-trip learning to complete the XML Cookbook.

More examples of Read/Write rules are in the FrameMaker installation, inside the *Structure* folder.

Details and examples are also included in the *OnlineManuals* folder in a PDF called *Structure_Dev_Guide.pdf*, which serves as a reference for structure designers.

Other Application Components

In addition to your template and DTD, you may insert paths to many other files. These are shown in Figure 14–8.

This particular chapter does not deal with all of the available Application elements. These elements were explained in Chapter 11.

Reading Your Application

Once you have set up your structured application within the *structapps.fm* file, you need to save it and then have FrameMaker scan through it—read it—so that your applications may be used.

After making changes and additions, save the *structapps.fm* file. Then, click *File>Structure Tools>Read Application Definitions*.

Figure 14–8. The Element Catalog shows other elements used in Applications.

Testing Your Application

After you have done the read, you can then use your Application. Test this by opening an XML document or by saving an existing structured document as XML. When prompted, you should see your new Applications on the list (if you have just modified an existing application, you will not see any difference in the application choices).

1. Select *File>Open*, browse, and select one of your XML documents.

2. Click the *Open* button.

3. When prompted, select your Application from the list.

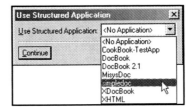

4. Click *Continue*.

Your file should open and you should see a formatted file that uses your XML tags and displays your XML document content. If your Application specifies a template, then the document will use that template.

To see the Application again, try saving the open document as XML and select from the list on the way out. Your Application should be available in both directions.

Assigning Your Application to a Structured FrameMaker Document

If a structured template is available and listed in the Application, the FrameMaker formatting can be applied when an XML document is opened. If a DTD is available and referenced in the XML, validation can be done against the DTD.

Rather than selecting your Application from the list, you can assign it to your FrameMaker structured documents. Then, when the XML is created, it will have extra information in it so that the Application is used on the way out, and again on the way into FrameMaker

To set the structured Application for your file, select *File>Set Structured Application* with the file open. Then, select the desired Application from the list and click *Set*. That is all there is to it.

Another way to set the structured Application is to specify it within the EDD. The appropriate element may be seen in Figure, which shows the beginnings of an EDD. In the Element Catalog, the StructuredApplication element would be selected and inserted to set the Application for all structured documents that end up using the EDD.

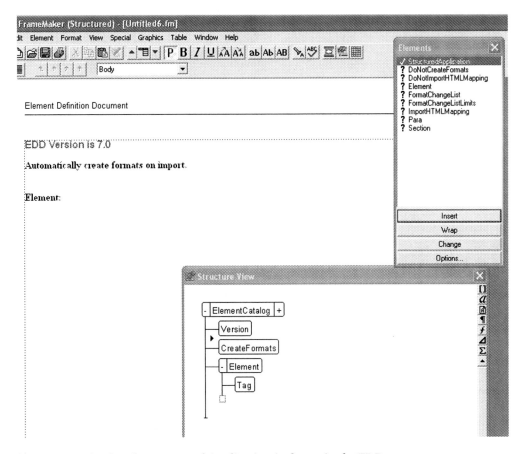

Figure 14–9.   Setting the structured Application is shown in the EDD.

Summary

Creating an Application is really is no more difficult for a FrameMaker user than creating a FrameMaker book. You just need to know where your files are, insert the paths to them, and then tell FrameMaker the Application exists.

CHAPTER 15

Resources for XML and Structured FrameMaker

THIS CHAPTER INCLUDES websites and other resources that relate to XML, FrameMaker, or both. These may help you expand on your knowledge as you move forward.

DTDs, XML, and Plug-ins

World Wide Web Consortium (W3C)

The W3C creates and maintains information technology for the World Wide Web. Their site is worth a visit, and includes everything from specifications to tutorials to news. Check them out at *www.w3c.org*.

W3Schools

The *www.w3schools.com* website is also very useful. It includes tutorials on many XML-related technologies. Tutorials are quick to complete and written in very beginner-friendly terminology.

XML.org

This website includes information on XML technologies and XML resources, such as books and training. *XML.org* also includes an events list, which may help you locate conferences and other happenings in your area.

DocBook and DocBook Slides

There are many sites with DocBook information. Norm Walsh's DocBook information site is strongly suggested. The site, *sourceforge.net/projects/docbook/*, includes example files, tutorials, DTDs, style sheets, and documentation. This is a good place to go if you want to get started with DocBook or create presentations using Norm's DocBook Slides DTD and example style sheets.

CUDSPAN

This site provides various no-cost plug-ins for FrameMaker users. The plug-ins are easy to install, add high-value functionality to FrameMaker, and include documentation. The site is provided by Chris Despopoulos (the C.U.D. of CUDSPAN), with the plug-ins provided free as a resource for his fellow FrameUsers.

According to the website, Chris creates the tools for his own use and then shares them without charge, license, or warranty. The website is *www.telecable.es/personales/cud/*.

Some of the great plug-ins included here are PrintTree (for printing structure views) and HuntOverrides (for locating overrides to formatting).

Mekon

This UK-based consulting firm creates custom plug-ins for FrameMaker. They are well-versed in XML and understand complex publishing environments. Check them out at *www.mekon.com*. Their latest autoconstruct plug-in allows users to pull graphics out of the main flow but maintain their attachment to structure.

Mekon is the creator of FrameAC™, a tool for writing VBscripts to work with FrameMaker. This allows you to enhance and extend FrameMaker's own capabilities.

Frank Elmore

Frank is the creator of FrameScript—a tool for writing scripts. This allows you to add functionality to FrameMaker. Check out *www.framescript.com* for more information.

FrameMaker Templates and Other Files

Bright Path Solutions

Bright Path Solutions provides information relating to publishing and XML. This book's author, Kay Ethier, is a consultant for Bright Path Solutions. The site includes downloadable FrameMaker templates and structured Application files, in addition to the other resources mentioned here. The Bright Path Solutions website is *www.travelthepath.com.*

MicroType

The MicroType corporate website has some of the best "list of…" resource links available for FrameMaker. Many of the resources and articles are free at *www.microtype.com.*

The MicroType site—run by Shlomo Perets—includes printable short cut lists, a free customization kit (to optimize your menus), and many tutorials.

Text Structure Consulting (Lynne Price)

Lynne Price, who runs Text Structure Consulting, provides free downloads of key FrameMaker structure files in an *enhanced* form. Lynne has modified the FrameMaker EDD structure to make it more efficient. She has also created a structured version of the Read/Write rules file for FrameMaker. Both of these downloads are quite helpful and can be implemented fairly easily in your FrameMaker installation. Lynne's website is *www.txstruct.com*.

FrameMaker Installation

Within the FrameMaker installation, there are various structured templates. Some are available through the FrameMaker Template Browser, which is accessed by selecting *File>New>Document* and clicking the *Explore Standard Templates* button. Additional templates are located in the following folders:

    FrameMaker7.x\samples\
    FrameMaker7.x\samples\MoreSamples\
    FrameMaker7.x\templates\
    FrameMaker7.x\structure\

DocSys CERN Templates

The DocSys site provides CERN document templates.Visit *docsys.web.cern.ch/docsys/framemaker/templates/welcome.html* to download the templates.

Society for Technical Communication's Rocky Mountain Chapter

This group has several templates available at *stcrmc.org/Samples_and_Templates/FrameMakerTemplates.htm*.

Books

XML Cookbook

This Adobe tutorial can be found in the FrameMaker 7.0 or 7.1 installation folders. Check your installation folders for a *XMLCookbook* subfolder. Print the tutorial (a PDF) found in that folder, then open the cookbook sample files as instructed by the tutorial.

Adobe Enterprise Publishing Guide

Published by Adobe and included in their FrameMaker 7 Solutions CD, this guide provides information on publishing with FrameMaker and XML. The book includes a list of Adobe-known XML and FrameMaker experts (the author is pleased to note that of the companies named worldwide, Bright Path Solutions is one of Adobe's selected few).

Advanced FrameMaker (book)

Published by TIPS Technical Publishing, this 500-page book provides FrameMaker users with techniques and tips for doing complex publishing. Chapter topics include running header/footers, XML round trip, generated lists, and many more. Purchases may be made via *www.technicalpublishing.com*.

Oracle XSQL

Published by Wiley, Michael D. Thomas' book includes a great hidden tutorial on XSLT.

XSLT

Published by O'Reilly, Douglas Tidwell's book covers XSLT and XML publishing options.

Conferences

In the conference name, 20XX indicates that the conference name includes the year and changes annually. Because there are a number of XML conferences worldwide, it is recommended that you search the Web for more current information.

XML 20XX

Run by IdeAlliance, *www.xmlconference.org* has information on this conference as well as other XML-related conferences that IdeAlliance runs. Information on their conferences may also be found at *www.idealliance.org*.

Extreme Markup Languages

This conference is also run by IdeAlliance and info can be found on the websites mentioned under XML 20XX.

Tri-XML 20XX Conference

This small, regional conference is held in the Research Triangle Park (RTP) in Morrisville, North Carolina. Because of the many XML experts living in the RTP area, this conference's schedule can rival some of the larger, national conferences. Information is at *www.trixml.org*.

FrameUsers Conference

Held each Fall in North America, this conference brings together experts and users from around the world for three days of presentations. Managed by FrameMaker expert Brad Anderson, this conference has been held since 1999 and is the only large conference of FrameMaker users.

Starting in 2004, a European FrameUsers Conference is planned annually in the Spring.

XML and FrameMaker User Groups

XML Eastern Alliance of User Groups

This Alliance has its own listserve and includes some of the groups mentioned below:

- *North Carolina USA*   Triangle area XML users (Tri-XML) information is at *www.trixml.org.*

- *New York USA*   Rochester SGML/XML user group website is *www.rnysxug.com.*

- *Washington DC USA*   Washington Area SGML/XML User Group has their website at *http://www.eccnet.com/xmlug.*

- *Pittsburgh PA USA*   Pittsburgh Markup Language users' (PittMark) website is *www.pittmark.org.*

- *Belgium*   The SGML/XML BeLux User Group website is *russell.bim.be/BeLuxweb/.*

- *Sweden*   Swedish SGML/XML User Group has their website at *info.admin.kth.se/SGML/.*

- *Finland*   SGML/XML User Group Finland *www.vtt.fi/SGMLUG*

FrameUsers

The *www.frameusers.com* site provides a variety of resources. You may join a listserve, peruse an event calendar, sign up for an annual conference, and peruse a list of worldwide user groups (called FUN, or FrameUsers Network).

Adobe Forum

The Adobe website—*www.adobe.com*—includes a Forum where you can post questions, answer questions posted by others, or review the archives for answers you need.

Quadralay Forum

Quadralay Corporation, makers of WebWorks Publisher and other tools, hosts a forum on their corporate site. Users may sign up for user group forums or topic-specific forums. Quadralay's website is *www.webworks.com.*

Index

forums.apress.com

FOR PROFESSIONALS BY PROFESSIONALS™

JOIN THE APRESS FORUMS AND BE PART OF OUR COMMUNITY. You'll find discussions that cover topics of interest to IT professionals, programmers, and enthusiasts just like you. If you post a query to one of our forums, you can expect that some of the best minds in the business—especially Apress authors, who all write with *The Expert's Voice*™—will chime in to help you. Why not aim to become one of our most valuable participants (MVPs) and win cool stuff? Here's a sampling of what you'll find:

DATABASES

Data drives everything.

Share information, exchange ideas, and discuss any database programming or administration issues.

INTERNET TECHNOLOGIES AND NETWORKING

Try living without plumbing (and eventually IPv6).

Talk about networking topics including protocols, design, administration, wireless, wired, storage, backup, certifications, trends, and new technologies.

JAVA

We've come a long way from the old Oak tree.

Hang out and discuss Java in whatever flavor you choose: J2SE, J2EE, J2ME, Jakarta, and so on.

MAC OS X

All about the Zen of OS X.

OS X is both the present and the future for Mac apps. Make suggestions, offer up ideas, or boast about your new hardware.

OPEN SOURCE

Source code is good; understanding (open) source is better.

Discuss open source technologies and related topics such as PHP, MySQL, Linux, Perl, Apache, Python, and more.

PROGRAMMING/BUSINESS

Unfortunately, it is.

Talk about the Apress line of books that cover software methodology, best practices, and how programmers interact with the "suits."

WEB DEVELOPMENT/DESIGN

Ugly doesn't cut it anymore, and CGI is absurd.

Help is in sight for your site. Find design solutions for your projects and get ideas for building an interactive Web site.

SECURITY

Lots of bad guys out there—the good guys need help.

Discuss computer and network security issues here. Just don't let anyone else know the answers!

TECHNOLOGY IN ACTION

Cool things. Fun things.

It's after hours. It's time to play. Whether you're into LEGO® MINDSTORMS™ or turning an old PC into a DVR, this is where technology turns into fun.

WINDOWS

No defenestration here.

Ask questions about all aspects of Windows programming, get help on Microsoft technologies covered in Apress books, or provide feedback on any Apress Windows book.

HOW TO PARTICIPATE:

Go to the Apress Forums site at **http://forums.apress.com/**.
Click the New User link.

Printed in the United States
113883LV00004B/175-178/A